1978

W9-CLF-696

# The
# Book of Oriental Literature

# The
# Book of Oriental Literature

### Edited by
## The Sirdar Ikbal Ali Shah

✳

THE OCTAGON PRESS

LONDON

First published 1937
First Impression in this Edition 1975

SBN: 900860 42 1 (cloth)
SBN: 900860 43 X (paper)

Printed by
Tonbridge Printers Limited,
Peach Hall Works, Shipbourne Road, Tonbridge, Kent.

# DEDICATION

DEDICATED TO THOSE WHOSE WORK IS
INCLUDED IN THIS VOLUME, FOR MAKING
LIFE RICH, WITH THE OUTPOURINGS OF
THEIR SOUL IN POETRY AND PROSE

# INTRODUCTION

*T*HE task of making this anthology has been a labour of love to me, for since my early days I have striven to interpret the East to the West, and Europe to Asia. Through this, I believe, lies the way of mutual sympathy between the nations; and such can only be accomplished by means of reading the effusions of one another's Great Minds; because if we but endeavour to understand about our fellow men, goodwill can come as the gentle dawn of peace. Years of study devoted to this work are as noble friends to me, whose memory, like precious odours, will abide with me to the last.

I make grateful acknowledgements to the following for inclusion of passages in this work: Messrs. William & Norgate; Colonial Press; British Academy; R. A. Society; Sir R. Burton (H. J. Cook, Esq.); James Madden, Esq.; The Commercial Press; The French Bookstore (Henry H. Hart, Esq.); J. F. Davis, Esq.; Ralph T. H. Griffith, Esq. (Lazarus & Co.); M. N. Dutt, Esq.; Sir William Jones; E. J. Robinson, Esq. (Wesleyan Conference Office); P. E. More, Esq.; Sir Mohamed Iqbal; Professor Macdonald; Francis H. Skrine, Esq.; Sir Rabindranath Tagore; T. D. Broughton, Esq.; Dr. Adams; Messrs. Arthur Probsthain & Co. (Professor C. E. Wilson); S. Robinson, Esq.; Edward FitzGerald, Esq.; Miss G. Bell; San Kaka Sha (F. Victor Dickins, Esq.); Messrs. Fisher Unwin; Messrs. Wright & Brown; to which must be added my unqualified indebtedness to Professor Sir Denison Ross, Dr. Randell and his staff at the India Office Library, to Mr. Probsthain and Bibliotheque Sino-Internationale of Geneva for great encouragement and guidance during the progress of the work; and no mere words can adequately thank that great patron of Asia's "Noble Things"—The Aga Khan.

*London* : 1937.  IKBAL ALI SHAH.

# CONTENTS

## AFGHANISTAN:

## ARABIA:

## CHINA:

# Contents

## INDIA:

# Contents

# Contents

Afghanistan

# AFGHAN LITERATURE

ALL truly great literature whether in poetry or prose must essentially interpret the soul of a people. The Afghan poetry does so in its Poshto language. Not having been born amidst the luxuries of life, their outlook on life is both austere and devout. In the following translations by H. G. Raverty of sixteenth and nineteenth century Afghan poets, benevolent sentiments are shown with their full measure of Sufi thought—a common heritage of Middle Eastern thinkers of all times.

## AN ODE

### BY ISMAT

*Y*ESTERDAY, half inebriated, I passed by the quarter
the wine-sellers dwell,
To seek out the daughter of an infidel, who is a vendor
of wine.

At the end of the street, a damsel, with a fairy's cheek,
advanced before me,
Who, pagan-like, wore her tresses dishevelled over
her shoulders, like the sacerdotal thread.

I said, " O thou, to the arch of whose eyebrows the
new moon is a shame!
What quarter is this, and where is thy place of abode ?"

'Cast," she replied, " thy rosary on the ground, and
lay the thread of paganism thy shoulder upon ;
Cast stones at the glass of piety ; and from an o'er-
flowing goblet quaff the wine.

After that draw near me, that I may whisper one
word in thine ear ;
For thou wilt accomplish thy journey, if thou hearken
to my words."

Abandoning my heart altogether, and in ecstasy wrapt,
I followed her,
'Till I came to a place, where, alike, reason and
religion forsook me.

At a distance, I beheld a company, all inebriated and
beside themselves,
Who came all frenzied, and boiling with ardour from
the wine of love ;

Without lutes, or cymbals, or viols; yet all full of
mirth and melody—
Without wine, or goblet, or flask; yet all drinking
unceasingly.

When the thread of restraint slipped away from my
hand,
I desired to ask her one question, but she said unto
me, " SILENCE! "

" This is no square temple whose gate thou canst pre-
cipitately attain;
This is no mosque which thou canst reach with tumult,
but without knowledge:

This is the banquet-house of infidels, and all within it
are intoxicated—
All, from eternity's dawn to the day of doom, in
astonishment lost!

Depart, then, from the cloister, and towards the
tavern bend thy steps;
Cast away the cloak of the darwesh, and don thou
the libertine's robe! "

I obeyed; and if thou desire, with ISMAT, the same
hue and colour to acquire,
Imitate him; and both this and the next world sell
for one drop of pure wine!

## A POEM

### BY MIRZA KHAN, ANSARI

How shall I define what thing I am?
　Wholly existent, and non-existent, thro' Him, I am.

Whatever becometh naught out of entity,
The signification of that nothingness am I.

Sometimes a mote in the disc of the sun;
At others, a ripple on the water's surface.

Now I fly about on the wind of association:
Now I am a bird of the incorporeal world.

By the name of ice I also style myself:
Congealed in the winter season am I.

I have enveloped myself in the four elements:
I am the clouds on the face of the sky.

From unity I have come into infinity:
Indeed, nothing existeth, that I am not.

My vitality is, from life's source itself;
And I am the speech, every mouth within.

I am the hearing-sense within ever ear;
And also the sight of every eye am I.

I am the potentiality in every thing:
I am the perception every one within.

My will and inclination are with all;
With mine own acts, also, satisfied am I.

Unto the sinful and vicious, I am evil;
But unto the good beneficent am I.

In the lot of the devoted, I am the honey:
In the soul of the impious, the sting.

I am with every one, and in all things;
Without imperfection—immaculate I am.

'Tis by the mouth of MIRZA that I speak:
An enlightened heart, without similitude, I am.

# A POEM

BY ABDUL-HAMID

*O* NECESSITY! what a terrible calamity art thou,
That changest man's nature into that of the dog!

The Muhammadan, thou makest follow Hindu rites,
And the Hindu, the usages of the Faithful to observe.

Kings and Princes thou makest stand at the door,
Of their crowns deprived, and from their thrones
driven.

Even the free and unrestrained birds of the air also,
Thou entanglest, helpless and paralyzed in the net.

The tutor likewise, in the sight of his own scholar,
Thou makest even more contemptible than the fowl.

Since by them, man cannot be exempted
From the tax of necessity's urgent demands,

Say then, from all power and dominion soever,
And in empire's sway, what advantage is there?

Unto the opulent, infinite Deity, this is exclusive,
That he is wanting in nothing, whatsoever it be.

The raising up of HAMID, too, shall be effected,
From out of the waves of affliction, and of grief!

# A POEM

### BY ABDUL-HAMID

ALTHOUGH free from grief and sorrow, am I never;
Still, that I meddled in love's affairs, regret I never.

Though my goods be plundered, and my neck stricken,
The one to turn from the moon-faced, am I never.

In the acquirement of a single straw's weight of love,
To be obstructed, by either faith or religion, am I
never.

Whether my head be firmly placed, or be it severed,
The one to rejoice or grieve thereat, am I never.

Though I stake both life and goods, on the heart-
ravishers,
Reproached therefrom, the world before, am I never.

Like one bereaved of his senses, in love's affairs,
Thinking of mine own profit or injury, am I never.

To me, O monitor! say naught regarding patience;
For the ear-giver, unto such speeches, am I never.

Whose sweet face hath not, thus, amazed me ever,
On such a charmer yet, set eyes have I never.

Why should my dear one, on HAMID a kiss bestow,
When, of such beneficence as this, worthy am I never.

∽∾∽∾∽∾∽∾∽∾∽∾∽∾∽∾∽∾∽∾∽∾∽∾

# A POEM

## BY KHUSHHAL KHAN, KHATTAK

By the laughter of the happy and the gay, I vow!
   And by the lamentations of the woe-begone, I
   vow!

By the inebriation of the intoxicated with wine;
And by the piety and abstinence of the monk, I vow!

By the hundred transports of meeting and association,
And by the thousand miseries of separation, I vow!

By the beautiful and fragrant roses of the spring,
And by the sweet melodies of the nightingales, I vow!

Compared to which the graceful cypress is as nothing,
By that tall stature, and form symmetrical, I vow!

That are tinged with the antimony of expression,
By those dark narcissus-like eyes, I vow!

That which is more slender, even than a hair,
By that delicately slight waist of thine, I vow!

On account of which, lovers pine away and die,
By that beauty, and by that elegance, I vow!

By that which cometh from the direction of the
   beloved—
By the balmy breath of the morning breeze I vow!

Who is the bearer of the message for an interview,
By the footsteps of that bearer of glad tidings, I vow!

.    .    .    .    .

With the whole of these many oaths and protestations,
A hundred thousand times again and again, I vow

That I love thee far more dearly than life itself;
And this, by thyself, I, KHUSHHAL, KHATTAK, vow!

## A POEM

### BY ASHRAF KHAN, KHATTAK

Account as wind or as dust, the world's pains
and pleasures:
The free man is not disquieted, by either its troubles
or its cares.

Their coming, and their going, are more speedy than
the dawn;
For I have, myself, experienced the heat and the cold
of time.

Show thou no hankering for the fare on the board of
fortune;
For there is not a morsel thereon, free from bitterness
and woe.

In a moment it produceth forms and figures of mani-
fold fashions—
As a mere throw of the dice account the revolutions
of fate.

Whoso may plume himself on a lucky turn of good
fortune,
It dealeth him a painful wound, at the moment of
exulting thereon.

If, with the eye of understanding, its sorrows and
joys be viewed,
The permanence of their duration is, than that of
the flower no more.

# A POEM

## BY KAZIM KHAN, KHATTAK

OBTAIN for thy requirements the dun steed of the
waves!
In the arena of the flood, practice the horsemanship
of the waves!

The meek and humble, like the oyster, have the pearl
acquired;
But naught of pearl's merchandise, beareth the caravan
of the waves.

The lowly and humble are more powerful than the
haughty and proud:
In the bonds of ocean, for ever confined, will be the
rolling of the waves.

The obstinate and refractory are by the meek and
humble subdued:
The ground-kisser unto the sea-shore is the tempest
of the waves.

See, at what time they will swallow the dark earth
altogether,
On the water's rolling throne seated, the kings of the
waves.

Trouble not the inexperienced and incompetent with
thy affairs:
For upon the target of the waters, become bent the
arrows of waves.

Woe and affliction are salutary to the mind of the
heart-broken;
For firmly fixed, the flood upon, is the foundation of
the waves.

They are the ups and downs of the world : O SHAIDA,
   behold them!
Rising and falling, without ceasing, is the world of
   the waves!

Arabia

# ARABIC LITERATURE

*I*F pre-Islamic poetry in Arabia up to A.D. 622 soared to heights unattained by Singers of a later age, it was not due to the reason that the Arab mind loved and possessed the freedom of thought in any less degree. To whatever age, therefore compositions in Arabic may belong, they show a deep appreciation of the realistic tendencies of human soul "passionately adoring what is of man—his sentiments of love and hate," and ultimately his silent communion to the matters spiritual, which the following translations and compositions by J. D. Carlyle, Ibn Amjed, Sir Charles Lyall, H. W. Freeland, Theodore Preston, W. F. Kirby and Sir Richard Burton amply prove.

~~~~~~~~~~~~~~~~~~~~~~~~~~~~~~~~~~~~~~~~

## THE BATTLE OF SABLA

### BY JAAFER BEN ALBA

SABLA, thou saw'st th' exulting foe
  In fancied triumphs crown'd;
Thou heard'st their frantic females throw
  These galling taunts around :—

" Make now your choice—the terms we give,
  Desponding victims, hear;
These fetters on your hand receive,
  Or in your hearts the spear."

" And is the conflict o'er," we cried,
  " And lie we at your feet?
And dare you vauntingly decide
  The fortune we must meet?

" A brighter day we soon shall see,
  Tho' now the prospect lowers,
And conquest, peace, and liberty
  Shall gild our future hours."

The foe advanc'd :—in firm array
  We rush'd o'er Sabla's sands,
And the red sabre mark'd our way
  Amidst their yielding bands.

Then, as they writh'd in death's cold grasp,
  We cried, " Our choice is made,
These hands the sabre's hilt shall clasp,
  Your hearts shall have the blade."

## MASHDUD ON THE MONKS OF KHABBET

*T*ENANTS of yon hallow'd fane!
　　Let me your devotions share,
There increasing raptures reign—
　　None are ever sober there.

Crowded gardens, festive bowers
　　Ne'er shall claim a thought of mine;
You can give in Khabbet's towers—
　　Purer joys and brighter wine.

Tho' your pallid faces prove
　　How you nightly vigils keep,
'Tis but that you ever love
　　Flowing goblets more than sleep.

Tho' your eye-balls dim and sunk
　　Stream in penitential guise,
'Tis but that the wine you've drunk
　　Bubbles over from your eyes.


## A FRIEND'S BIRTHDAY

*W*HEN born in tears we saw thee drown'd,
　　While thine assembled friends around,
　　With smiles their joy confest;
So live, that at thy parting hour,
They may the flood of sorrow pour,
　　And thou in smiles be drest!

## ON THE VICISSITUDES OF LIFE
### BY THE CALIPH RADHI BILLAH

Mortal joys, however pure,
    Soon their turbid source betray;
Mortal bliss, however sure,
    Soon must totter and decay.

Ye who now, with footsteps keen,
    Range through hope's delusive field,
Tell us what the smiling scene
    To your ardent grasp can yield?

Other youths have oft before
    Deem'd their joys would never fade,
Till themselves were seen no more
    Swept into oblivion's shade.

Who, with health and pleasure gay,
    E'er his fragile state could know,
Were not age and pain to say
    Man is but the child of woe?

## THE VALE OF BOZAA

### BY AHMED BEN YOUSEF ALMENAZY

THE intertwining boughs for thee
 Have wove, sweet dell, a verdant vest,
And thou in turn shalt give to me
 A verdant couch upon thy breast.

To shield me from day's fervid glare
 Thine oaks their fostering arms extend,
As anxious o'er her infant care
 I've seen a watchful mother bend.

A brighter cup, a sweeter draught,
 I gather from that rill of thine,
Than maddening drunkards ever quaff'd,
 Than all the treasures of the vine.

So smooth the pebbles on its shore,
 That not a maid can thither stray,
But counts her strings of jewels o'er,
 And thinks the pearls have slipp'd away.

∽∽∽∽∽∽∽∽∽∽∽∽∽∽∽∽∽∽∽∽∽∽∽∽∽

## TO YOUTH

### BY EBN ALRABIA

*Y*ES, youth, thou'rt fled, and I am left,
 Like yonder desolated bower,
By winter's ruthless hand bereft
 Of every leaf and every flower.

With heaving heart and streaming eyes
 I woo'd thee to prolong thy stay,
But vain were all my tears and sighs,
 Thou only fled'st more fast away.

Yet tho' thou fled'st away so fast,
 I can recall thee if I will;
For I can talk of what is past,
 And while I talk, enjoy thee still.

## AL-FIND OF THE BANU ZIMMAN

*F*ORGIVENESS had we for Hind's sons:
 we said: "The men our brothers are:
The Days may bring that yet again
 they be the folk that once they were."

But when the Ill stood clear and plain,
 and naked Wrong was bare to-day,
And nought was left but bitter Hate—
 we paid them in the coin they gave.

We strode as stalks a lion forth
 at dawn, a lion wrathful-eyed;
Blows rained we, dealing shame on shame,
 and humbling pomp and quelling pride.

Too kind a man may be with fools,
 and move them but to flout him more;
And Mischief oft may bring thee peace
 when Mildness works not Folly's cure.

## BASHAMAH SON OF HAZN OF NAHSHAL

WE give thee greeting, O Salmá: do thou give us greeting back; and if thou givest the cup to the noblest, reach it to us!

And if thou callest one day to a mighty and valiant deed the chiefest of noble men, let thy call go forth to us.

Sons of Nahshal are we: no father we claim but him, nor would he sell us for any other sons.

When a goal of glory is set and the runners rush forth thereto, of us shalt thou find in the race the foremost and the next.

And never there comes to die a mighty man of our line, but we wean among us a boy to be mighty in his stead.

Cheap do we hold our lives when the day of dread befalls; but if we should set them for sale in peace, they would cost men dear.

White are our foreheads and worn: for ever our cauldrons boil: we heal with our rich store the wounds our hands have made.

I come of a house whose elders have fallen one by one as they sprang to the cry of the fighters—" Where are the helpers now?"

If there should be among a thousand but one of us, and men should call—" Ho! a knight!" he would think that they meant him.

When the fighters blench and quail before the deadly stroke of the sword-edge, we leap forth and catch it in our hands.

Never shalt thou see them, though their loss be great and sore, weeping among the weepers over him that is dead!

Many a time we bestride the steed of peril and death, but our valour bears us back safe, and the swords that help us well.

〜〜〜〜〜〜〜〜〜〜〜〜〜〜〜〜〜〜〜〜〜〜〜

# HITTAN SON OF AL-MU'ALLA OF TAYYI

FORTUNE has brought me down—her wonted way—
   from station great and high to low estate;
Fortune has rent away my plenteous store;
   of all my wealth honour alone is left.
Fortune has turned my joy to tears; how oft
   did Fortune make me laugh with what she gave!
But for these girls, the *kata's* downy brood,
   unkindly thrust from door to door as hard—
Far would I roam and wide to seek my bread
   in Earth that has no lack of breadth and length.
Nay, but our children in our midst, what else
   but our hearts are they, walking on the ground?
If but the breeze blow harsh on one of them,
   mine eye says no to slumber all night long.

## SA'D SON OF MALIK, OF THE TRIBE
## OF KAIS SON OF THA'LABAH, OF
## BAKR

How evil a thing is War, that bows men to shameful
rest!
War burns away in her blaze all glory and boasting of
men :
Nought stands but the valiant heart to face pain, the hard-
hoofed steed,
The ring-mail set close and firm, the nail-crowned helms
and the spears,
And onset again after rout, when men shrink from the
serried array—
Then, then, fall away all the vile, the hirelings, and Shame
is strong!
War girds up her skirts before them, and Evil unmixed
is bare.
For their hearts were for maidens veiled, not for driving
the gathered spoil :
Yea, evil the heirs we leave, sons of Yashkur and al-Lakah!

But let flee her fires who will, no flinching for me, son
of Kais!
O children of Kais, stand firm before her, gain peace or
give :
Who seeks flight before her hear, his Doom stands and
bars the road.
Away! Death allows no quitting of place, and brands are
bare!
What is life for us when the Uplands and valleys are ours
no more ?
Ah, where are the mighty now, the spears and the generous
hands ?

## IYAS SON OF AL-ARATT, OF TAYYA

*C*OME friend and fellow, come—for sometimes is
　Folly sweet! so come, let us greet our band of
　drinkers aglow with wine,
And wash from our hearts sour speech of wisdom with
　cups abrim, and cut short the ills of Life with laughter
　and jest and joy!
Yea, when once a moment comes of rest from the whirl,
　be quick and grasp it : for Time's tooth bites and quits
　not, and mischief waits ;
And sure, if a bright hour lifts thy soul to a little peace,
　enough in thy path there lies of shadow and grief and
　pain!

## FROM THE DIWAN OF AN-NABIGHAH

He had dwelt long at the court of an-Nu'man son of al-Mundhir, the last
king of al-Hirah, who greatly admired his poems; but the king having been
led by the malice of the poet's enemies to withdraw his favour from him, an-
Nabighah fearing for his life fled from al-Hirah to his home; thence he betook
himself to the court of Ghassan in Syria, where he praised the king, 'Amr son
of al-Harith al-A'raj, in this poem.

Leave me alone, O Umaimah—alone with my sleepless
    pain—alone with the lifelong night and its wearily
    lingering stars ;
It draws on its length of gloom ; methinks it will never
    end, nor ever the Star-herd lead his flock to their fold
    for rest ;
——Alone with a breast whose griefs that roamed far
    afield by day the darkness has all brought home : in
    legions they throng around.


A favour I have with 'Amr, a favour his father bore
    toward me of old, a grace that carried no scorpion's
    sting.
I swear, and my word is true—an oath that has no reserve,
    and nought in my heart is hid save fair thought of him
    my friend—
If those twain his fathers were who lie in their graves,
    the one at Jillik, the other there at Saida by Harib's side,
And Harith of Jafnah's line, the Lord of his folk of old—
    yea, surely his might shall reach the home of his
    enemy!
In him hope is sure of help when men say—" The host
    is sped, the horsemen of Ghassan's line unblemished,
    no hireling herd,
His cousins, all near of kin, their chief 'Amr, 'Amir's son
    —a people are they whose might in battle shall never
    fail! "
When goes forth their host to war, above them in circles
    wheel battalions of eagles, pointing the path to bat-
    talions more :

Their friendship is old and tried—fast comrades in foray, bred to look unafraid on blood, as hounds to the chase well trained.

Behold them, how they sit there, behind where the armies meet, watching with eyes askance, like elders in grey furs wrapt,

Intent: for they know full well that those whom they follow, when the clash of the hosts shall come, will bear off the victory.

Ay, well is their custom known, a usage that Time has proved, when lances are laid in rest on withers of steeds arow—

Of steeds in the spear-play killed, with lips for the fight drawn back, their bodies with wounds all scarred, some bleeding and some half-healed.

And down leap the riders where the battle is strait and stern, and spring in the face of Death like stallions amid the herd;

Between them they give and take deep draughts of the wine of Doom as their hands ply the white swords, thin and keen in the smiting-edge.

In shards fall the morions, burst by the fury of blow on blow, and down to the eyebrows cleft fly shattered beneath the skulls.

In them no defect is found, save only that in their swords are notches a many, gained from smiting of host on host;

An heirloom of old, those blades, from the fight of Halimah's Day, and many the mellay fierce that since has their temper proved;

Therewith do they cleave in twain the haulberk of double woof, and kindle the rock beneath to fire ere the stroke is done.

A nature is theirs, God gives the like to no other men— a wisdom that never sleeps, a bounty that never fails.

Their home is in God's own land, His chosen of old; their faith is steadfast; their hope is set on nought but the World to come.

Their sandals are solf and fine, and girded with chastity
their welcome with garlands sweet the dawn of the
Feast of Palms.

There greets them when they come home full many a
handmaid fair, and ready on trestles hang the mantles
of scarlet silk;

Yes, softly they wrap their limbs, well knowing of wealth
and ease, in rich raiment, white-sleeved, green at the
shoulder in royal guise,

They look not on Weal as men who know not that Woe
comes too: they look not on evil days as though they
should never mend.


Lo, this was my gift of praise to Ghassan, what time I
sought my people, and all my paths were darkened,
and strait my ways.

## LAMENT FOR LOSS OF SIGHT

### BY AL-ASWAD BIN JAFAR

IF now thou seest me a wreck, worn out and minished
of sight, and all my limbs without strength to bear my
body along,

And I am deaf to the calls of love and lightness of youth,
and follow wisdom in meekness, my steps easy to guide—

Time was I went every night, hair combed, to sellers of
wine, and squandered lightly my wealth, compliant,
easy of mood.

Yea, once I played, and enjoyed the sweetest flavour of
youth, my wine the first of the grape, mingled with
purest of rain—

Wine bought from one with a twang in his speech, and
rings in his ears, a belt girt round him; he brought
forth for good silver coin.

A boy deals it to our guests, girt up, two pearls in his
ears, his fingers ruddy, as though stained deep with
mulberry juice,

And women white like the moon or statues stately to see,
that softly carry around great cups filled full with the
wine—

White women, dainty, that shoot the hearts of men with
their eyes, fair as a nest full of ostrich eggs betwixt rock
and sand.

Kind words they speak, and their limbs are soft and smooth
to the touch, their faces bright, and their hearts to lovers
gentle and mild.

Low speech they murmur, in tones that bear no secrets
abroad; they gain their ends without toil, and need no
shouting to win.

I lie as though Time had shot my shape with darts un-
awares winged sure to pierce me, unfeathered, sent
from no bow-string.

What man can hope for a guard against the Daughters of
Time? what spells avail to defeat the fated onset of
Doom?

They closed my eyes—but it was not sleep that held them from sight: one said who stood by—" He's gone, the Son of al-Khadhdhaq! "

They combed my hair—but it was not because it hung unkempt, and then they clad me in clothes that bore no signs of wear.

They sprayed sweet odours on me, and said—" How goodly a man! " then wrapped my form in a white sheet closely folded around;

And then they sent of their best, young men of gentle descent, to lay my limbs in a grave dug deep out there in the dust.

Grieve not for me overmuch: let sorrow pass as it will; the wealth I left shall rejoice—why not?—the heart of my heir.

# GLEANINGS FROM THE ARABIC
## PARAPHRASE

### THE LAMENT OF MAISUN, THE BEDOUIN WIFE OF
### MUAWIYA

*J* GIVE thee all the treacherous brightness
    Of glittering robes which grace the fair,
Then give me back my young heart's lightness
    And simple vest of Camel's hair.
The tent on which free winds are beating
    Is dearer to the Desert's child
Than Palaces and kingly greeting—
    O bear me to my desert wild!
More dear than swift mule softly treading,
    While gentlest hands his speed control,
Are camels rough their lone way threading
    Where caravans through deserts roll.
On couch of silken ease reclining
    I watch the kitten's sportive play,
But feel the while my young heart pining
    For desert guests and watch-dog's bay.
The frugal desert's banquet slender,
    The simple crust which tents afford,
Are dearer than the courtly splendour
    And sweets which grace a monarch's board.
And dearer far the voices pealing
    From winds which sweep the desert round
Than Pomp and Power their pride revealing
    In noisy timbrel's measur'd sound.
Then bear me far from kingly dwelling,
    From Luxury's cold and pamper'd child,
To seek a heart with freedom swelling,
    A kindred heart in deserts wild.

# THE FOOD OF PARADISE

## By Ibn Amjed

*I*N the school founded by the Caliph for the study of divine things sat the devout Mullah Ibrahim, his hands folded in his lap, in an attitude of meditation. Ibrahim taught students from all the countries of Islam, but the work was thankless and ill-paid. And as he sat there he thought on his state for the first time in many years.

"Why is it," he said to himself, "that a man so holy as I am must toil so hard to instruct a pack of blockheads, when others who have merited nothing through piety or attention to the commands of Allah fare sumptuously every day and neither toil nor spin? O, Compassionate One, is not this thing unjust? Whereof should Thy servant be burdened, like an ass in the market-place, which carries two panniers both filled to the top and stumbles at every blow of the driver's stick?"

And as he considered, Ibrahim the Wise, as men called him, brought to mind that verse in the Holy Literature in which it says: "Allah will not let any one starve." And taking deeper counsel with himself, he said: "May it not be that those whom I have blamed for their sloth and inactivity are, after all, the better Moslems, that they have greater faith than I? For, perusing this passage, they may have said to themselves: 'I will cast myself upon the mercy of Allah, which in this text is surely extended to all men. Allah in his bounty will surely feed and maintain me.' Why then toil and strive as the faithless do? It is those who have faith that are the elect."

At that moment a great pasha halted before the gates of the seminary, in his piety alighting from his palanquin to give alms to a beggar, as all good Moslems do. And as Ibrahim watched him through the lattice, he thought: " Does not the condition of the beggar as well as that of this pasha prove the justice of the text upon which I have been meditating? Neither starves, but the wealthier man is assuredly the more devout, for he is the giver and not the receiver, and for this very purpose has been blest with the goods of this world. Why do I hesitate, wretched man that I am? Shall I not, as the Book ordains, cast myself on the bounty of Allah and free myself for ever from the intolerable burden of instructing fools in a wisdom they can never understand?"

So saying, Ibrahim the Sage arose from his place in the College of the Caliph, and walked out of the City of Baghdad where he had dwelt for many years. It was evening, and betaking himself to the banks of the river, he selected a dry and shady spot beneath a spreading cypress tree, and, awaiting the bounty of Allah, fell fast asleep in the certainty that the Lord of all Compassion would not fail him.

When he awoke, it was early morning, and a divine hush lay upon everything. Ibrahim lazily speculated as to the manner in which he would be sustained. Would the birds of the air bring him sustenance, would the fishes from the stream leap ashore, offering themselves for the assuagement of his growing hunger? In what way did those who merited the help of Allah first receive it, if not in some miraculous manner? True, the wealthy were bequeathed riches by their parents. But there must be a beginning. A pasha might sail down the river in his barge and supply his wants out of golden dishes and silver cups.

But morning blossomed into day and day into night and still the miracle remained unaccomplished. More than one pasha glided past him in his gilded barge, but these made only the customary salutations and gave no other sign. On the road above pilgrims and travellers passed, but without taking the least notice of him. Hunger gnawed

at his vitals, and he thought with envy of the millet por-
ridge with goats' milk the mullahs would now be enjoying
at the seminary. Still was he trustful, and, as he made the
customary ablutions in the river, his faith had abated not
one jot.

Again he slept, and once more day dawned in scarlet
and silver beauty. By this time he felt so faint as scarcely
to be able to stand. The hours crept slowly onward, yet
no sign came that his hunger was to be satisfied.

At last, as midday approached with its stifling heat,
something floating upon the surface of the water caught
his eye. It seemed like a mass of leaves wrapped up with
fibre, and wading into the river he succeeded in catching
it. Back he splashed with his prize to the bank, and sitting
down on the sward, he opened the packet. It contained a
quantity of the most delicious-looking *halwa*, that famous
marzipan, of the making of which only Baghdad knows
the secret, a sweetmeat composed of sugar mingled with
paste of almonds and attar of roses and other delicate and
savoury essences.

After gorging himself with the delightful fare, Ibrahim
the Wise drank deeply from the river, and lolled on the
sward, sure that his prayer had been answered, and that
he would never have to toil more. There was sufficient
of the ambrosial food to serve for three meals a day, and
on each day after the hour of midday prayer a similar
packet of *halwa* came floating down the stream as though
placed there by the hands of angels.

"Surely," said the Mullah, "the promises of Allah are
true, and the man who trusts in Him will not be deceived.
Truly I did well to leave the seminary, where, day-in,
day-out, I had perforce to cram divine knowledge into
the heads of idiots incapable of repeating a verse correctly
even at the fifteenth attempt."

Months passed, and Ibrahim continued to receive the
food that Allah had promised with unfailing regularity.
Then, quite naturally, he began to speculate whence it
came. If he could find the spot where it was deposited

on the surface of the stream, surely he must witness a miracle, and as he had never done so, he felt greatly desirous of attaining the merit such a consummation would undoubtedly add to his fame as a holy man.

So one morning, after eating the last of the *halwa* he had received on the preceding day, he girded up his loins, and taking his staff, began slowly to walk up-stream. " Now," said he, " if what I suppose be true, I will to-day receive my luscious food at an earlier hour than usual, as I shall be nearer the place where it is deposited on the water, and indeed on each day I shall receive at an even earlier hour, until at last I come to the spot where some divine seraph, sent by Allah from Paradise, drops the savoury food of heaven upon the stream in justification of my trust in the most Merciful."

For some days Ibrahim walked up-stream, keeping carefully to the bank of the river and fixing his eyes on its surface in case he should fail to discern the packet of *halwa*. But every day at an ever earlier hour, it floated regularly past him, carried by the current so near to the shore that he could easily wade out and secure it. At nights he slept beneath a convenient tree, and as men perceived him to be a mullah and a sacred man, no one thought of molesting him.

It was on the fourth day of his journey that he observed the river had widened. In a large island in the midst of the stream rose a fair castle. The island composed a princely domain of noble meadow-land and rich garden, crossed and interlaced by the silver of narrow streams, and was backed by the blue and jagged peaks of great mountains. The castle itself was built of marble white as sculptured ice, and its green and shady lawns sloped down to a silent and forlorn shore of golden sand.

And when night descended this wondrous region was illuminated by the romance of moonlight into an almost unearthly radiance, so that Ibrahim in all his piety was forced to compare it with Paradise itself. The white castle on its dark rocks seemed like day pedestalled upon night, and from the sea-green of the shadow of myrtles rose the peaks of pavilions whence came the sound of guitars and lutes and voices more ravishingly sweet than Ibrahim, the son of the seminary, had ever believed earth could hold.

And as Ibrahim gazed spellbound at the wondrous spectacle and drank in the sounds of ecstasy which arose from the garden, wondering whether he were not already dead and in the purlieus of Heaven, a harsh voice hailed him at his very elbow, asking him what he did there. He turned swiftly, to see standing beside him an ancient man in the garb of a hermit, with long matted hair and tangled beard.

" Salaam, good father," he said, much relieved, for, like all men of peace, he feared violence. " The peace of Allah, the Merciful, the Compassionate, be upon you."

" And upon you, my son," replied the anchorite. " But what do you here at this hour of the night, when all such as you should be asleep ? "

" Like yourself, I am a holy man," replied Ibrahim, with unction, " but I travel on a quest the nature of which I may not divulge to any. Passing this spot, I was attracted by the unusual appearance of yonder castle and its surroundings, and would learn its history, if that is known to you."

" It is, though in part only," rejoined the hermit, " for I have dwelt many years in this neighbourhood, but have little converse with men. Know, then, that the place you behold is called the Silver Castle. It was built by a pasha now dead, who was greatly enamoured of a certain princess, whose father refused him her hand in marriage. But, not to be gainsaid, so fierce and unruly a thing is love in some men, he built this strength in the midst of the river as you see, and placed upon it so many dark and terrible spells of magic that none could cross to or from it without his sanction. Then, abducting the princess, he espoused her and placed her in yonder tower. The King, her father, came with an army to besiege the place, but so potent were the necromancies the pasha had surrounded it with that he was compelled to raise the siege and leave his daughter in the hands of his enemy."

"You amaze me," cried Ibrahim. "And does this princess remain here still?"

"No, brother," replied the hermit, "like her lord she has passed away, but they have left behind them a daughter who governs the castle, a lady of surpassing beauty, who spends her days in pleasure and in spending the wealth her father bequeathed her. But she has but one sorrow, and that is that none can dissolve the spells woven by her father the pasha, so that no one may either gain admittance to the castle or leave it. Her companions are therefore either the very aged or those born on the island and no other, which, for a young and beautiful woman, must be wearisome. But you will pardon me, brother, I am going on a pilgrimage to a certain shrine in Baghdad, where I betake myself once a year to acquire merit. Meanwhile, if you choose to rest, you may dwell in my humble cell yonder until I return in seven days' time."

Ibrahim gladly accepted the hermit's offer, and when he had gone, sat down to ponder over the tale he had told him. Now, among other wisdoms, he had acquired during his years of study a deep knowledge of the magical art, and he bethought him that it might be given to him to rid the castle and its inhabitants of the spells which held them prisoner on the island.

But in the midst of his thoughts he fell asleep, and did not waken until the sun was high in the heavens. Then he made his ablutions, and betook himself to the banks of the river, where he sat and watched the surface of the water for a sign of the appearance of the delicious food he received daily.

And as he watched, he beheld a curious thing. Some three hours before midday a very beautiful woman appeared on the marble battlements which overhung the river. So fair was she that the Mullah gasped with surprise at the radiance of her beauty, which was that of the houris of Paradise. For her hair was as golden wire which is drawn thin by the cunning of the goldsmith, her eyes were yellow, and bright as topazes found on Mount Ararat, and the colour of her cheeks was as that of the roses of Isfahan. And as for the flesh of her body, it shone with the lustre of silver, so brightly polished it was.

" Can this be the Princess ? " thought Ibrahim, " or an angel from heaven ? Nay, surely it is she, for this woman, though beautiful surpassingly, is still a mortal."

And as Ibrahim stood beholding her, she raised her arm and cast something into the river. And when she had done so, she withdrew from the battlements and disappeared like a planet behind clouds.

The Mullah kept his eyes fixed on that which she had cast into the stream, and in a little perceived that it was the very packet of leaves which he was wont to receive daily. Wading into the stream he secured it, unwrapped it, and found it full of the delicious *halwa*, as usual.

" Ha," said he, as he devoured the savoury sweetmeat. " So now I know at last that radiant being by whose hands Allah, the Just, the Merciful, has ordained I shall be fed daily. Truly, the Compassionate must have put it into the heart of this divine princess to cast this luscious food on the breast of the stream at the self-same hour each day. And shall I not seek to repay her the distinguished kindness she has done me by freeing her from the spells by which she is encompassed, and which keep her prisoner, she who should be wed to a Sultan at least and should reign in Baghdad itself ? "

And with these grateful thoughts, he sat down to consider by what means the spells which surrounded the castle might be broken. And, casting himself into a deep trance, he walked in spirit in the Land of the Jinn, where, as a holy man, he could come to no harm. And coming to the house of one of the Jinn, whom he knew and whose name was Adhem, he summoned him and had speech with him.

" Hail, holy man," said Adhem, making low obeisance. " I am your servant. In what way can I serve you ? "

Ibrahim acquainted him with the reason for his presence there, at which the Jinn assumed an air of the greatest concern.

"What you ask is indeed hard, most wise Ibrahim," he said doubtfully. "But I will take counsel of my brethren on the matter without delay, and shall let you know the result of our deliberations by a speedy and trusty messenger. No more can I say or do at present."

With this Ibrahim departed and soon after awoke from his trance. He seemed only to have been an hour in the Land of the Jinn, but it must have been five hours or more, for the sun was high in the heavens when he fell asleep, and now moonlight was sparkling on the waters of the river. And the same exquisite music he had heard before arose from the gardens of the castle, as though from the lips of peris.

And as Ibrahim listened entranced, a shape scarcely more solid than the moonlight rose slowly out of the river and stood before him in the shadowy likeness of a Jinn. Three times it made obeisance before him, then it spoke.

"Most wise and holy Ibrahim," it said, "my master Adhem, a prince among the people of the Jinn, has sent me to acquaint you with the decision of his counsellors. They proffer you this ring set with the diamond which men call adamant, and in whose shining surface if you will gaze, you shall behold the nature of those spells which keep the Princess and her train prisoners in yonder castle. And, having discovered the nature of those spells, if you summon our people to your aid in such shapes as will dissolve or break them they will come in such guise as will set the Princess free."

With those words the Jinn vanished into the river whence he had come. And, without delay, Ibrahim took the ring which the spirit had cast on the grass at his feet, and peered into the shining stone it held.

And straightway he beheld the first spell. Close to the shore of the river arose a mighty bastion as of stone, invisible to mortal eyes, which surrounded the castle from shore to shore. And Ibrahim summoned to him the hosts of the Jinn in the guise of sappers, with picks and hammers, and on this wall they fell mightily in their myriads, so that without sound or clamour of any sort, they reduced it to dust ere a man could count a hundred.

Then Ibrahim looked once more in the surface of the diamond, and saw a great web like that of a spider hanging in the air round the castle. And he summoned the hosts of the Jinn in the shape of eagles, which so rent at the invisible web with their strong beaks that in less time than it takes to tell of it, almost, it fell in fragments into the stream.

Once more Ibrahim gazed into the stone, and this time he saw an army of viewless giants, with spear and scimitar in hand, drawn up in array of war on the shores of the island. And he called the Jinn people to him in the likeness of greater and more powerful giants, who did battle with those on the island. Terrible was the strife, and Ibrahim trembled mightily as he watched it. But soon the Jinn prevailed over the giants of the island, and put them to flight.

The spells which had surrounded the castle were now removed, and as day had dawned, Ibrahim cast about for some means of reaching the castle. No sooner had he wished this than by the power of the Jinn a bridge rose out of the stream by which he was enabled to cross to the island. And when he had done so, he was accosted by an old man who held a bared scimitar in his hand, and who asked him by what means he had been enabled to reach the island, which had so long been under enchantment.

"That I may tell only to your lady, the Princess," said Ibrahim. "Admit me to her presence without delay."

The guard, marvelling, ushered him through the great gate of the castle, and across a spacious court where fountains sang mellifluously. Entering a magnificent hall, the floor of which was inlaid with squares of blue and white marble and the walls with lapis lazuli and other rare stones, he gave the Mullah into the keeping of a black eunuch, who requested the holy man to follow him.

Upon a dais sat the incomparable Princess whom Ibrahim had beheld on the battlements, and who daily cast the packet of *halwa* on the waters of the river. To her the Mullah made obeisance, and, kneeling before her, told his tale.

"And what, most wise Ibrahim, do you ask in recompense of your so notable offices on my behalf?" asked the Princess. "Speak, and it shall be granted to you, even to the half of my inheritance."

"Nay, noble lady," exclaimed Ibrahim. "For have I not reason enow to be grateful to your Highness for the delicious food with which you have fed me daily? That *halwa* which you cast every morning from the battlements, and which has floated down the stream I have eaten with thankfulness. Surely only an angel from Paradise could have put it into your heart to despatch it."

The Princess blushed so deeply that her heightened colour could be seen even beneath her veil.

"Alas, good Mullah!" she cried, wringing her hands. "What is this you tell me? Curses on the day on which I first cast that *halwa* as you call it, on the waters of the river. Know, that each morning it is my custom to take a bath of milk, after which I anoint and rub my limbs with essence of almonds, sugar and sweet-scented cosmetics. These, then, I remove from my nakedness and, wrapping them in leaves, cast them into the stream."

"Ah, now, Princess, I see who has been blind," cried Ibrahim, with a wry countenance. "Allah surely gives food to everyone; but its quality and kind are dictated by what man deserves!"

# THE KASÎDAH OF HÂJÎ ABÛ
## AL-YAZDI

THE hour is nigh; the waning Queen walks forth
    to rule the later night;
Crown'd with the sparkle of a Star, and throned on orb
    of ashen light:

The Wolf-tail sweeps the paling East to leave a deeper
    gloom behind,
And Dawn uprears her shining head, sighing with sem-
    blance of a wind:

The highlands catch yon Orient gleam, while purpling
    still the lowlands lie;
And pearly mists, the morning-pride, soar incense-like to
    greet the sky.

The horses neigh, the camels groan, the torches gleam, the
    cressets flare;
The town of canvas falls, and man with din and dint
    invadeth air:

The Golden Gates swing right and left; up springs the
    Sun with flamy brow;
The dew-cloud melts in gush of light; brown Earth is
    bathed in morning-glow.

Slowly they wind athwart the wild, and while young Day
    his anthem swells,
Sad falls upon my yearning ear the tinkling of the Camel-
    bells:

O'er fiery waste and frozen wold, o'er horrid hill and
    gloomy glen,
The home of grisly beast and Ghûl, the haunts of wilder,
    grislier men;—

With the brief gladness of the Palms, that tower and sway
    o'er seething plain,
Fraught with the thoughts of rustling shade, and welling
    spring, and rushing rain;

With the short solace of the ridge, by gentle zephyrs
    played upon,
Whose breezy head and bosky side front seas of cooly
    celadon;—

'Tis theirs to pass with joy and hope, whose souls shall
    ever thrill and fill
Dreams of the Birthplace and the Tomb,—visions of
    Allah's Holy Hill.

But we? Another shift of scene, another pang to rack
    the heart;
Why meet we on the bridge of Time to 'change one
    greeting and to part?

We meet to part; yet asks my sprite, Part we to meet?
    Ah! is it so?
Man's fancy-made Omniscience knows, who made Om-
    niscience nought can know.

Why must we meet, why must we part, why must we
    bear this yoke of MUST,
Without our leave or askt or given, by tyrant Fate on
    victim thrust?

That Eve so gay, so bright, so glad; this Morn so dim,
    and sad, and grey;
Strange that life's Registrar should write this day a day,
    that day a day!

Mine eyes, my brain, my heart, are sad,—sad is the very
    core of me;
All wearies, changes, passes, ends; alas! the Birthday's
    injury!

Friends of my youth, a last adieu! haply some day we
meet again;
Yet ne'er the self-same men shall meet; the years shall
make us other men:

The light of morn has grown to noon, has paled with
eve, and now farewell!
Go, vanish from my Life as dies the tinkling of the Camel's
bell.

   .    .    .    .    .

In these drear wastes of sea-born land, these wilds where
none may dwell but He,
What visionary Pasts revive, what process of the Years
we see:

Gazing beyond the thin blue line that rims the far horizon-
ring,
Our sadden'd sight why haunt these ghosts, whence do
these spectral shadows spring?

What endless questions vex the thought, of Whence and
Whither, When and How?
What fond and foolish strife to read the Scripture writ
on human brow;

As stand we percht on point of Time, betwixt the two
Eternities,
Whose awful secrets gathering round with black profound
oppress our eyes.

" This gloomy night, these grisly waves, these winds and
whirlpools loud and dread.
What reck they of our wretched plight who Safety's shore
so lightly tread? "

Thus quoth the Bard of Love and Wine, whose dream of
Heaven ne'er could rise
Beyond the brimming Kausar-cup and Houris with the
white-black eyes;

Ah me! my race of threescore years is short, but long
    enough to pall
My senses with joyless joys as these, with Love and
    Houris, Wine and all.

Another boasts he would divorce old barren Reason from
    his bed,
And wed the Vine-maid in her stead;—fools who believe
    a word he said!

And "'Dust thou art to dust returning,' ne'er was spoke
    of human soul,"
The Sûfi cries, 'tis well for him that hath such gift to ask
    its goal.

"And this is all, for this we're born to weep a little and
    to die!"
So sings the shallow bard whose life still labours at the
    letter "I."

"Ear never heard, Eye never saw the bliss of those who
    enter in
My heavenly kingdom," Isâ said, who wailed our sorrows
    and our sin:

Too much of words or yet too few! What to thy God-
    head easier than
One little glimpse of Paradise to ope the eyes and ears of
    man?

"I am the Truth! I am the Truth!" we hear the God-
    drunk gnostic cry
"The microcosm abides in ME; Eternal Allah's nought
    but I!"

Mansûr was wise, but wiser they who smote him with the
    hurlèd stoned;
And, though his blood a witness bore, no wisdom-might
    could mend his bones.

" Eat, drink, and sport; the rest of life's not worth a
fillip," quoth the King;
Methinks the saying saith too much : the swine would say
the self-same thing!

Two-footed beasts that browse through life, by Death
to serve as soil design'd,
Bow prone to Earth whereof they be, and there the proper
pleasures find :

But you of finer, nobler stuff, ye, whom to Higher leads
the High,
What binds your hearts in common bond with creatures
of the stall and sty?

" In certain hope of Life-to-come I journey through this
shifting scene "
The Zâhid snarls and saunters down his Vale of Tears
with confi'dent mien.

Wiser than Amrân's Son art thou, who ken'st so well the
world-to-be,
The Future when the Past is not, the Present merest
dreamery ;

What know'st thou, man, of Life? and yet, for ever
twixt the womb, the grave,
Thou pratest of the Coming Life, of Heav'n and Hell
thou fain must rave."

The world is old and thou art young; the world is large
and thou art small;
Cease, atom of a moment's span, to hold thyself an
All-in-All!

Fie, fie! you visionary things, ye motes that dance in
sunny glow,
Who base and build Eternities on briefest moment here
below;

Who pass through Life like cagèd birds, the captives of
    a despot will;
Still wond'ring How and When and Why, and Whence
    and Whither, wond'ring still;

Still wond'ring how the Marvel came because two coupling
    mammals chose
To slake the thirst of fleshly love, and thus the " Immortal
    Being " rose;

Wond'ring the Babe with staring eyes, perforce compel'd
    from night to day,
Gript on the giant grasp of Life like gale-born dust or
    wind-wrung spray;

Who comes imbecile to the world 'mid double danger,
    groans, and tears;
The toy, the sport, the waif and stray of passions, error,
    wrath and fears;

Who knows not Whence he came nor Why, who kens
    not Whither bound and When,
Yet such is Allah's choicest gift, the blessing dreamt by
    foolish men;

Who step by step perforce returns to countless youth,
    wan, white, and cold,
Lisping again his broken words till all the tale be fully
    told.

# ED-DIMIRYAHT

## Book I—The Kingdom of Jinneesthan

### *Canto III*

#### THE COUNCIL OF KINGS

*E*L Hahrith from his throne at length arose,
And all was silence, and his voice alone
In that wide hall was heard, as thus he spoke:
"King of the Jinn, the son of Jarjarees
Before you stands; my elder brethren fell
By Allah's minions murdered, in the fight
In which my father died. Remember ye
How mighty was the strength of Jarjarees,
And how he must have overcome his foes,
If some who meanly dreaded Allah's wrath,
And some who feared that Jarjarees would seize
The kingdoms which they ne'er deserved to rule,
Had not in fear or malice, kept aloof
Far from the din of war? On them be shame!
The power of Jarjarees was overthrown,
And since his death no king has ever dared
To war with Allah, or proclaim himself
The leader of the monarchs of the Jinn.
Kings, hither called by me, I bid you choose
A Chieftain who shall fill my father's throne,
And wage with Allah never-ceasing war.
Whom therefore should you choose beside myself,
The sole surviving son of Jarjarees?
My father's magic armour I possess,
And you shall swear to aid me with your arms,
Till Allah and his servants perish all,
Or abdicate in fear their thrones of light,
And vainly seek to hide from us in Hell.
Take then the oath. My troops are all around,
And no one shall refuse, for am not I
The only hero who refused to stoop
Before a thing of earth which Allah made?

And think you with an army at my back,
That such as I will brook the insolence,
Of any monarch here who dares rebel
Against the son of Mighty Jarjarees?
Kings of the Jinn, ye take the oath or die!"
    The Kings who served his father crowded round
And bent the knee before him, but the Kings
Who would not follow Jarjarees to war,
And those who never knew that rebel Chief,
Stood all irresolute; they did not dare
To war with Allah, yet the troops around
Stood waiting but the word to slay them all.
    Thus long had Ed-Dimiryaht silent stood,
But now he stepped among the wavering kings,
And thus addressed them: "Princes, do not fear
The threats of Iblees. I am sent from Heaven
To save you from his vengeance, and I grasp
The sword of Azraeel."
                    Then he forced his way
Among the amazed and unresisting guards,
Until he stood before the throne, where sat
The rebel Iblees, when again he spoke:
"El Hahrith, though your soul is black with sin,
Yet Allah's pardon waits for you if you come,
And yield to him in peace. Reflect awhile.
Almighty is the King whom once you served,
And how shall you oppose him? Know you not,
That had the righteous monarchs of the Jinn
Declared themselves allies of Jarjarees,
Yet Allah's forces must have conquered all?
You may indeed maintain your ground awhile,
Though struggling blindly in the hand of God,
For he may wisely let you rule awhile,
That greater good from evil may result.
But fear you not the Trumpet? Fear you not
The Sword of Azraeel?"
                    Iblees heard, and sat
A moment silent, while a smile of scorn

Flashed like the lurid lightning o'er his face:
"I reck not what befalls," at length he cried,
"For Allah is my mortal enemy.
But lo, before you, monarchs of the Jinn,
You see a greater God than Allah's self,
In me. O Ed-Dimiryaht, dare you come
To counsel me to stoop before a King
Whom I despise? But you shall see my power,
For I have here a prisoner who has lain
In chains to wait my wrath. Prepare yourselves,
O ye rebellious Kings, to yield or die.
Go, bring Marjahneh hither!"
                  Thus he spoke,
And Ed-Dimiryaht deigned not to reply:
But round him thronged the Kings who would not stoop
To Iblees, and with no divided voice,
Proclaimed him King of the Believing Jinn.
The troops of Iblees every sword unsheathed,
Expecting his command to hew them down,
When harsh the clanking of a chain was heard,
And calm and self-collected even then,
Marjahneh stood before them. On her brow
They saw a streak of fire, where jagged rocks
Had touched her, and her hair disordered hung
Around her, and her plumes were crushed and bruised
By the great weight of stone. Then Dahsim rose,
And turning to his daughter he exclaimed:
"Jinneeyeh, will you yield to Iblees now?
If Allah could protect his wretched slaves,
You perhaps might hope assistance at his hands:
Lo, every monarch of the Jinn has sworn
To yield to Iblees, and shall you refuse?
Has insufficient punishment been yours,
Or will you still provoke us till we rise,
And slay you as an enemy of all
Who bow before the son of Jarjarees?"

  "Think not," she answered, "that I am alone.
Though all the monarchs of the Jinn rebel

Against the might of Allah, he is here
To strengthen me to meet whate'er befalls."
She looked around her and perceived the Kings
Who stood by Ed-Dimiryaht. "Kings, behold
How Iblees, tyrant as he is, can treat
Those who defy his power! O trust not him!
Dahsim, behold the Kings who will not yield
To Iblees! See, I do not stand alone,
For these are not his slaves, and in the midst
Stands Ed-Dimiryaht, who has never stooped
To any King but Allah!"
                        While she spoke,
A wrathful murmur rose among the Kings,
And every sword was drawn and tightly grasped
Although they wished not to commence the fight,
Till Iblees forced it on them in his ire.
    Then Iblees spoke. "Bring here the magic arms
Of Jarjarees, and soon the Kings shall own
His son's resistless might. I'll slay them all,
And wrest the Sword of Azraeel from the grasp
Of Ed-Dimiryaht, who alone has dared
To rouse the rebels to resist their King."
In haste he donned the arms, and raised his spear,
When Ed-Dimiryaht bade the Kings retire,
And leave him single-handed to oppose
His fearful foe. The way was scarcely clear,
When Iblees rushed against him. Up he raised
The Sword of Azraeel sheathed, and with the sheath
He smote his enemy. The clashing arms
Fell before Ed-Dimiryaht. Iblees fled
In terror and confusion to his throne:
When Ed-Dimiryaht took the enchanted arms,
And in the sight of Iblees girt them on.
    While Iblees sat confounded, Dahsim felt
An anger by reflection uncontrolled,
And with the anger of a baffled Chief
Who wreaks his bootless rage on all around,
He turned upon Marjahneh in his wrath,

And cried in furious accents, "Will you yield
To Iblees now? Reflect upon your doom.
The upper worlds are beautiful and bright,
But this is an awful chaos. You shall pine
For ever in our dungeons hopelessly,
For if you will not yield to Iblees now,
I'll break your wings, and chain you in a cave."
Bright was the light that flashed amid the hall,
For all the foes of Iblees clothed their forms
In wreaths of flame, prepared for utmost strife.
Speechless with anger Ed-Dimiryaht stood
A moment, then he drew a flaming sword
Steeped in the burning drops of gall which cause
Death, paleness, putrefaction. On he sprang,
And lifting up his blade in act to strike,
He held the fearful sword o'er Dahsim's head,
And cried, "O Dahsim, speak another word.
And over you I shed the dews of death,
And the Siraht would sink beneath your weight."
Dahsim recoiled in terror, while the chains
Marjahneh wore, fell clanking to the ground,
And she was freed, and Ed-Dimiryaht turned,
And led her to the Kings. O mournfully
Her answer to her father smote the ear!

     "O woe to me, for fatherless am I!
The tyranny of those who league themselves
Against the might of Allah, never yet
Devised a greater punishment than this.
To me, your daughter, you employed the threat,
And I renounce you till the day when God
Shall lead you from your sins. Alas, alas,
Before the fall of Iblees, who would think
That I could thus address you! Though I live
Until the Trumpet's Second Blast resounds,
I never can forget that you were once
My father, but unworthy as you are,
I call you so no longer. All is changed.
O Dahsim, I would gladly die for you,

And would not grudge life, liberty, or wings,
If you from your apostasy would turn.
We once were friends in Heaven, but never more
We meet in love again. Alas for me,
For truly worse than fatherless am I!"
Her voice was lost in sobs; when Iblees rose,
And called his sons around and prepared
To rush against his enemies. They charged,
When Ed-Dimiryaht raised the Archangel's sword
And waved it round his head. His foes fell back,
Senseless as though a shooting star had struck
Their flames of fire. He called the faithful Kings:
" Quit, quit for ever this accursed world!
The highest Earth is like a lower Heaven;
And we will found a mighty empire there
And call it Jinneesthan. Abandon now
Their palace to the wicked."
                    Then he sprang
Swift from the hall, attended by his troops,
Nor did they set their feet upon the ground,
Till they alighted on the highest Earth.


## Book III—Suleymahn Ibn Dahood

### Canto VI

#### THE CITY OF AMBER

ALONE within the Amber City stands
    The Wezeer Ahssaf, and its golden gleam,
Though dimmed by endless twilight, is as bright
As man can bear. The Diving Jinn have gone
To fight the deadliest foes of Jinneesthan;
And he, a human hero, stands alone,
At what a depth he knows not, on the bed
Of that vast sea that circles round the world.
O Ahssaf, dost thou fear? An awful fate
For man to visit such a place as this,

It must be! Brave was Ahssaf, yet he felt
Both fear and awe. Around him he beheld
Huge palaces of amber, which arose
High in the brightening waters, while the suns
Would gleam, perchance, upon a coral dome,
Or on a tower of amber, set with pearls.
Nor these were unadorned. Around them waved
The sea-grass, and the gorgeous purple weeds,
And green and olive. Here the ocean zones
Restrict not aught that's lovely in their bounds,
And let them rove no further; everywhere
The ocean plants are spread, and 'mid them coiled,
The glorious worms of green and gold and red,
Entwine their glittering rainbow-dress of hair
Among the fronds; and flowers of every hue
Expand their living petals. Surely earth
Possesses not the beauties of the sea!

And Ahssaf, as he looked on all around,
Exclaimed, " The care of God is o'er me here :
He smiles on me from all his glorious works,
And I am not alone beneath the sea! "
He knelt and prayed, not for himself alone,
But for those mighty Kings, his dearest friends,
One wandering like a beggar, known to none :
One struggling with remorseless, deadly foes,
Who armed with more than demon-power, had sought
To bind the virtuous in the snares of Hell.

Then on the grass he laid him down and slept,
Exhausted by the wonders of the day,
And when he woke, he felt refreshed, and rose
Restored to strength, and walked the shining streets,
And every sight seemed lovelier than the last.

At length he reached a palace in the midst
Of Amberabahd. As far as eye could reach
Vast domes of amber and coral rose
In the bright sparkling waters, and o'er all,
The waving splendour of the seaweeds spread ;
And there pourtrayed by seaweeds, shells, and flowers,

Appeared the history both of men and Jinn.
Among them, too, were mystic emblems traced,
Which stretched their meanings into future years,
And Ahssaf saw but understood them not.
He saw the conflicts of a western world,
Of which he little knew; and he perceived
Emblems of future peaceful arts displayed,
Nor guessed their meanings, though with straining eyes
He sought to pierce the mysteries that they veiled,
Till he was forced to look away for rest.
Bright jewels, too, abounded; but for these
The Divers cared not; and they would not change
E'en for the blinding glories than enwrap
Joharahbahd, their lovelier city here:
For Amberabahd, to moonlight tempered down,
By the deep waters of the sea that flows
Within the coral reed of Jinneesthan,
Is fitter for the eyes of Diving Jinn,
Who only painfully endure the light
Wherein the higher races sport and play,
With ever new and ever freshening zest.
      As Ahssaf looked on Sahleh's glorious home,
Well might he feel how weak and frail was man!
But he looked proudly up, and he exclaimed,
" What if we have not now the exalted powers,
In which the angels and the Jinn rejoice?
Thank God, the life of man is but a day!
How wretched were a life of centuries
Upon the gloomy earth from whence I came!
We soon should weary of a life like ours,
If it were long continued. God be praised,
The life of man is only as a day,
And glories that surpass Joharahbahd:
Await us in the eternal worlds above!"
      But now the fight was ended, and the Jinn
Returned to Amberabahd. King Sahleh saw
The Wezeer Ahssaf, and his guards he sent,
Commanding them to bring before his throne,

E                          53

The unwonted human stranger. " Who art thou ? "
The King demanded, " wherefore canst thou tread
The ocean waters fearlessly, and live ? "
    King Sahleh spoke and Ahssaf thus replied :
" Behold Suleymahn's Wezeer, Ahssaf, here !
By Ed-Dimiryaht's influence, I defied
The rebel Faktash, who possessed the Seal,
And therefore Ed-Dimiryaht placed me here,
To wait till King Suleymahn shall regain
The throne that he has lost. Behold, O King,
'Tis therefore I presume to tread unharmed
The floor of ocean.—Tell me, if you know,
How went the contest at Joharahbahd :
    " When all seemed lost, did Azraeel's sword decide
The victory in our favour, yet we left
Whole squadrons of our friends in ashes laid
Upon the shattered walls of adamant,
That vainly might oppose Suleymahn's Seal."
    " Does Ed-Dimiryaht live ? " the Wezeer asked,
" For surely he with Faktash' self would fight,
All desperate as he knew such strife to be."
    " Few fought as valiantly as did the King."
He answered, " when he fought with Faktash first,
King Ed-Dimiryaht stunned him at a blow,
Although he could not wound him while he wore
Suleymahn's awful Seal ; but after that,
The Efreet pierced the shoulder of the King,
And Ed-Dimiryaht was not conquered then !
He stood amid the ashes, and he fought
As if he were unhurt, till Azraeel came,
And chased our foes away from Jinneesthan,
And healed our wounded. One alone had strength,
Protected by a mighty angel's power,
To cope with Faktash, for she fought unarmed,
And surely we were fools to fight with arms
'Gainst that divinest spell. Meymooneh knew
All arms were worse than useless, and alone
She fought against the fiend who wore the Seal,

And drove him back: all else who dared oppose
The awful spell, were wounded or were slain:
But she, who trusted only in her God,
And in her pure and spotless innocence,
That never knew temptation, sin, or woe,
Prevailed against the most resistless spell,
(Though robbed of half its force in wicked hands),
That ever yet compelled our race to yield.
Ahssaf, Suleymahn's Wezeer, be my guest,
For you oppose our common enemies,
And serve Suleymahn, he who rules us all;
And the believing Jinn, and men alike,
Are subjects of a mightier King than he!"

"I hear and I obey!" the Wezeer cried,
"And I rejoice that I, although a man,
Can view your splendid city. Scarce, I deem,
Joharahbahd can boast a lovelier glow!"

"We Divers," answered Sahleh with a smile,
"Prefer our city to Joharahbahd:
But should you ask the Flying Jinn, be sure
That they will praise their glorious city most.
You can behold the glories that we love,
Around us, for our city lies entombed
Deep in a tranquil sea; but never man
Shall see Joharahbahd, until the Blast
Of Consternation shakes it from its base!"

So Ahssaf dwelt with Sahleh, and he viewed
That glorious city of the Diving Jinn:
But, had he stayed in ocean all his life,
He surely could not even then have seen
One half the wonders that around him spread.
Thus quickly passed the forty days away,
When, darting through the water to the ground,
King Ed-Dimiryaht's messengers arrived.

"Ahssaf, Suleymahn is not yet restored.
But Ed-Dimiryaht occupies the throne,
Until Suleymahn shall again return.
The Efreet flung the Seal away, and waits

Suleymahn's wrath in chains. We came at once,
To bid you to Jerusalem again."
 King Sahleh cried, "I also will be there,
For when Suleymahn shall regain his throne,
Perchance he needs my service. Ahssaf, go:
I through the water seek Jerusalem,
Your bearers through the air, a vaster sea
Than this!"
    The Wezeer instantly replied,
"Farewell, O Sahleh! I shall ne'er forget
The kindness you have shown me!"
       Then he sprang
Into the palankeen his bearers held,
And they at once commenced their upward course.
Now have they passed the highest amber towers,
And brighter shines the dazzling light above:
A moment, and like lightning on them burst
The unclouded suns of Jinneesthan, concealed
No longer by the water; then away
The Jinnees darted to the World of Men.
Again the flash of many-coloured light:
Again the tumult of the Outer Sea:
And when the Wezeer dared to raise his head,
The desert lay below him. As he gazed,
The desert vanished, and the Jinnees sank
Before Suleymahn's throne. The journey o'er,
The wondering Wezeer left the palankeen,
And looked around and knew Jerusalem.

## BOOK VI—THE CLOSE OF A CYCLE

### *Canto IV*

#### THE CONSUMMATION

TIME is no more and Love has conquered Hell,
  And every evil world is swept away,
And Heaven extends throughout the universe.
No longer matter, time, and space are chains:
Their temporal might is gone for evermore.
Nor do the races sprung from light and fire,
And those from earth, as formerly, remain
Apart, for all distinctions are destroyed.
Now is the veil uplifted from the Throne,
And a transparent light beams over all,
That nothing can compare with, nor produce,
Except the Throne, an emblem as it is,
Of the great omnipresent primal Soul.
But even Eesa sees no form revealed.
Around the happy this eternal light
Is spread, and they with God converse in soul,
For all can feel the Universal Life
That mingles with their souls, and feel with awe
That God himself is speaking to their hearts,
In close communion, never more to cease.
The deadliest foes on earth are greatest friends,
And every heart is open; all can see
The inmost feelings of another's soul,
E'en as on earth we see a human face!
The power to live for self is all unknown,
For in promoting joy, but virtue more,
They but promote their own. No talisman
Is needed to control the race of Jinn;
For having passed through Hell's terrific flames,
The wicked all their wickedness have lost.
And ever speaks the eternal Mind of God,
To all in Heaven: " Continue in the way
Of righteousness and progress evermore!

All obstacles are gone, and ye are now
The sons of God for ever. Nought can touch
Your spotless virtue. That itself ye feel,
Reward enough for all the cares of earth."

Those who on earth have felt the eternal Mind,
The most, are greatest now, and strive to raise
Those who are yet below them in the scale
Of joy and virtue, higher than the point
That they themselves have reached. For ever on !
Development and progress never cease,
In Heaven or Earth ; and this eternal law,
The mainspring of this glorious universe,
Unchanged shall last throughout eternity.

To God in His infinity, rolls on
The endless progress of immortal souls :
And infinite as God Himself its course,
For to His greatness it may ne'er approach,
The Archangels still grow nobler than before :
The angels and the sons of earth and fire,
Alike. The dread solemnity has left
The face of Azraeel, and no more 'tis said,
That he of all the angels ne'er can smile :
For all acknowledge that his golden Key,
Though formed from his resistless Sword of flame,
For them unbarred the eternal gates of Heaven.
The former Heaven was all unlike to this,
To which e'en angels had to pass through death,
And cross the dread Siraht, the Bridge of Breadth.

Nearest to God Himself works Eesa still,
And subject but to Him alone, he rules,
The race of Adam, now no longer weak ;
And Ed-Dimiryaht rules the race of Jinn ;
The Archangels rule the angels ; but they rule
As best and noblest of the assembled worlds,
Which thus they govern, not by fear but love.

But e'en the Archangels yield to Eesa's power ;
The power of goodness : yet not he is King,
But God alone, who speaks to every heart,

And trains it to obedience to His will.
Yet is this not subservience; love alone
Directs the universe from which is cleansed
Whate'er had power to clog its endless course:
For mutual love and virtues are the joys
That Heaven presents to all. On these alone,
The order of the universe depends,
E'en now; and when all sin and woe are gone,
How mightily shall love and virtue rule!
　　What are the afflictions of a life on earth?
E'en as the faded blossoms of a tree,
Which must be scattered, ere the immortal fruit
Can spring to all luxuriance in the sun
Of God's eternal goodness, and the love
Which he bestows on all in Earth and Heaven,
And all in all the worlds that he has sown
Through endless space, beyond our twilight sphere.
　　And while God's children work thus gloriously,
Shall Eesa and his Father gaze on all,
In love and joy and glory none can speak.
Eternally the work of all shall last,
Eternal as their innocence and joy,
Which must endure, while with unbounded love,
Shall God and Eesa watch the assembled worlds,
And approbation upon all things smile.
And God shall see His creatures in their joy,
And as His voice shall speak them " very good! "
Shall Eesa, with a heart that overflows
With love to all, reflect the immortal smile
Of God upon the eternal universe,
Brightening for ever in His changeless love!

# THE MAKAMAH
# OF THE
# MOSQUE BENI HARAAM

### THE WORDS OF ABOU-ZAID OF SEROUG

SINCE the day when I first equipped my camel,
  And journeyed away from my wife and my children,
I was always as eager as the oppressed for deliverance
To make a visit in person to the city of Basra,
The high repute of its remarkable sites and learned men,
And the traditional renown of its shrines and martyrs
Having been confirmed to me by the united testimony of all
Who possessed accurate knowledge, or corrections in
  reporting:
And I ceased not to pray God to let me tread on its soil,
That I might enjoy the delightful prospect of it,
And to entreat Him to place me within its precincts,
That I might be able to explore every quarter of it.
  Now when good fortune had at last brought me to it,
And my eyes had surveyed it in every direction,
I found there whatever could fill the eye with cheerfulness,
Or beguile a stranger from the recollection of his home.
So one morning, when the shades of night were dis-
  appearing,
And the bird of announcement was calling to the sleepers,
I arose early to explore the streets of the town,
And to satisfy my desire of penetrating into the midst of it;
And by traversing it, and walking to and fro throughout it,
I was brought at last to a quarter remarkable for its
  sanctity,
And named after the tribe Benou-Haraam who occupied it,
Which contained mosques that were much frequented,
And fountains that were much resorted to,
And well-constructed buildings, and agreeable dwellings,
That possessed peculiar excellences and many advantages;
There thy companions thou mayst choose
                    From every class and kind;

For some there are who still devote
              To pleasure all their mind,
And some, in true devotion's path
              Who all their pleasure find;
Some choral music loving best,
              Some on Koran to muse;
Some skilled to extract from hardest books
              The meaning most abstruse,
Some swift to extricate the mean
              From hardship and abuse;
Some who, though dear it cost their eyes,
              No toil in reading spare,
And some who spare no cost that guests
              The ready meal may share;
'Tis there that liberal arts abound,
              And best of sages meet,
'Tis there that bounty's liberal hand
              Bestows her blessings sweet,
And there that beauty's tuneful band
              The hearer sweetly greet;
And there thou mayst a playful friend,
              Or prayerful, freely choose,
Improve a wise man's company,
              Or cups of wine abuse.
Now while I explored the streets and surveyed their
    beauty,
Until the westering of the sun and the approach of evening,
I observed a remarkably excellent and well-frequented
    mosque,
Where the people were discussing the interchangeable
    letters,
And coursing along as it were in the arena of controversy;
So I turned aside to them, intending to solicit their bounty,
Not from any desire to learn their opinions on grammar;
But sooner than a person in haste can snatch a firebrand
The calls of the Muezzins were heard summoning to
    prayer,
And the appearance of the Imaum followed their call;

So that the discussion was necessarily interrupted,
And the people bestirred themselves to rise and stand up.

And I was thus diverted by the duties of devotion
From endeavouring to procure the means of maintenance,
And prevented by God's worship from seeking man's
    bounty.
But when our obligatory prayers were finished,
And the congregation was about to disperse,
There came from the midst of them a man of sweet elo-
    quence.
Who united with a graceful manner and address
Fluency of speech and consummate power of rhetoric;
Who thus addressed us,
" O my neighbours, whom I preferred above my country-
    men,
And whose land I chose as my place of refuge,
And whom I made my most intimate confidants
And the depositaries of my every secret,
And whom, both in my presence and in my absence,
I have constituted my only provision and resource,
Know that the garb of truth is brighter than robes of pomp,
That the disgrace of this world is lighter than that of the
    next,
That real religion is to give sincere counsel to others,
That the indication of true faith is to guide others aright,
That he whom we consult is the depositary of our confi-
    dence,
That he who solicits our guidance has a right to our
    advice,
That a brother is he who reproves thee, not who excuses
    thee,
And that a real friend is he who tells thee the truth,
Not he who always allows that thou art right."
And those present replied, " O most affectionate friend,
O thou who hast been our most beloved companion,
Tell us the hidden meaning of thy ambiguous words,
And the real purport of thy concise address to us ;

And as for that which thou desirest from us,
It shall speedily be fulfilled, however difficult it be;
For by Him who conferred thy friendship upon us,
And made us of thy sincerest wellwishers,
We will not fail to give thee our best advice,
Nor withhold from thee our aid or protection."
  And he replied,
" May you be rewarded with good and saved from evil;
For you are men from whom no insincerity ever proceeds,
And of whom no companion ever has cause to complain,
By whom no reasonable expectation is ever frustrated,
And from whom no secret need ever be concealed.
I will tell you at once what distresses my breast,
And consult you on that whereby my patience is over-
    come :
Know then that while my means were straitened,
And while fortune continued to be averse from me,
I was sincere in my purpose of covenant with God,
And gave Him the pledge of a solemn vow,
That I would never buy wine, nor carouse with com-
    panions,
Nor quaff strong drink, nor array myself in drunkenness;
And yet my misleading propensity and deluding appetite
Seduced me to enter the company of profligates,
And there to pass round among us flagons of wine,
And lay aside restraint and suck the juice of the grape,
And indulge freely in intoxicating potations,
With no more thought about repentance than about the
    dead.
Nor was I content with having done once as I tell you,
In yielding obedience to the Father of Evil,
    But even indulged in old wine on a fifth day of the
    week,
And became inebriated therewith on our holy eve.
And, behold, I now avow contrition for my neglect of
    piety,
And am very penitent for having given myself to wine,
While I greatly dread the consequences of my broken vow,

And openly confess my transgression in quaffing the
  strong.
Is there then, my friends, any atonement that you know,
That may remove my guilt far away from me,
And bring me near again to my Lord?"
Now when he had thus explicitly unfolded his narration,
And given vent to the complaints of anxious grief,
I said to myself, "Abou-Zaid! this is thy opportunity,
Now, therefore, prepare thyself for vigorous exertion":
So I sprang up from my seat, like a brave champion,
And I started forth from my row like an arrow,
And said—
"My most illustrious friend, in noble rank,
And high distinction proudly eminent,
Who seekest one to guide thee to a path
That may thy final happiness ensure;
Thou soon wilt find a cure for thy distress,
The sore remorse that robs thee of repose,
If thou'lt but listen while I tell of ills,
That left me plunged in dire perplexity.
Know then, Seroug was once my dwelling-place,
Where purest faith is practised and professed;
I there was wealthy, honoured, and obeyed;
My house a hall of hospitality,
And all my goods expended on my guests;
Their liberal praise by generous acts I won,
And by unceasing bounty still retained;
Nor cared to hoard my gains, but spent them all
With lavish hand, in large munificence;
And, though the sordid quench that welcome light,
A beacon-fire I ever kindled high,
That guided wanderers to find in me
Their best resource, and refuge most secure:
For none complained that, when they sought my aid,
They 'vainly looked for showers to slake their thirst,
To summer clouds, whose lightning falsely gleamed';
Or that, whene'er my proffered boons they claimed,
They 'struck on flints that failed to yield a spark';

But, while my fortune smiled, I still appeared
To all around a source of affluence;
Though soon, alas! my lot was doomed to change;
For lo! a feud with foreign foes appeared,
And God permitted infidels of Roum
To seize our lands and dwellings, and enslave
The families of all who there professed
A simple faith in Allah's unity.
They took whate'er was mine of great or small;
And since that day an outcast I have been,
Still roaming far and wide, and craving aid
From those who once besought it at my hand,
And sunk so deep in hopeless indigence,
That death I now should deem a welcome boon;
Nay more—The same disaster ruinous,
That scattered from me all that cheered my life,
Has stolen too at one fell swoop away
My only daughter, whom they captive led,
A ransom claiming that I cannot pay.
O look then on my woe, and stretch thy hand
To save me from this worst calamity,
This foulest wrong, by adverse fortune wrought,
And aid me to redeem my child from thrall.
For if to Pity's call thou'lt lend an ear,
And Mercy's hest devote thyself to obey,
Thereby thou shalt a full remission gain
Of errors past, and if to good resolves
Relapse succeed, and bring thee fresh remorse,
Repentance shall renewed acceptance find.
And though in verse my counsel I've exprest,
Reject it not as vain; for e'en in verse
I oft enforce the words of timely truth.
Then gladly welcome this sincere advice,
With gratitude to one who thus would guide
Thy steps in wisdom's path; and freely give
Whate'er of recompense thou hast at hand,
That so thou may'st my thankful praises win."
Now when I had rapidly delivered this long reply,

The person solicited being inspired with belief of my
　　words,
Desire to display bounty incited him to become my
　　benefactor,
And zeal to undertake the performance of onerous duties
Made him eager to engage in the relief of my difficulties;
So he gave me on the spot what little he had with him,
And was also profuse in his promises of more:
So that I returned home exulting in my prosperous artifice,
Having easily succeeded by the scheme that I had devised
In swallowing, as it were, the sop that I had sought for,
And readily attained by the poem that I had woven
To a deglutition of the dainties that I had desired.
Whereupon Hareth said to me, "By Him who created thee!
How wonderfully ingenious are thy wiles!"
But I only laughed heartily, and indited fluently,
　" Since all mankind in selfish fraud
　　　　　　　　With tigers seem to vie,
　By guile among them ever live,
　　　　　　　　And turn its channel sly
　To move the wheel of life, that so
　　　　　　　　The millstone round may fly.
　At eagles aim thy shafts, and seek
　　　　　　　　Each noblest prize t'obtain;
　For if thou but their plumage graze,
　　　　　　　　Thou may'st some feathers gain;
　And strive the fairest fruits to pluck,
　　　　　　　　Since haply may remain
　Some leaves, at least, within thy grasp
　　　　　　　　If fruit thou seek in vain.
　Thou wayward fortune thwart thee now,
　　　　　　　　Or treat thee with disdain,
　Thy heart from all distracting thoughts
　　　　　　　　And anxious fears refrain;
　For e'en the changeful course of time
　　　　　　　　A promise may contain,
　That soon the state of life will change,
　　　　　　　　That makes thee now complain."

China

## CHINESE LITERATURE

*T*HE Chinese may perhaps be called the Grand Masters of Oriental literature, because since Confucius in B.C. 500 gathered together the "Book of Odes," down almost to modern times China has not ceased to produce great verse and prose. Unlike much other Eastern poetry the Chinese Singers have adopted a more direct method of expression, there is allegory and metaphor, but in every direction the treatment is objective. The following are from the translations of Henry H. Hart— W. J. B. Fletcher and J. F. Davis and the Confucian Analects from Dr. Legge.

## GRIEF

### BY LI PO

*M*y lady has rolled up the curtains of pearl,
    And sits with a frown on her eyebrows apart.
Wet traces of tears can be seen as they curl.
    But who knows for whom is the grief in her heart?

## THAT PARTING AT CH'ANG-KAN

### BY LI PO

WHEN first o'er maiden brows my hair I tied,
 In sport I plucked the blooms before the door.
You riding came on hobby-horse astride,
 And wreathed my bed with green-gage branches o'er.
At Ch'ang-kan Village long together dwelt
 We children twain, and knew no petty strife.
 At fourteen years, lo! I became thy wife.
Yet ah! the modest shyness that I felt!

 My shamefaced head I in a corner hung;
Nor to long calling answered word of mine.
 At fifteen years my heart's gate open sprung,
And I was glad to mix my dust with thine.
 My troth to thee till death I keep for aye:
My eyes still gaze adoring on my lord.
 When I was but sixteen you went away.
In Chü-t'ang Gorge how Yen-yü's billows roared!

 For five long months with you I cannot meet.
The gibbon's wail re-echoes to the sky!
 Before the door, where stood your parting feet,
The prints with verdant moss are covered high.
 Deep is that moss! it will not brush away.
In early autumn's gale the leaflets fall.
 September now!—the butterflies so gay
Disport on grasses by our garden wall.

 The sight my heart disturbs with longing woe.
I sit and wail, my red cheeks growing old.
 Early and late I to the gorges go,
Waiting for news that of thy coming told.
 How short will seem the way, if we but meet!
 Across the sand the wind flies straight to greet.

## WE THREE

### BY LI PO

ONE pot of wine amid the Flowers
    Alone I pour, and none with me.
The cup I lift; the Moon invite;
    Who with my shadow makes us three.
The Moon then drinks without a pause.
    The shadow does what I begin.
The shadow, Moon and I in fere
    Rejoice until the Spring come in.
I sing: and wavers time the Moon.
    I dance: the shadow antics too.
Our joys we share while sober still.
    When drunk, we part and bid adieu.
Of loveless outing this the pact,
    Which we all swear to keep for aye.
The next time that we meet shall be
    Beside yon distant Milky Way.

## THE MOON OVER THE PASS

### BY LI PO

O'ER Altai's range the Moon arises bright
    Floating in vasty seas of cloud and night.
O'er boundless plains the shrill wind hither blows,
And whistles as o'er Yü-mên Pass it goes.
Beneath the Milky Way there stretches white
The road that leads to yonder tower-crowned height.
The eager Tartars search each hollow bay
Of Tsaidam's sea. Nor see I come away
One mortal soul of all who went to fight.
They dwell in arms; and backward gazing pine
For frontier towns; and longing to return
O'er sad worn faces draws a bitter line.
To-night, as from his lofty tower I yearn,
No voice re-echoes back these sighs of mine.

## HARD ARE THE WAYS OF SZECHWAN

### BY LI PO

*L*o! how huge! how mighty!
 Sheer and towering high!
Hard are the ways of Szechwan,
 Harder than scaling the sky!
Monstrous surely the country
Ts'an-ts'ung and Yu-fu won . . .
Ages a thousand are past and done,
Yet through the Gorge of Ch'in, as then,
It access gives to worlds of men.

Westward is T'ai-po Hill,
 Free to the birds alone,
Joining with Omi Mountain,
 By winding paths unknown.
The earth caved in ; and the hill
Snapped; and the Mighty died.
Thereafter the steps of the sky
 Were joined by bridges of stone.

Above on Kao-piao Mountain
 Six dragons bear back the sun.
Beneath it, a piled-up fountain,
 Bursting, wild billows run.
Never attain this height
The yellow cranes in flight :
 Apes are sickened of climbing,
Wearied their nervous might.

Twisted, contorted, cragged,
 Winds Ch'ing-ni range afar.
Stretch from thy summit ragged ;
 Pluck thee a shining star!
Sitting, aloud I sigh.
 My hands beat on my breast.
When come ye back, I cry,
 From wandering in the West ?

Roads so fearsome o'er peaks so rent
   Cannot be grasped, I fear.
Wailing about old trees so bent
   But sad-voiced birds I hear.
Male pursuing the female
   Around the woods in flight . . .
Hark! how the goatsucker's moan
   Sobs to the Moon by night!
Wailing its mate . . . A-hone!

Through vacant hills alone :
   " Hard are the ways of Szechwan,
     Harder than scaling the sky! " . . .

A fresh young face grows withered
   Hearing its mournful cry.
Peaks join on to the heavens,
   Scarcely a foot between.
Hollow old firs o'er-drooping
   Chasms of depth unseen.
Torrents and cascades rushing
   Rage with a stunning roar.
Boulders whirling before them
   In thundering caverns pour.

Dangers such as are here . . .
   Wanderers, ah! from afar! . . .
Why come to this scene of fear ?
   Why come to this world of war ?
Buttressed on towering rock
   The Hall of Swords ascends.
Thousands can never shock
   This Pass, if one defends.

Mate to some bandit keeps it . . .
   Some werewolf, jackal he . . .
Shun the fierce tiger at dawn !
   At eve from serpents flee!

Teeth-gnashing, blood-sucking slayers!
   The people in masses fall.
Ch'eng-tu a pleasant dwelling?
   Perchance. Yet better than all,
Return to thy home while early,
   For fear you may hear the cry:—
" Hard are the ways of Szechwan!
   Harder than scaling the sky!" . . .

Turned to yon western country,
   Sadly and long I sigh.

# A DREAM OF LI PO

## BY TU FU

THE clouds flying over me travel all day.
But long since the wanderer travelled this way!
Three nights in succession I dreamèd of thee.
Your meaning I know; for our thoughts aye agree.
When you bid me farewell, you are forced to, alas!
And painful that road is, not easy to pass.
The waters with storm and with billows are tossed;
And I fear lest the oars of your skiff may be lost.
You scratch your grey head, when you go out, as then,
As if you still bore the sad burdens of men.
Official retinues the capital throng;
Yet *this* man alone wanders sadly along!
That God's mills grind surely, who ventures to say,
While age yet increases the load of the day?
The name that a myriad ages shall last
Is but a dull mock when our lifetime is past!

## A FAREWELL ODE TO CHENG SHIH ERH ON HIS RETIRING FROM THE WORLD TO THE LU SHAN

### BY LIU CHANG-CH'ING

By Kiukiang a house you have with half an acre
   ground,
  To which you now return to close its wicket 'gainst the
    world.
You enter in that valley; and there is no one found.
  A barrier about the door the Autumn grass has curled.
Of Time and Space unheeding, now are your simples
   sold;
  And, speechless, on your ragged staff you wend your
    homeward way,
To find those bamboo-shoots are grown to chilly trees
   and old,
  Where from the hill your vacant rooms oppose the
    dying day.
Beneath your cottage trickles by a little singing rill.
  The clouds you see are sailing past to visit men below.
The blooms of Immortality with fragrance clothe the
   hill:
  A bunch of which I pluck to send for greeting as you
    go.

# THE BALLAD OF ENDLESS WOE
## BY PO CHÜ-I

THE Lord of Han loved beauty;
  In love's desire he pined.
For years within his palace
  Such love he could not find.

A maiden in the house of Yang
  To wedlock's age had grown.
Brought up within the harem,
  And to the world unknown.

A lovely form of Heaven's mould
  Is never cast aside.
And so this maid was chosen
  To be a Prince's bride.

If she but turned her smiling,
  A hundred loves were born.
There are no arts, no graces,
  But by her looked forlorn.

'Twas in the chilly Springtime,
  They bathed in Hua-ch'ing Lake;
And in the tepid waters
  The crusted winter slake.

When thence attendants bore her,
  So helpless and so fair;
Then first beat in her Prince's breast
  Desire and tender care.

With cloud-like hair and flower-like face
  Her tinkling footsteps ring.
How warm in her pure curtains
  To pass a night of Spring!

The nights of Spring are short, alas!
  Too soon the sunlit dawn!
From then no longer held the Prince
  His Court at early morn.

But steeped in love, at banquet's side,
  No other business knew.
One Spring behind another came.
  One night the next renew.

Although within his palace
  Three thousand beauties dwelt,
His love for these three thousand
  Did on one bosom melt.

When dressed, in secret chamber
  Her beauty served the night.
In gilded hall, the banquet done,
  The wine brought love's delight.

Her brothers and her sisters
  Were ranked on steps of fame.
And all her humble cottage
  Was lit with honour's flame.

Until throughout the Empire
  All parents hailed with joy
The birth of some fair maiden;
  And wanted not a boy.

The lofty palace balconies
  Amid blue clouds abide,
Their fairy storm of sweet delights
  Goes echoing far and wide.

'Twas wanton song, lascivious dance,
  And stringèd music's fire.
The whole day long the Emperor gazed,
  And never seemed to tire.

When like an earthquake came the boom
  Of drums and war's alarms,
To shatter that sweet rainbow song
  Of Beauty in Love's arms.

The clouds of dust rolled gloomily
  About the palace doors,
As chariots, troops of horsemen,
  Went westward to the wars.

That lady fair would go with him.
  And then she stayed again.
At last she came for forty miles ;
  And lodged her on the plain.

Alas! the armies will not start.
  No hope is there at all,
Till those persuasive eyebrows
  Before the chargers fall.

Her ornaments the earth receives ;
  Neglected there they lie.
Her feathers, golden hair clasp,
  And pins her blood-stains dye.

Her Lord now cannot rescue.
  His mantle hides his face.
With that last look the tears of blood
  In trickling sorrow race.

The yellow dust is scattered wide,
  And desolate the wind,
As up a spiral bridge of cloud
  She leaves the earth behind.

Below great Omi Mountain
  But rarely people go ;
And dimly falls the sunlight ;
  And dull the banners flow.

Are green the streams of Szechwan;
  And verdant Szechwan's hills.
Yet morn by morn and night by night
  What grief his bosom fills!

When from his tent the Moon he sees,
  His breast is charged with woe.
The rain of night, the watches' bell,
  Like torments through him go.

But loud rebellion's din resounds.
  He to his chariot fares.
With steps unequal came he there;
  And halting thence repairs.

Beneath the slope of Ma-wei,
  And hidden in the soil,
He cannot see that lovely face
  That death has made its spoil.

The Prince gazed on his Ministers.
  Their tears together flow.
They eastward saw the city;
  And turned their steeds to go.

Her lake, her garden still were there;
  Unchangèd were they all:
The lotus in the T'ai-yeh Lake,
  The willow by the hall.

The lotus seemed her face to be.
  Her brows the willows seem.
The sight of them made gush again
  His tears in bitter stream.

When plum and peach the spring renewed,
  And blossoms opened well;
When *wu-t'ung* leaves in autumn rain
  Before the breezes fell.

Within the courts unheeded grew
  And rank the autumn grass;
And all the steps were red with leaves,
  Ne'er swept for him to pass.

The tresses of her comrades
  Were newly streaked with grey.
The eunuchs of her palace
  And women pined away.

The firefly flitting through the room
  Her spirit seemed to be;
The whole wick of his lamp he trimmed,
  Yet sleep his eyes would flee.

How slowly through the dreary night
  The bell the watches tolled.
How sleepless blinked the Milky Way,
  Ere dawn the light unrolled!

When chill the roof where true love dwelt,
  How thick the frost flakes form!
When cold the halcyon's coverlet,
  Who then can make it warm?

In dreary gloom his life wore on;
  And years have passed, I deem;
But never yet her spirit came
  To soothe him in a dream.

By chance there came a wandering priest,
  Was steeped in magic lore,
And skilled to call the spirit home
  That dwelt on Pluto's shore.

In pity for the Prince's grief,
  That never let him rest,
He, Fang-Shih, sent to seek her;
  And bade him do his best.

The driving power of air he fixed,
    Like lightning thence he flew.
The highest heaven, the lowest earth
    He searchèd through and through.

Above he searched the azure vault,
    The yellow Styx below;
Both stretched in gloomy emptiness,
    Nor traces of her show.

And then he learnt that on the sea
    There was a fairy hill.
It stood upon the void obscure,
    That glamour covers still.

Fair, glinting, high its turrets rose,
    And spanned with rainbow hair;
Where many fairies stood about,
    So modestly and fair.

And one among them, T'ai-chên called,
    Than all the rest more rare,
So white her skin, so sweet her face,
    None could with her compare.

He knocked him on the fairy door,
    The palace western hall;
And bade the young attendants
    That lady fair to call.

And when she heard that tidings
    From Han Huang waited by,
From out the silken curtains
    Her dream did swiftly fly.

She thrust aside the pillow;
    Her garments hurried on;
And through the rich-set doorway
    Her wav'ring steps have gone.

Her cloud-like hair hung all awry,
  So fresh from sleep the dame.
With coronal all slanted,
  Into the hall she came.

Her fairy sleeves the wind blew up,
  They floated on the air.
Like rainbows seemed her raiment,
  Like wings her garment fair.

Her lovely face looked wist and sad,
  And tears were in her eyes.
She seemed a sweet plum blossom
  Where spring rain pearling lies.

Her heart she stilled; her glances veiled;
  And thanked her Emperor's care.
"My voice," she said, "since parting,
  My face my sorrows wear.

"In Chao-yang Court my love remains.
  It knows no other sway.
Through palaces of Fairyland
  But slowly drags the day.

"When I would turn my head to view
  The world of men below,
I never can see Chang-an;
  So thick the mist wreaths flow.

"But take the former things I had,
  To show my love how true.
This ornament and golden pin
  To take him, give I you.

"One half this golden pin I keep
  Now broken in my grasp.
The other half to him I send,
  With half this golden clasp.

"And tell him that my heart is fixed,
　As true as is the gold.
In heaven mortals meet again.
　I wait him purely bold."

The messenger was going thence.
　He asked one word again.
"There is one thing," she said to him,
　"Known only to us twain.

"The seventh moon, the seventh day
　We stood in Chang-sheng Hall.
'Twas night, and none beside us;
　We two were all in all.

"We swore that in the heaven above
　We never would dispart:
One tomb on earth enclose of us
　The frail and mortal part."

.　　.　　.　　.　　.

The heaven is vast; and earth is old;
　And Time will wear away.
But this their endless sorrow
　Shall never know decay.

# THE SONG OF THE WANDERING SON

## BY MÊNG HSIAO

In tender mother's hands the thread
　　Made clothes to garb her parting son.
Before he left, how hard she spun,
How diligently wove; in dread
　　Ere he return long years might run!
Such life-long mother's love how may
One simple little heart repay?


# RICHES

## BY MRS. TU CH'IU

If you will take advice, my friend,
　　For wealth you will not care.
But while fresh youth is in you,
　　Each precious moment spare.
When flowers are fit for culling,
　　Then pluck them as you may.
Ah! wait not till the bloom be gone,
　　To bear a twig away.

## A SONG OF KIANG-NAN

### BY LI I

*A* TRADER of Ch'ü-t'ang I married;
  And daily monotony rue.
Had I know Love's streams never miscarried,
  I had married a boat-boy—like you!


## WISE AGE TO YOUTH

### BY TU CHIU NIANG

*W* EAR your gold and silken garments;
  Store not one of them away;
Flaunt them in your years of beauty
Ere the world grows old and gray.

Pluck the blossoms in the springtime
When they open to the sun,
For you'll find but withered branches
When bright youth and love are done.

# THE DOCTRINE OF THE MEAN
## (*Confucian Analects*)

TSZE-LU asked about energy.

The Master said, " Do you mean the energy of the South, the Energy of the North, or the energy which you should cultivate yourself ? "

" To show forbearance and gentleness in teaching others : and not to revenge unreasonable conduct :— this is the energy of the Southern regions, and the good man makes it his study.

" To lie under arms : and meet death without regret :— this is the energy of the Northern regions, and the forceful make it their study.

" Therefore, the superior man cultivates a friendly harmony, without being weak—How firm is he in his energy! He stands erect in the middle, without inclining to either side. How firm is he in his energy! When good principles prevail in the government of his country, he does not change from what he was in retirement. When bad principles prevail in his country, he maintains his course to death without changing. How firm is his energy!

# THE SUPERIOR MAN
## *(Confucian Analects)*

THE superior man does what is proper to the station in which he is; he does not desire to go beyond this.

In a position of wealth and honour, he does what is proper to a position of wealth and honour. In a poor and low position, he does what is proper to a poor and low position. Situated among barbarous tribes, he does what is proper to a situation among barbarous tribes. In a position of sorrow and difficulty, he does what is proper to a position of sorrow and difficulty. The superior man can find himself in no situation in which he is not himself.

In a high situation, he does not treat with contempt his inferiors. In a low situation, he does not court the favour of his superiors. He rectifies himself, and seeks for nothing from others, so that he has no dissatisfaction. He does not murmur against Heaven, nor grumble against men.

Thus it is that the superior man is quiet and calm, waiting for the appointments of Heaven. While the mean man walks in dangerous paths, looking for lucky occurrences.

The Master said : " In archery we have something like the way of the superior man. When the archer misses the centre of the target, he turns round and seeks for the cause of his failure in himself."

The way of the superior man may be compared to what takes place in travelling, when to go to a distance we must first traverse the space that is near, and in ascending a height, when we must begin from the lower ground.

# A LETTER

### BY LI SHANG YIN

You ask
  When I intend to return?
Not yet, old friend.
I lack the time.

Do you remember that night,
How, at Pa Shan,
The first autumn rain
Came down like a cloudburst,
And flooded the pool?
And how we sat the livelong night,
And talked, and talked,
The while rising to snuff
The candles
That guttered and sputtered
In the west window?

Oh! To be back again
At Pa Shan,
On that night of rain,
With you,
Old friend!

# FAREWELL TO A FRIEND

### BY LI TAI PO

WHERE misty blue mountains loom dim in the north,
And the eastern wall rears its high gate,
Where down the green stream drops a lone fisher craft,
There I watched you ride off to your fate.

The clouds drifted lazily far overhead,
Snow-white sails on an ocean of blue.
Your horse bore you from me for ever and aye,
As I waved a last farewell to you.

Hot tears my eyes blinded,
And dim grew the sun ;
From the mountains the north wind blew chill.
The glad day was ended, swift came on black night,
As you vanished from sight o'er the hill.

# A LETTER

### BY CHANG CHI

PEARLS!
　Twin pearls,
Bright gems of ocean,
To me, a married woman,
You have sent!

Yet you know I have a husband
In attendance in the palace,
On the Lord of Light, the Emperor,
May he live ten thousand years!

But the thought that prompted you
I cherish
In my bosom with the jewels.
There they've lain hidden till this hour,
In the soft, enfolding silk.

I know—you need not tell me—
That your thoughts are pure as moonlight,
Or as the glowing sun at midday,
Overhead.

My home lies noble in its gardens.
There the marriage oath I've taken,
And I ever shall be faithful,
Even past the gates of death.

So——!
The twin pearls are in this letter.
I send them back to you in sadness,
With a sigh.

If you look closely, you'll find with them
Two other twin gems lying,
Twin tears fallen from my eyelids,
Telling of a breaking heart.

Alas! that perverse Life so willed it
That we met too late, after
I had crossed my husband's threshold
On that fateful wedding day!

# A HAPPY OLD MAN

### BY LIU TZU HUI

THE water murmurs
   In the old stone well,
And, a rippling mirror,
Gives back the clear blue sky.
The river roars,
Swollen with the late rains
Of Spring.
On the cool, jade-green grass
The golden sunshine splashes.

Sometimes, at early dawn,
I climb,
Even as far as Lien Shan Temple.
In the Spring I plough
The thirsty field,
That it may drink
New life.
I eat a little,
I work a little,
My hair grows daily thinner,
And, it seems,
I lean ever a bit more heavily
On my old thornwood cane.

# WRITTEN ON A DOOR-POST

### BY LIU SHÊN SHÜ

*T*HROUGH the turquoise-blue sky drifts a cloud on the
    breeze ;
The little brook laughs on its way.
The birds warble and call in the pink-blossomed trees,
Like voice of children at play.

The sweet fragrance, distilled by the sun and the rain,
Pervades the warm, crystal-clear air,
As I wend my blithe way up the little-used lane,
Light-hearted and free from all care.

There I seek the cool shade of the green willow-grove,
Shut off from the world and its strife,
And alone with the birds and the books that I love,
I find the real treasures of life.

Where the grass whispers softly to answering leaves,
I meet with the sages of old,
While the sun's dancing light patterns magical waves,
And showers my garments with gold.

## SAN-YU-LOW
### OR THE
## THREE DEDICATED ROOMS

### Section I

#### The Ode says,

" My house, having changed its owner, now belongs to
a rich man.

I therefore bundle my kin and my books under my arm,
and go over to another village.

The lofty rooms, which I built myself, I myself dispose
of ;

Unwilling to ruin my posterity, by leaving them such
extensive possessions."

#### Again,

" Within the period of an hundred years, it must have
belonged to some other person ;

And it is surely better to sell it while new, than when
become old.

The pine trees, the bamboos, and the Mei flowers must
enter the account ;

But my kin and my books, my dogs and my chickens,
shall accompany me.

The scraps of old verses stuck against the walls ;—for
these he may fix his price.

For the wet weather clothes, hanging without, it is not
worth while to bargain.

Hereafter, when I may perhaps come, during my leisure,
to pay a visit ;

The former master will be called the honoured guest."

. . . . .

The above detached lines, together with the regular
stanza, were composed by an eminent person, in the
Dynasty of Ming, who sold his house and built another.
Selling one's house, however, is a troublesome sort of
business ; it cannot sufficiently be regretted. What is

there of pleasure in it, that a man should compose all sorts of verses and rhymes on such a subject?

If you wish to know the nature of property in this world, it is altogether transitory. There is no river or hill which remains unchanged for a thousand years; but there is not a house which remains unsold for an hundred. If you give it into the hands of your children and grand-children, they will deliver to other persons with its value diminished. It is better oneself to seek a purchaser, before it is altogether destroyed; then if you cannot sell it for its price, you still leave behind you the reputation of liber-ality. It will be said, " He knew well enough it was expen-sive, and therefore let it go cheap. He did it as a favour; it was not that he was taken in." If, on the contrary, your children or grandchildren happen to sell it low, there soon arise plenty of discussions. It is said, " He has wasted the patrimony of his fathers; and is undutiful. He has dismembered what his ancestors loved; and is wicked. He knows not the difficulty of laying the founda-tion of a fortune; he is a fool. These three bad names, are all that his ancestors, who founded the family, and accumulated the property, have delivered down to him. It is better to have not a single brick left you. Though the man, who has not enough land to stick an awl into, is the cause of his posterity acquiring their fortune with empty hands, they still obtain the credit of not having had an inch of ground as a step towards it. Those men, therefore, who are fathers and grandfathers, when they have arrived at the end of their days, should turn round their heads and give a look at those who are coming after them. If, upon examination, they appear by their conduct to be unworthy children, it is better to get rid of the property at once; thus preventing their becoming the Prodigal Sons of a frugal father, and receiving the ridicule of mankind.

From ancient times down to the present, of those persons who have been particularly eminent for such good sense, there have been only two. The one was named Tang-yew; the other Yu-shin. They, seeing that their sons were degenerate, and that afterwards their property must inevitably be given up to other persons in a ruined state, thought it better to dispose of it with their own hands. There are still two lines of an old Ode, which allude to this,—they say,

" Give splendid arms to grace the soldier's side ;
  Give paints and patches to the beauteous bride."

If their posterity, they thought, disposed of it for them, it was most probable that they would not find a good receiver. Most inevitably one would contend and another tug, until they fought about it. To say nothing about their sons and wives having no place to live in, their very graves and tombs would not be secure from disturbance. If such then is the case with those who possess the Empire, how much more so with the common people.

I am now going to speak of one person, who was eminent for sense, and of another who was deficient ; that they may serve as examples to the world. The patrimony of these two persons could not be compared to a tile of Tang-yew's house, or to a brick on Yu-shin's wall. But why do I, in speaking of these two inferior men, make use of such a lofty comparison ? The reason is, because of these two, the surname of one was Tang, of the other Yu. Every one said, they were the descendants of Tang-yew, and Yu-shin ; that they took the national appellation of those Emperors for their surnames ; that they were descended in a line from them. I therefore borrow the ancestors in delineating the descendants, in order to do justice to the original source.

The sensible man had all his ancestor's disposition ; the stupid fellow had very little of the character of his family. They mutually diverged from each other, as the heavens from the abyss. How dissimilar branches sprung from the same stem will be perceived.

During the reign of Kea-tsing, of the Dynasty of Ming ; in the province of Sze-chuen, the Foo of Ching-too, and the Heen of Ching-too ; there lived a rich man in increasing circumstances. His surname was Tang ; his epithet, Yo-chuen. This man had an immense quantity of land. Whenever he got any money, he delighted only in buying fields and purchasing ground. But he would build no houses ; and of those family utensils which are in constant use, he would not buy one too many. With regard to clothes and food, they had no weight with him. His disposition was to make money by all sorts of means. As to his extensive property in rich lands, no sooner did they enter into his possession than the profits came in. They increased daily as the moon towards her plenitude. Houses and furniture (he thought) are not only unprofitable, but there is a fear lest the God of fire should destroy them, and in a moment they should become annihilated. If all the family had fine garments, there immediately come unpleasant fellows to borrow clothes. If there are plenty of victuals, one soon has people claiming acquaintance, and taking their seats, in quest of food. There is nothing like being contented with coarse articles ; people in that case will not be begging them.

He took fast hold of this idea, and, in addition to not buying any thing but houses, would not spend a candareen or a cash. The state of his mind being thus, he could not be at rest with his niggardliness, but wanted also to steal a great name. He said, that he was descended from the Emperor Tang-yew ; and that his ancestors had great celebrity. That they lived in a thatched house with mud steps ;—that what they lived upon was broth and Yuen wine ;—that they used earthen jars and pots ;—and that their garments were of cloth and deer skins. The father being thus economical, his sons could not but obey his precepts. People seeing him (the father) parsimonious in the extreme, began to scrutinize him behind his back, saying ; " There is an ancient proverb, which says, ' If a man is very economical he must have a prodigal son.' He must inevitably have a successor who will turn things upside down ; so that Tang's disposition to save will not descend." Unexpectedly, however, the son imitated his father. From his earliest years he commenced a scholar, seeking preferment by all sorts of means; and was a titular Sew-tsac. In his eating and drinking he did not seek for luxury; in his clothes he wished not for a super-abundance; in his instruments of amusement he did not aim at the best. It was only on the subject of houses that he differed from his other desires. There, indeed, he was not contented with economy. To look at the house in which he lived, it was like any rich man's necessary. He was quite ashamed of it. He wanted to be building fine houses; but was afraid to begin, lest the means could not be obtained. He had heard people say that to buy an old house was better than to build a new one; therefore, in a consultation with his father, he said, " If we can buy a handsome house, which will be fit for us to live in, we may then look for a garden, and build a library in it, such as may suit our wish." Yö-chuen, desiring much to become a Fung-keun, wished only to flatter his son, and, without being aware, deviated from his constant opinion. He said in answer, " There is no necessity to be in a hurry; in this street is a handsome house and garden. It is not yet completely built; but the day of its being finished must inevitably be the day of its sale; you and I will just wait a while." The son said, " When people want to sell houses, they do not build: when they build houses, they do not intend to sell them. Where is the probability that, when they have finished building, they intend to sell the house?" Yö-chuen said, " Pray where did you get that crochet? The man who possesses ten thousand pieces of gold may build a house which costs him only one thousand. But if a man's possessions in houses and lands are half and half, he may be said to be a large tree without a root, which must inevitably be blown down when the wind comes. Then how much more may this man, who, without possessing an hundred acres in land, suddenly builds a house with a thousand rooms, be called a tree without a root? He truly will not wait for the wind's blowing, but will tumble down of himself! How can there be any question about it ? "

The son, hearing these words, said that they were very true ; and, as before, accorded with his father. He went seeking only for land, and did not come to ask about houses. He wished that the other man would soon have finished building ; in order that the present owner being gone, he might give the finishing stroke instead of him. The rich man's plans proved successful : the result justified his words. There are two lines of the " She-king," which are applicable to the case.

" The nest one bird constructs with anxious toil,
    'Ere long another seizes as her spoil."

He who was building the house was descended from Chung-hwa. His surname was Yu, his name Haou, and his epithet Soo-chin. He was one who delighted in reading books of poetry ; but did not seek to be an eminent scholar. From the indolence of his disposition, he had a great aversion to any office ; and was not cut out for being a mandarin. He therefore detached his thoughts from a great name, and entirely gave himself up to odes and wine ; and by these means could not but be reduced to beggary.

During his whole life he had scarcely any other delight than in arranging and building gardens and summer houses. From the beginning of the year to the end, not a day passed without his advancing the work. The house which he was now building he wished to be of the highest perfection, and not of the common order ; he said, " Let other men have their fine fields and their numerous acres ; pleasures and riches were the concerns of others ; on him they had no influence." There were only three things in which he truly took an interest, and which he was determined to have of the best quality. These three were, the house which he inhabited in the day, the bed in which he slept at night, and the coffin in which he was to be laid after death. Having these ideas in his breast, he went on with the work of earth and wood, labouring continually at it in an indefatigable manner.

Tang Yö-chuen's son, having waited several years without seeing him finish the business, was a little vexed and angry at heart ; and said to his father, " Why have we waited such a long time ? That man's house is not yet finished, nor is his money yet expended. From this it would appear that he is a fellow of ways and means. With regard to the business of his selling it hereafter, that seems to be a little uncertain." Yö-chuen replied, " Every day later makes it a day more certain ; and each day make it more advantageous for us. There is no occasion for you to fret about it. The reason why his house is not finished is merely this ; when it is completed, the appearance does not hit his wish ; and he wants to take it to pieces, in order to build again. If it is excellent, he seeks for still higher excellence ; so that of every day, during which it is delayed, the alterations and improvements are wholly for our own advantage. The reason of his money not being completely wasted is because the usurers and the workmen, seeing he is building it very high, wishing to take and lend to him on credit. The labourers do not sue him for their food and debts, because they think that by every additional day of work they get a day's wages ; while, if they were to press him hard, he would certainly stop the work for a couple of days, and they would have no employment. It is thus that his money is not all expended. This may be called ' taking flesh to feed an ulcer.' It is not that he is possessed of ways and means. When he has arrived at the period when he can draw together no more, those persons who have him in their books will inevitably press him all together, and begin to curse him. There is no fear that he will not seek, in the first place, to sell what he has in land ; and as that will not suffice to pay them, he will certainly think about his house. If he now begins to collect, at an early period, while his debts are not large, he can wait for a good price in order to sell it, and therefore will not let it go cheap. The right way will be to wait till a later day, when his debts are a little increased; and, anxious to sell, he will be willing to come down with the terms. This is all the very making of us; why go and obstinately fret about it?"

The son, hearing this, still more applauded and acquiesced. Indeed, after a few years, Yu-soo-chin's debts by degrees accumulated, and his creditors every day came before his doors to claim them; and there were some who would not go away again. The house which he was building could not be finished; and he at last wanted to seek a man to buy it.

All those who are selling houses are differently circumstanced from the vendors of lands. They must necessarily wish to find out a purchaser in some neighbouring situation, that he may have either his foundations contiguous, or his windows opposite. If some distant person wishes to buy, he will want to enquire of those in the neighbourhood. Should the neighbours utter a word of disadvantage, he, who wanted to purchase, will not be willing to do it. Not like lands, or hills, or fish ponds, in the midst of an empty desert, which any one can manage. Therefore in selling a house, it is certainly desirable to sell to some one in the neighbourhood.

Tang-yö-chuen was a monied man; it would not do to trifle with him. The people of the house of course went to ask him first. Both the father and son, though at their hearts they greedily coveted it, merely returned for answer, that "They did not want it." They waited till he entreated them earnestly; and then went over,—just to give a look. As if disliking it, they said that "He had built it but indifferently. The apartments were not fit for a gentleman; and the winding avenues would only impede business. The fine carved doors, when they were required to keep out thieves, would have no strength. Rooms, which should be different, were like each other. The ground and the air were very damp. No wonder that it would fetch no money. The flowers and bamboos were like plantations of mulberry and hemp. Those who came to saunter here must inevitably be constantly served with wine and eatables. Such a house as this was fit only to be turned into a nunnery, or a jos-house. If one wished to make inner apartments for one's children, it would never do."

Yu-soo-chin had during his whole life spent his heart's blood upon it; and now, seeing that it did not obtain approbation, but that they shewed a dislike and contempt towards it, was not altogether pleased. But, as besides this man there was no one who could buy the house, it was as well not to quarrel with him.

The people present advised Yö-chuen not to say too much against it. The price altogether was not high; and even if he took it to pieces and built it again, it would pay for the workmen and their maintenance. Yö-chuen and his son of course praised and dispraised it, till they brought it down to an exceeding low price; not above one fifth of the value.

Yu-soo-chin had no alternative; and must bear the pain of selling it. State rooms, pavilions, and fish ponds, were all delivered over in the bonds. There was only one set of rooms which he had been at all his life, and had brought exactly to fit his taste. This he would not write down in the bonds, but wanted to build a partition wall, and make another entrance, in order that he might inhabit it till his death.

The son decidedly wanted to force him to sell it altogether, in order that it might be complete. Yö-chuen seemed to agree with the rest of the people. Screwing up his mouth, he said, "Let him sell it, or not sell it; where is the use of forcing him? He only wishes to keep this small shred, that it may be the means of recovering the property hereafter, when he has improved his circumstances. It will then, as of old, revert to its original master, which will be a very good thing." When the people heard this, they all said that it was the speech of a benevolent man. How should they know that it was far otherwise; that it was altogether the language of contempt! He concluded that it could never be recovered, and therefore left him this shred. Indeed it was quite useless; and the whole must inevitably become one house; the only difference being, whether sooner or later. He therefore listened to his requisitions, and entirely accorded with him in words. Accordingly they took the whole house and divided it into two compartments. The new master obtained nine parts and the old possessor, one.

It seems that these few studies were in the style of a pagoda, consisting altogether of three stories. In each story was a tablet, written upon by eminent persons, all of whom he could name. In the lowest room were carved lattices, crooked railings, bamboo seats, and flower-stands. It was the place where he received people. Upon the front of the tablet were written four characters to this effect:

" DEDICATED TO MEN."

The middle story had bright tables and clear windows; with some toothpicks and pictures. It was the place where he was accustomed to read and write. Upon the tablet were four characters, saying:

" DEDICATED TO THE ANCIENTS."

The highest story was empty and light. There was nothing besides a chafing dish of incense, and a sacred book. This was where he retreated from the crowd, retired from noise, divided himself from men, and shut out example. On the front of the tablet were four characters to this effect:

" DEDICATED TO HEAVEN."

Having divided the building into compartments for these three different uses, he likewise took them unitedly, and formed a tablet, calling them:

" THE THREE DEDICATED ROOMS."

Before he had parted with the rest of his property, those three appellations, though well chosen, were still vainly applied. The rooms had not yet been really made use of.

The lowest apartment only could be excepted; for as he was exceedingly fond of guests, and, if a person from a distance visited him, immediately placed a bed in it, the appellation of, " Dedicated to men," was certainly applicable. As to the two upper apartments, he had not hitherto been in them. Now that his summer houses were gone, besides the apartment " Dedicated to the Ancients," he had no place to read or write in; and, except that " Dedicated to Heaven," no place to which he could retire from noise, or retreat from the crowd. All the day long he sat in them, and the names which he had dedicated became truly applicable. He then fully understood that in a small house a great deal might be done; and that it was better to despise the name and assume the reality. These four popular lines are not inapplicable,

> " Lord of ten thousand acres, blooming fair,
>   A few small morsels quell thy appetite;
> A thousand spreading roofs demand thy care,
>   And, lo! six feet suffice thee ev'ry night."

Hitherto the little strength which he had possessed, had all been dissipated in vain. He henceforth applied his enterprising and extensively operating genius, collectively at a single point; and caused these apartments to be decorated to an extraordinary degree. Residing in the midst of them, Yu-soo-chin not only did not feel the misery of parting with his garden, being, on the contrary, very much relieved by the absence of that burden; but also did not suffer from a violent neighbour at his side. How he could live securely in this habitation, will be shewn in the next section, where it is explained.

## SECTION II

After Yö-chuen and his son had bought the pleasure ground, the rich man's taste unavoidably proved different from that of the former owner; and he wanted to alter it once again. But it was not necessary to transpose the beams, or to change the pillars; and make it altogether unlike its former appearance. It was like a handsome landscape, where the only thing requisite was to add a blade of grass, or take away a tree. The appearance did not suit his idea of a picture. When he had worked at it for a time, he found that he had missed his original intention of turning iron into gold, and, contrary to his expectation, was turning gold into iron.

The persons who came to see it, all said that, " This pleasure ground was large and unsuitable. That, after all, it was not to be compared with those studies; though if they were united, it would be well enough. That it was no wonder the other retained the small part and despised the large one; or that he held it tenaciously, and would not sell it. That the partition turned out to be that of one inch of gold to ten cubits of iron."

Yö-chuen and his son, hearing these sayings, inadvertently became angry and repentant of the bargain; they then knew that a man may be rich and yet not comfortable. They applied to the brokers; and going over to annoy him, required that he should insert it in the deeds, and give the whole over to them. Yo-soo-chin, since selling the pleasure grounds, had employed no workmen, and had certainly not been extravagant. As he owed no private debts, and was short neither of money nor food, how should he wish to sell his property? He therefore said to them in answer, " When this habitation was gone, tell me where I should repose myself? But if you should even cause me to be short of sustenance and destitute of clothing, I will still hold out." How much more determined was he now, when his circumstances were improved.

The brokers came over and spoke about it to Yö-chuen's son. He could not help taking his father to task, and said that, " He had been all his life time studying men, but had on this occasion, for once not formed a right judgment." Yö-chuen answered, " That fellow may be violent while he is alive, but he cannot be violent after he is dead.

He is now rather an old man, and without heirs. When the breath is out of his body, all his wives, mistresses, and servants, will inevitably revert to others. How much more then, these few rooms. The whole family, and all that they carry with them, will come over to us; there is no fear of their flying away up to heaven." The son hearing this said that "Though his words were true, still this man's duration seemed to be without limit; there was no waiting for him; and the sooner they got the whole of the property the better." From this time hence, they made Yu-soo-chin the chief subject of their thoughts, and did not so much curse him that he might die soon, as they hoped that he would soon become poor; for when he had arrived at the period when he should be short of sustenance and destitute of clothings (they thought), he certainly could not hold out.

Who could have conceived that, when men had such virtuous wishes, heaven would not accord with them! He not only did not become impoverished, with all their hoping; but also did not die, in spite of all their cursing. On the contrary, he hereafter grew stronger as he became older. He was neither troubled with a want of clothes, nor did his sustenance fail him; and he had no necessity to sell his apartments.

Yö-chuen and his son were enraged and vexed beyond measure; and concerted a plan. They went over and applied to the brokers, insisting that he should redeem back the whole. They said, "Two families cannot live in one garden. Exalted in his dedicated rooms on high, he looks down upon that summer house of ours. He can see into our private rooms, while we cannot view his women's apartments. This unequal sort of business will never answer."

Yu-soo-chin heard these words, but knew that their wish to be off the bargain was feigned, and that the real truth was, they greedily desired to get the whole. He repeated his former words, and returned a sharp and decisive answer.

Yö-chuen and his son were exceedingly angry, and it only remained for them to oppress him with the mandarin's power. They wrote a document, announcing, in open hall, their wish to undo the bargain; hoping that, by a little bribery, they might buy over and manage the mandarin, and through him get the whole property.

They little thought that that officer was incorruptible; that he had formerly been a poor scholar, and had been cheated and insulted by a person of property. He said, "That is an indigent man; how, then, can he redeem it? Yours is evidently a plot to ruin and devour him. You are persons of property, and want to be rich without being virtuous; I, who am a magistrate, wish to be virtuous without being rich." Then, in open hall, he rebuked them for a while; and tearing up the deed, turned them both out.

Yu-soo-chin had a friend, bound to him by the first principles of honour. He was a man from a distant part of the country, and possessed great wealth. It was his delight to make light of riches in performing acts of benevolence. He happened one day to come and converse with Yu-soo-chin. Seeing that he had sold his garden and pavilion, he heaved a deep sigh. When he heard, also, that persons had been plotting against him, and that he could not live securely even in this little nest, but must hereafter give it up entirely, he wanted immediately to produce the money and redeem it for Yu-soo-chin.

The latter was a man unequalled for his independent spirit. To say nothing of his unwillingness to put another to inconvenience for some hundreds or thousands; if a man offered him but one tael or five mace, without shewing he had some claim to it, he would refuse to accept it. Having heard what his friend had to say, he told him that his warm-heartedness was all in vain. He was mistaken in his view of the subject. Of the possessions of this world, where was that which remained a thousand years without being sold? One might indeed take care of it during life-time; but there was no securing it after death. "Though now (said he) you interest yourself in my cause, and advance large sums of money to redeem a small portion of it, I cannot live above a few years; and some of these days, when I die without heirs, every brick and tile of it must revert to other persons. Though now, from a generous motive, you are willing to make light of your money, I am afraid that you cannot assist me twice. Though now, alas! you may redeem the property for me, wait till a little while hence, and you cannot be of any service to my ghost." The friend, seeing that he assumed this mode of plain thinking, was unwilling to press him.

He lodged with him several nights in the "Three Dedicated Rooms," and afterwards, when he took leave, in order to return home, addressed Yu-soo-chin thus, previous to commencing his journey. "At night, while I was reposing in the lowest room, I perceived a white rat, which ran about, and then suddenly darted into the floor. Some wealth is, no doubt, concealed there. On no account sell this house to any one. A little time hence you may, perhaps, dig up some treasure; but I will not say positively." Yu-soo-chin, hearing these words, only gave a sort of cold laugh, and said, "Thank ye"; they then separated.

The old saying says well, that "No wealth even fell by chance to him, whose destiny was to be poor." It is only the wealthy purchasers of houses who dig up hidden treasures. There never yet has been seen a person selling his property, who has found half a vile cash in his own ground. Yu-soo-chin was a knowing man; how should he have the folly to indulge any such ideas! Hence, when he had heard what his friend had to say, he merely gave a sort of cold laugh; and did not begin to rout up the bricks and dig the earth.

Yö-chuen and his son, since they had experienced the mandarin's wrath, had let shame succeed to resentment. They were still more busy with their plots; and hoped that Yu-soo-chin would soon die; that he would soon become a lonesome ghost. They might then enter his house with a good face.

Who could have thought that when a rich man had been right in all his conjectures, there should only be the two circumstances of life and death, which would not acknowledge his control! Yu-soo-chin not only did not die, but having arrived at upwards of sixty years, became suddenly quite brisk, and got a son.

There immediately came great numbers of congratulatory guests, and assembled in the "Three Dedicated Rooms." They all said that "Now was the opportunity to get back the property." When Yö-chuen and his son heard of the event, they were very much disturbed. They were, before, only afraid of not obtaining a portion, but, now, were apprehensive that they should lose the whole; and were anxious beyond measure.

After a month had elapsed, there unexpectedly came over to them several brokers, saying that Yu-soo-chin, after the birth of his son, had been reduced to poverty by his guests; they had eaten his salt clean and his vinegar dry. He had now no means of subsistence left, and could only think of the house he lived in. He had issued the cards for selling it, and the bills were all on the doors. They ought not to let slip this opportunity, but should pounce upon it as quickly as possible."

When Yö-chuen and his son heard this, they were mad with joy. Their only apprehension was, that he would remember and hate them for the circumstances which were passed; that he would prefer selling it to some other person, and would not wish to have any dealings with them.

They little thought that Yu-soo-chin's way of thinking was altogether different from their own. He said, "The descendants of the two families of Tang and Yu are very different from those of others. His ancestor, Te-yao, conferred the Empire on my forefather, who had nothing to give in recompense. Now, since the obligation has descended to his posterity, to take this small property, and bestow it for nothing, would not be improper; how much more, then, when I get a price for it. I will not, for a little resentment of the present day, obliterate the great favours of former times. Tell him not to be anxious ; just let him trust to me to fix some small price for it, and give it over to him altogether.

Yö-chuen, as well as his son, when he heard of this, was happy beyond measure. He said, " I always delighted in dwelling upon my ancestors, and have ever received their favourable influence. If it had not been for their ancient generosity, how should I have obtained this magnificent residence. Thus it is that men may rejoice in having virtuous forefathers!" He then went over with the brokers and settled the bargain. He had hitherto delighted in seeking for an advantage ; but now, when old things had been brought forward, he wished to confer the obligations to the last. Yu-soo-chin, on the other hand, did not higgle about it ; but imitated Yö-chuen's ancestor, who had given up his throne and his kingdom ; and accordingly sought some thatched cottage, in which he might live, having parted with the whole of the concern.

There were a few honest friends who could not justify Yu-soo-chin. They said, " When you had your house, where was the objection to selling it to some other person, that you should wish to dispose of it to him, who envied and plotted against you. He has now succeeded ; and both father and son will go about to every one chattering and exulting. Before you had a son, you would not abate in your resentment. Now that you had got a son, he might have proved a foundation for recovering the whole ; and even though you had not recovered it, that which you have, would have sufficed. Why then take the possession, which remained to you, and give them over to Yö-chuen ? "

Yu-soo-chin, having heard what they had to say, gave a sort of laugh, and then said in answer, " Your intentions, gentlemen, are very good ; but you regard merely what is before your eyes, without considering the hereafter. I judge that his plans will eventually benefit me.

If I had wanted to redeem the whole property, I must have waited till my son was grown up. When he had arrived at manhood, it might then have been possible to get it all back. I, however, am an old man, and conceive that I cannot last until he is grown up; and who can tell that after my death my son would not have sold it to Yö-chuen. Having waited till the son had parted with it, he would then have laughed at and abused the father. It is better that the father should sell the property, and then people will compassionate the son.

"But even this would have been but a small matter. It is ten thousand to one that I shall soon have died; and my son would not have been grown up. My wife, being content to strive with hunger, would not have parted with the property to Yö-chuen. He, seeing that the new would not come into his hands, and fearing, also, that the old might be redeemed, would inevitably have laid plots to cut off my heir. Thus, I am fearful that, not only the property would not have been recovered, but my son also would have been sacrificed. This indeed might be called a loss! By selling it cheap to him now, I have merely deposited a part with him, and have made him incur a debt which will be paid into the hands of my son. If he does not pay it, there are others who will. The old proverb says, "To endure injuries is the sure policy."

Having heard him thus far, the people, though they were a little startled, said, "That he was very unsafe," Yu-soo-chin unexpectedly died a few years after having sold the property; and left his son, a child, under the protection of his widow, who possessed scarcely anything. Their sole reliance was on the price of the house, which produced a little interest, just enough to subsist upon. Tang-yö-chuen's possessions became every day greater. He knew how to make money, and his son knew how to take care of it. Everything came in; nothing went out. The property which he had bought was so secure, that it might last for a thousand years. Every one arraigned the wisdom of Heaven, saying, "The descendants of those persons, who were liberal and just, had little or nothing; while the progeny of those, who enriched their families by unworthy means, were able to heap up riches." The saying, however, of the ancients is very true, " That when virtue and vice have arrived at their full, they must finally be recompensed; the only difference being, whether soon or late." These words are constantly in men's mouths, but leave very little impression on their hearts. If the recompense comes late, it is just the same as if it came early; and doubtless his lot who waits for it is the worst.

If you wish to understand the subject of late and early recompenses, it very much resembles laying out money and receiving the interest. If you receive it back one day sooner, you receive one day's less interest. If you leave it for one year more, you receive one year's additional interest. If you look for a recompense with an anxious heart, Heaven will not conclude the matter with you; and it will appear as if there were no recompense. Heaven will wait till you have lost all expectation, and, when you have utterly given up the idea, will then suddenly send it. Just as a bad debt of many years standing which, when the lender has entirely forgotten it, arrives unexpectedly at his door, with an exceedingly large accumulation of interest. How much superior in advantage to lending out and receiving it back immediately!

When Yu-see-chin's son had attained to the age of seventeen or eighteen, he suddenly acquired a literary title. His name was Yu-tsze-chin; his epithet Ke-woo. He was created a Hëen, and being chosen to go to Peking, was raised to the office of Chang-ko. He was a man who dared to speak in the cause of rectitude, and became a great favourite with the Emperor Tsung.

At length, when his mother became old, he requested leave to retire and support her. As he was making the best of his way home, and was some miles from it, he saw a woman, not much more than twenty, with a document in her hand, kneeling by the wayside, and crying out aloud, "I entreat that my Lord, Yu, will receive and examine this." Ke-woo told her to come into the boat, and taking the deed, looked at it. It turned out to be in the name of her husband, who wanted, with his family and effects, to come under his protection, and become his slaves. Ke-woo said to her, "By your appearance you seem to be of a good family. Why do you wish to throw yourselves under my protection? Why, too, does your husband not shew himself; but desire that you, a woman, should expose yourself, and come to the wayside, crying out aloud?"

The woman said, "I am descended from an ancient family; but my father-in-law, during his lifetime, was fond of buying lands; and every acre of land, and every house which adjoined to his own, he always endeavoured to add to the stock. Those people who parted with their property did not part with it willingly; but every one of them hated him in their hearts. Before my father-in-law died, they happened, in the first place, to be favourable times, which prevented him from breaking in upon his wealth. Secondly, he was a person of rank; and, therefore, if a mandarin had anything against him, it was only necessary to spend a little money, and he could still live unmolested. At length the favourable times no longer existed; and before half a year was over, my father-in-law died. My husband was young, and likewise possessed no rank. Those persecutors of the orphan and the widow rushed upon him all in a body, and all went before the Hëen with charges against him; so that within a year, he experienced a great many different actions; and the larger half of his property was expended. But now there has befallen him a still greater evil, which is not yet got over. My husband is at present in prison, and it is not money which will get him out. He who can speak in his behalf must be a person of eminence. If such a person concerns himself in his cause, and manages the business as if it were his own, he may then be liberated. He who in this place at present answers to this description can only be your Lordship; besides which, this business has some relation to you. Although it is my husband's cause, it is truly the same as if it were your Lordship's. He therefore wrote this letter, and directed me to come before you, and throw ourselves upon your support; presenting to you all our property and our persons, and only entreating that your Lordship will not reject them as worthless, but accept of them as soon as possible."

Ke-woo, hearing these words, could not overcome his surprise. He asked her, "What can that business be, which you have not yet got over, and which concerns me? Without doubt, while I have been absent from home, my slaves have been creating a piece of work, and, in conjunction with you and your husband, produced this evil. This has led you to throw yourselves upon my support. Do you want me to take a parcel of strangers, to recognize them as belonging to a family of rank, and by protecting them, to incur guilt, through an unjust stretch of power?"

The woman said, "It is by no means thus. In the midst of our place is a tall building, called 'The Three Dedicated Rooms.' It was originally your Lordship's property; but was sold away. We lived in it for several years without molestation. Lately, however, some unknown enemy unexpectedly presented an anonymous petition, saying that my husband was one of a nest of robbers; and that the three generations, from the grandfather to the grandson, were all rogues. That there were now twenty pieces of treasure deposited under the 'Three Dedicated Rooms,' and that when the hoard was taken up, the particulars would be understood. The mandarin having seen this document, quietly sent some thief-takers forward, to raise up the hoard. Contrary to all expectation they sure enough produced from under the flooring twenty pieces of treasure. My husband was then apprehended, and taken to the mandarin's court. He was pointed out as a harbourer of thieves, and punished severely with torture and beating, in order that he might discover his associates, together with the rest of the spoil which they might have taken.

"My husband endeavoured, with all his might, to solve this business, but could not make it out clear. This money not only was not his, but he knew not from whence it had flown thither. As the circumstances of its coming were not plain, it was impossible to unravel the cause. We might, however, still rejoice that no one appeared to have lost it. The mandarin committed my husband on suspicion, and has not yet decided on the nature of his crime. My husband daily pondered the subject, and considered that as this property originally belonged to your Lordship's family, it was possible that your grandfather formerly deposited the treasure in the ground, and your father, not knowing of the circumstance, did not take it away. Hence, that which ought to have been a profitable concern, turned out to be a source of misfortune.

"It is not at present to be discussed whether this be so or not. We only entreat that your Lordship will claim it ; this money will then be disposed of. When the money is once disposed of, my husband will, in the midst of death, be restored to life. As it will be your Lordship who restores his existence, all our property ought to become yours. How much more, then, this pleasure ground, and these few apartments, which were constructed by your father with infinite pains and labour. Everything has its owner. These, then, truly, ought to revert to your family. There cannot remain the least dissatisfaction on our part. We entreat that your Lordship will not reject them."

Ke-woo, having heard these words, felt very suspicious. He then said in answer, "My family has of old observed a maxim, not to receive the offers of the common people. As to your throwing yourselves upon my support, we will say nothing about that. It is true enough that the pleasure ground and the apartments were all of them originally possessed by my family. They were, however, sold with all the proper forms of brokers and deeds, and were not conjured away by your relations. Therefore, if I want them again, I must take the original price and pay it back to you. Then, indeed, I may have them; but there is no reason why you should give them back for nothing. As to the treasure, it has no concern with me whatever; and it will not be proper for me to claim it. Do you now go and wait till I have had a meeting with the Hëen. I will then desire him to be careful in examining the case, as it is highly necessary to have a clear adjudgment. If the charges are not true, your husband will of course be released from prison; and doubtless, will not be put to death unjustly."

When the woman had heard these words, she rejoiced exceedingly, and having returned him ten thousand thanks, took her departure.

But it is not known from whence these misfortunes arose, or whether they were afterwards got the better of. There remains only one section; examine it a little, and you will learn.

### SECTION III

Ke-woo, having heard what the woman had to say, returned home. He then fancied himself to be the examining Magistrate, and again and again considered the matter in different lights, saying, "Not to mention that this treasure is not the patrimony of my ancestors, yet, allowing that it were so, how came their son to know nothing about it; nor my kindred to contend for its possession? On the contrary, it was a person out of the family who knew of it, and presented a petition on the subject. As the petition was without a name, it is plain that he must be an enemy; I have no doubt about it. At the same time, supposing that he had some cause of disagreement, it surely was not well to charge the other with such a vile business, and to point him out as a harbourer of thieves. Then, again, at the time of taking up the treasure, the petitioner's words were verified, and it answered exactly to the amount specified in the document, without being more or less. It is difficult to conceive that he who presented the petition, for the sake of gratifying a secret enmity, should be willing to risk such a vast sum, and having placed it in another's ground, should go and carry on such a foolish business."

He considered it for several days, but could make nothing of the matter. It was the constant subject of his thoughts, and during his sleep, and in his dreams, he cried out, and muttered broken sentences. His mother, hearing him, asked what was the matter. He then took the woman's words, and recounted them minutely. When she first heard him, his mother, likewise, was very suspicious; but having considered for a time, discovered it, and exclaimed, "It must be, it must be! This treasure does indeed belong to my family; the man was right enough in his conjectures. When your father was alive, he had a friend who came from a distance. This friend remained several nights in the lowest of the Three Dedicated Rooms; and perceived a white rat, which ran about, and then darted into the floor. At the time of his departure, he spoke to your father, desiring him by no means to sell the apartment; for he might, hereafter, acquire some unlooked for treasure. By all appearances, this treasure has come to light. Your father, by not taking it, made it a source of misfortune to others; do you then go and recognize it, and thereby save the man's life."

Ke-woo answered, "There is something more to be said on this subject. Such an idle story as this is not fit for the mouth of a respectable personage; and when I talk about a white rat to the Hëen, who knows but he will suspect that I covet that large sum of money; and not liking to claim it, have trumped up this story, in order to impose upon simple people. Besides, neither was this white rat seen by the eyes of my father, nor was this idle story related by my father's mouth. The more I consider it, the more vain does it appear; it may indeed be called the dream of a fool. If it were the property of my family, my father should have seen it; or how happened it, that I myself perceived nothing of the kind, but that it should appear to another. The whole story is false; there is no occasion to believe it. Still, however, it will be proper to consult with the Hëen, and to clear up this doubtful business, in order to save a guiltless plebeian. This will be acting like a virtuous officer."

Just as he had done speaking, a servant suddenly announced that the Hëen had arrived to pay his respects. Ke-woo said, " I was just wishing to see him; make haste, and request that he will come in." When the Hëen had paid his respects, and talked a little on general subjects, he waited not till Ke-woo had opened his mouth, but took up the doubtful affair, and requested his instruction, saying, " Tang such a one, the possessor of the hoard, has again and again been closely examined, but the truth could not be obtained. He yesterday made a deposition saying that the place where the hoard was discovered originally belonged to your family; and that, therefore, the treasure must have been left by your ancestors. I accordingly came, in the first place, to pay my respects; and secondly, to request your instruction, not knowing whether such be the case or not."

Ke-woo said, " My family, for several successive generations, has been very poor; nor did my immediate predecessors accumulate anything. I, therefore, cannot rashly lay claim to the treasure; for by so doing I should acquire a bad name. There must be something else in this affair; nor is it necessary to say that it is a hoard accumulated by a nest of thieves. I entreat, sir, that you will still continue a clear investigation, and effect a decision of the business. If you can bring the crime home to the prisoner Tang, then well and good."

The Hëen said, " At the period when your father departed this life, though you, sir, was still a child, and therefore, perhaps, was not fully acquainted with former circumstances; yet, can we not ask your mother, whether, before the property was disposed of, she saw or heard of anything particular? "

Ke-woo answered, " I have already asked my mother,

but she talks a little at random; and it is not what my father said. As I am now, sir, speaking before you, it is not proper for me to say anything unadvisedly. I will therefore keep it to myself." The Hëen, hearing this, insisted upon his telling it out; but Kee-woo was determined to say nothing.

His mother was fortunately standing behind the screen, and wishing sincerely to do a good action, desired her steward to go out, and taking the story in question, recount it minutely for his master. When the Hëen heard it, he considered silently for some time, and then said to the steward, "I will trouble you to go in and ask, where is the dwelling house of him who saw the white rat; whether he is at present alive or not; whether his family is rich or poor; on what terms of intimacy was your master with him during his life time; and whether they were in the habit of rendering each other mutual assistance? I have to request that your lady will speak with precision; as the present day's enquiry may serve in the place of a formal trial; and, perhaps, in the course of the discussion, this obscure case may be cleared up."

The steward went in for a while, and coming back, answered, "My mistress says that the person who saw the white rat was from afar; and lived in such a Foo, and such a Hëen. He is not yet dead, and his fortune is very large. He is a man of great virtue; who sets a small value on riches, and was on terms of strictest friendship with my former master. Seeing that he had sold his pleasure ground, and that he must hereafter part with his rooms, he wanted to produce the money and redeem it for him. As my former master would not consent, his friend, therefore, went no farther. The words in question are those which he uttered at the period of his departure." The Hëen, having considered a little, directed the steward to go in and ask, saying, "Did he, after the death of your Ladyship's husband, come to pay his vows to the deceased, and then meet with your Ladyship? Pray mention any expression which you might have heard him utter."

The steward went in, and returned, saying, "When my master had been dead for upwards of ten years, his friend then knew of it, and came on purpose to pay honours to his memory. Seeing that the apartments were sold, he was very much surprised; and asked, 'After my departure, did you obtain that unlooked for treasure (which I predicted)?' My mistress answered that indeed they did not obtain it. He then sighed, and said, 'It is a fine thing for those who bought the property. Deceitful in their hearts, and contriving plots to get possession of the buildings, they have acquired wealth which they did not deserve. By and by, however, they will meet with an unlooked for calamity.' A very few days after his departure, some persons brought an accusation against the family of Tang, and gave rise to this business. My mistress constantly praised and admired him, saying that he was one who could see into futurity."

The Hëen, having heard thus far, laughed heartily, and going towards the screen, made a low bow, saying, "Many thanks to your Ladyship for your instruction, which has enabled me, a dull magistrate, to make out this extraordinary business. There is no necessity for further enquiry. I will trouble your messenger to bring a receipt, and will then send the twenty pieces of treasure to your house.

Ke-woo said, "What is your reason for so doing; I beg that you, sir, will instruct me on this subject. The Hëen answered, "These twenty pieces of treasure were neither left by your ancestors, nor were they plundered by the prisoner Tang. The fact was just this. That eminent personage wished to redeem the property for your father; but as your father possessed a very independent disposition, and tenaciously refused, his friend on this account deposited the money, giving it to him as the means of redeeming the property hereafter. As he did not wish to tell this plainly, he pretended the agency of some spirit; with the idea that, having waited till he was gone, your father would dig up the treasure. When he came to pay honours

to the deceased, seeing that he had not recovered the
pleasure ground, but had also sold his dwelling, your
friend then knew that the treasure was in the hands of the
enemy, and was vexed beyond measure. At his departure,
therefore, he left an anonymous petition, with the intention of waiting till the family was broken, and the property
dispersed. As the truth is now plain, your original possessions ought to be restored and presented back to you.
What is there to say against this?"

Ke-woo, having heard this, though in his heart he
applauded him, still had an objection to the measure,
from the suspicion which would accrue. He did not wish
to thank the Hëen in too great a hurry; but making him
a bow, said that "He had formed an excellent conclusion,
and must be possessed of admirable wisdom. That though
Lung-too himself were to re-appear, he could not equal
this. At the same time (said he), though you conclude
this treasure must have been left by our generous friend,
still there are no persons to bear witness to it, and it is
not well for me to put in a claim rashly. I entreat, sir,
that you will keep it in your treasury, to supply the wants
of the people during famine."

While he was still declining the acceptance of it, a
servant came in, with a red ticket in his hand, and in a
whisper, announced to his master, saying, "The person,
of whom you have just now been talking, is at the door.
He says that he has come from the distance of above a
thousand Lee, to pay his respects to my mistress. As the
Hëen is present, I ought not to announce him; but since
he is acquainted with the business, and has arrived at a
very lucky moment, I therefore let you know, sir, as you
may wish to request his entrance for the purpose of questioning him." Ke-woo rejoiced greatly, and informed the
Hëen. The latter was ready to dance with joy, and desired
that he might quickly be requested to enter.

He appeared to be a person of great respectability,
with a round face, and white locks. He paid his respects
to his friend, but only slightly regarded the Hëen, who

was a stranger to him; and having made a bow, advanced onward, saying, " The object of my coming to-day, was to see the wife of my deceased friend. I came not to court the rich and powerful; nor do your affairs concern me, a person from the country. I cannot presume to visit you; so shew me the way into the house, that I may go and see the lady."

Ke-woo said, " As my venerable friend has come from a distance, it is not right to treat him as a visitor. Since the Hëen, however, is concerned in a difficult affair, and wants to ask you some questions; and as it is a great occurrence to find you here, we entreat you will not object to sitting down for a moment."

The old gentleman, hearing these words, made his obeisance and sat down. The Hëen took some tea with him; and then, bowing, said, " About twenty years since, you performed, sir, an act of great virtue. No person at first knew of it. It has just now fallen to my lot to bring the matter to light. With respect to that treasure, which was given to your friend, without the least notice, except by some reference to the agency of spirits, pray, sir, was not you the author of it?"

When the old gentleman heard this, he was taken by surprise, and for sometime did not speak; having recovered his embarrassment, he said in answer, " How should such a rustic as I perform any act of great virtue? What, sir, can you mean by your question?"

Ke-woo said, " Some expressions, respecting a white rat, were heard to proceed, sir, from your mouth. On account of a certain suspicious affair, they were going to impute the crime of harbouring thieves to a worthy person. As I could not hear this, I requested the Hëen to set him at liberty. While we were talking about it, we, by degrees, got a clue to the subject; but since we are not certain whether the story of the white rat be true or false, we have to request a word from you, sir, to settle it."

The old gentleman determinedly refused, and would not speak; till a message came from the mistress of the house, begging him to give up all the truth, in order that a worthy person might be exculpated. He then laughed, and taking the circumstances which had been profoundly secreted in his breast for upwards of twenty years, let the whole out. They accorded to a tittle with what the Hëen had said. Having directed the people to bring the treasure, in order that they might examine the letters and marks upon its surface; all these particulars agreed exactly.

The Hëen and Ke-woo admired the old gentleman's great virtues; Ke-woo expatiated with the old gentleman on the penetrating genius of the Hëen; while the Hëen, again, with the old gentleman, dealt out their praises on the conduct of Ke-woo, who had conferred benefits instead of cherishing resentment. " Such actions as these," said they, " would be hereafter talked of far and wide; one might know this without divination."

They went on with their praises of each other without ceasing; and the attendants who were present, put their hands to their mouths in order to repress their laughter, saying that " The Hëen had issued orders to apprehend him, who had presented the anonymous petition. Now, when he had found him out, instead of giving him a beating, he was sitting down and conversing with him. This was quite a new thing! "

When the Hëen returned to his office, he sent a messenger to deliver the twenty pieces of treasure, as well as to procure a receipt for the same. Ke-woo, however, would not receive it. He wrote back a letter to the Hëen, requesting that he would give this money over to the family of Tang, and redeem the property with it. That, in the first place, this would be fulfilling the intentions of his father; secondly, it would accord with the wishes of his generous friend; and lastly, it would enable Tang's family to purchase some other residence. Thus, neither the givers, nor the receivers, would be injured in the least.

All parties praised such unexampled generosity. The Hëen, in compliance with the words of the letter, released the prisoner Tang from his confinement, and delivering to him the original price, received from him the two deeds, by which the property had been sold. A messenger being sent off with these, the pleasure ground, and the apartments, were delivered into the possession of the original master.

On the same day, in the highest of the " Three Dedicated Rooms," he offered up wine, as a token of gratitude to heaven; saying, " Thus amply has my father's virtue been rewarded; thus bitter has been the recompense of Tang's crimes. O! how is it that men are afraid of virtue; or how is it that they delight in being vicious ? "

Tang Yö-chuen's son and his wife made out a deed, as before, delivering up their persons, and together with the price of the house, which they had received from the Hëen, offered it to Ke-woo, entreating that he would accept of their services for the remainder of their lives. Ke-woo resolutely refused the acceptance; but at the same time quieted them with kind words. Then the husband and wife, having engraved a tablet, wishing him long life, took it home and made offerings to it. Though they could not prevail upon him to receive them into his service, they recognized him as their master. They not only endeavoured to recompense his past favours; but also wanted everybody to know that they belonged to the family of Yu; for then no person would venture to molest them.

In order to remember these circumstances, everyone had a stanza of verses, the object of which was to advise persons of opulence, not to be contriving schemes for the acquirement of their neighbours' property. The lines were to this effect :

" By want compell'd, he sold his house and land,
    Both house and land, and purchasers, return ;
Thus profit ends the course by virtue plann'd,
    While envious plotters their misfortunes mourn."

India

# *INDIAN LITERATURE*

*A*LL Indian literature dating as it does from 500 B.C. is one glorious garland of imaginative composition, soulful, exquisite and predominatively subjective—" in which the heart weeps in love ; or knees are bent in praise before a hero-king." It has great war-ballads, delicate love poems and allegorical tales of high fancy. The passages selected for this section are from the compositions and translations of Sir William Jones ; M. N. Dutt ; E. J. Robinson ; P. E. More ; Professor Macdonnell ; Sir Mohamed Iqbal ; R. T. H. Griffith ; Francis H. Skrine ; Sir Rabindranath Tagore and T. D. Broughton.

# THE PALACE OF FORTUNE,
## AN INDIAN TALE

MILD was the vernal gale, and calm the day,
When Maia near a crystal fountain lay,
Young Maia, fairest of the blue-eyed maids,
That rov'd at noon in Tibet's musky shades;
But, haply, wand'ring through the fields of air,
Some fiend had whisper'd,—Maia, thou art fair!
Hence, swelling pride had fill'd her simple breast,
And rising passions rob'd her mind of rest;
In courts and glitt'ring tow'rs she wish'd to dwell,
And scorn'd her lab'ring parents' lowly cell:
And now, as gazing o'er the glassy stream,
She saw her blooming cheek's reflected beam,
Her tresses brighter than the morning sky,
And the mild radiance of her sparkling eye,
Low sighs and trickling tears by turns she stole,
And thus discharg'd the anguish of her soul:
" Why glow those cheeks, if unadmir'd they glow?
Why flow those tresses, if unpraised they flow?
Why dart those eyes their liquid ray serene,
Unfelt their influence, and their light unseen?
Ye heavens! was that love-breathing bosom made
To warm dull groves, and cheer the lonely glade?
Ah, no: those blushes, that enchanting face
Some tap'stried hall or gilded bow'r might grace,
Might deck the scenes, where love and pleasure reign,
And fire with am'rous flames the youthful train."

While thus she spoke, a sudden blaze of light
Shot through the clouds, and struck her dazzled sight:
She rais'd her head, astonished, to the skies,
And veil'd with trembling hands her aching eyes;
When through the yielding air she saw from far
A goddess gliding in a golden car,
That soon descended on the flow'ry lawn,
By two fair yokes of starry peacocks drawn:

A thousand nymphs with many a sprightly glance
Form'd round the radiant wheels an airy dance,
Celestial shapes, in fluid light array'd;
Like twinkling stars their beamy sandals play'd:
Their lucid mantles glitter'd in the sun,
(Webs half so bright the silkworm never spun)
Transparent robes, that bore the rainbow's hue,
And finer than the nets of pearly dew
That morning spreads o'er ev'ry op'ning flow'r
When sportive summer decks his bridal bow'r.

The queen herself, too fair for mortal sight
Sat in the centre of encircling light.
Soon with soft touch she rais'd the trembling maid,
And by her side in silent slumber laid:
Straight the gay birds display'd their spangled train,
And flew refulgent through th' aerial plain;
The fairy band their shining pinions spread,
And as they rose fresh gales of sweetness shed;
Fan'd with their flowing skirts the sky was mild,
And heav'n's blue fields with brighter radiance smil'd.

Now in a garden deck'd with verdant bow'rs
The glitt'ring car descends on bending flow'rs:
The goddess still with looks divinely fair
Surveys the sleeping object of her care;
Then o'er her cheek her magick finger lays,
Soft as the gale that o'er a vi'let plays,
And thus in sounds, that favour'd mortals hear,
She gently whispers in her ravish'd ear:

" Awake, sweet maid, and view this charming scene
For ever beauteous, and for ever green;
Here living rills of purest nectar flow
O'er meads that with unfading flow'rets glow;
Here am'rous gales their scented wings display,
Mov'd by the breath of ever-blooming May;
Here in the lap of pleasure shalt thou rest,
Our lov'd companion, and our honour'd guest."

The damsel hears the heav'nly notes distil,
Like melting snow, or like a vernal rill;
She lifts her head, and, on her arm reclin'd,
Drinks the sweet accents in her grateful mind:
On all around she turns her roving eyes,
And views the splendid scene with glad surprise;
Fresh lawns, and sunny banks, and roseate bow'rs,
Hills white with flocks, and meadows gem'd with
      flow'rs;
Cool shades, a sure defence from summer's ray,
And silver brooks where wanton damsels play,
That with soft notes their dimpled crystal roll'd
O'er colour'd shells and sands of native gold:
A rising fountain play'd from ev'ry stream,
Smil'd as it rose, and cast a transient gleam,
Then gently falling in a vocal show'r
Bath'd ev'ry shrub, and sprinkled ev'ry flow'r
That on the banks, like many a lovely bride,
View'd in the liquid glass their blushing pride;
Whilst on each branch with purple blossoms hung
The sportful birds their joyous ditty sung.

While Maia thus entranc'd in sweet delight
With each gay object fed her eager sight,
The goddess mildly caught her willing hand,
And led her trembling oe'r the flow'ry land;
Soon she beheld where through an op'ning glade
A spacious lake its clear expanse display'd;
In mazy curls the flowing jasper wav'd
O'er its smooth bed with polish'd agate pav'd;
And on a rock of ice by magick rais'd
High in the midst a gorgeous palace blaz'd;
The sunbeams on the gilded portals glanc'd,
Played on the spires, and on the turrets danc'd;
To four bright gates four iv'ry bridges led,
With pearls illumin'd, and with roses spread:
And now, more radiant than the morning sun
Her easy way the gliding goddess won;

Still by her hand she held the fearful maid,
And as she pass'd the fairies homage paid:
They enter'd straight the sumptuous palace-hall,
Where silken tapestry emblaz'd the wall,
Refulgent tissue, of an heav'nly woof;
And gems unnumber'd sparkled on the roof,
On whose blue arch the flaming diamonds play'd,
As on a sky with living stars inlay'd:
Of precious diadems a regal store,
With globes and sceptres, strew'd the porph'ry floor;
Rich vests of eastern kings around were spread,
And glitt'ring zones a starry radiance shed:
But Maia most admir'd the pearly strings,
Gay bracelets, golden chains, and sparkling rings.

High in the centre of the palace shone,
Suspended in mid-air, an opal throne:
To this the queen ascends with royal pride,
And sets the favour'd damsel by her side.
Around the throne in mystick order stand
The fairy train, and wait her high command;
When thus she speaks: (the maid attentive sips
Each word that flows, like nectar, from her lips.)

"Fav'rite of heav'n, my much lov'd Maia, know,
From me all joys, all earthly blessings flow:
Me suppliant men imperial Fortune call,
The mighty empress of yon rolling ball:"
(She rais'd her finger, and the wond'ring maid
At distance hung the dusky globe survey'd,
Saw the round earth with foaming oceans vein'd,
And lab'ring clouds on mountain tops sustain'd.)
"To me has fate the pleasing task assign'd
To rule the various thoughts of humankind;
To catch each rising wish, each ardent pray'r,
And some to grant, and some to waste in air:
Know farther; as I rang'd the crystal sky,
I saw thee near the murm'ring fountain lie;

Mark'd the rough storm that gather'd in thy breast,
And knew what care thy joyless soul opprest.
Straight I resolved to bring thee quick relief,
Ease ev'ry weight, and soften ev'ry grief;
If in this court contented thou cans't live,
And taste the joys these happy gardens give:
But fill thy mind with vain desires no more,
And view without a wish yon shining store:
Soon shall a num'rous train before me bend,
And kneeling votaries my shrine attend;
Warn'd by their empty vanities beware,
And scorn the folly of each human pray'r."
She said; and straight a damsel of her train
With tender fingers touch'd a golden chain;
Now a soft bell delighted Maia hears
That sweetly trembles on her list'ning ears;
Through the calm air the melting numbers float,
And wanton echo lengthens every note.
Soon through the dome a mingled hum arose,
Like the swift stream that o'er a valley flows;
Now louder still it grew, and still more loud,
As distant thunder breaks the bursting cloud:
Through the four portals rush'd a various throng,
That like a wintry torrent pour'd along:
A crowd of ev'ry tongue, and ev'ry hue,
Tow'rd the bright throne with eager rapture flew.

A lovely stripling step'd before the rest
With hasty pace, and tow'rd the goddess prest;
His mien was graceful, and his looks were mild,
And in his eyes celestial sweetness smil'd:
Youth's purple glow, and beauty's rosy beam
O'er his smooth cheeks diffus'd a lively gleam;
The floating ringlets of his musky hair
Wav'd on the bosom of the wanton air:
With modest grace the goddess he addres't,
And thoughtless thus prefer'd his fond request.

" Queen of the world, whose wide extended sway,
Gay youth, firm manhood, and cold age obey,
Grant me while life's fresh blooming roses smile,
The day with varied pleasures to beguile;
Let me on beds of dewy flow'rs recline,
And quaff with glowing lips the sparkling wine;
Grant me to feed on beauty's rifled charms,
And clasp a willing damsel in my arms;
Her bosom fairer than a hill of snow,
And gently bounding like a playful roe,
Her lips more fragrant than the summer air,
And sweet as Scythian musk her hyacinthine hair:
Let new delights each dancing hour employ,
Sport follow sport, and joy succeed to joy."

The goddess grants the simple youth's request,
And mildly thus accosts her lovely guest:
" On that smooth mirror full of magick light
Awhile, dear Maia, fix thy wand'ring sight."
She looks; and in th'enchanted crystal sees
A bow'r o'er canopied with tufted trees:
The wanton stripling lies beneath the shade,
And by his side reclines a blooming maid;
O'er her fair limbs a silken mantle flows,
Through which her youthful beauty softly glows,
And part conceal'd, and part disclos'd to sight
Through the thin texture casts a ruddy light,
As the ripe clusters of the mantling vine
Beneath the verdant foliage faintly shine,
And, fearing to be view'd by envious day,
Their glowing tints unwillingly display.

The youth, while joy sits sparkling in his eyes,
Pants on her neck, and in her bosom dies;
From her smooth cheek nectareous dew he sips,
And all his soul comes breathing to his lips.
But Maia turns her modest eyes away,
And blushes to behold their am'rous play.

She looks again, and sees with sad surprise
On the clear glass far diff'rent scenes arise:
The bow'r, which late outshone the rosy morn,
O'er hung with weeds she saw, and rough with thorn;
With stings of asps the leafless plants were wreath'd,
And curling adders gales of venom breath'd:
Low sat the stripling on the faded ground,
And in a mournful knot his arms were bound;
His eyes, that shot before a sunny beam,
Now scarcely shed a sad'ning, dying gleam;
Faint as a glimm'ring taper's wafted light,
Of a dull ray that streaks the cloudy night:
His crystal vase was on the pavement roll'd
And from the bank was fall'n his cup of gold;
From which th' envenom'd dregs of deadly hue,
Flow'd on the ground in streams of baleful dew,
And, slowly stealing through the wither'd bow'r
Poison'd each plant, and blasted ev'ry flow'r:
Fled were his slaves, and fled his yielding fair,
And each gay phantom was dissolv'd in air;
Whilst in their place was left a joyless train,
Despair, and grief, remorse, and raging pain.

Aside the damsel turns her weeping eyes,
And sad reflections in her bosom rise;
To whom thus mildly speaks the radiant queen:
"Take sage example from this moral scene;
See how vain pleasures sting the lips they kiss,
How asps are hid beneath the bow'rs of bliss!
Whilst ever fair the flow'r of temp'rance blows,
Unchang'd her leaf and without thorn her rose,
Smiling she darts her glitt'ring branch on high,
And spreads her fragrant blossoms to the sky."

Next to the throne she saw a knight advance,
Erect he stood, and shook a quiv'ring lance;
A fiery dragon on his helmet shone,
And on his buckler beam'd a golden sun;

O'er his broad bosom blaz'd his jointed mail
With many a gem, and many a shining scale;
He trod the sounding floor with princely mien,
And thus with haughty words address'd the queen:
" Let falling kings beneath my jav'lin bleed,
And bind my temples with a victor's meed;
Let ev'ry realm that feels the solar ray,
Shrink at my frown, and own my regal sway:
Let Ind's rich banks declare my deathless fame,
And trembling Ganges dread my potent name."


The queen consented to the warrior's pray'r,
And his bright banners floated in the air:
He bade his darts in steely tempests fly,
Flames burst the clouds, and thunder shake the
     sky;
Death aim'd his lance, earth trembled at his nod,
And crimson conquest glow'd where'er he trod.


And now the damsel, fix'd in deep amaze,
Th'enchanted glass with eager look surveys:
She sees the hero in his dusky tent,
His guards retir'd, his glimm'ring taper spent;
His spear, vain instrument of dying praise,
On the rich floor with idle flute he lays:
His gory falchin near his pillow stood,
And stain'd the ground with drops of purple blood;
A busy page his nodding helm unlac'd,
And on the couch his scaly hauberk plac'd:
Now on the bed his weary limbs he throws
Bath'd in the balmy dew of soft repose:
In dreams he rushes o'er the gloomy field,
He sees new armies fly, new heroes yield;
Warm with the vig'rous conflict he appears,
And ev'n in slumber seems to move the spheres.
But lo! the faithless page with stealing tread
Advances to the champion's naked head:

~~~~~~~~~~~~~~~~~~~~~~~~~~~~~~~~~~~~

With a sharp dagger wounds his bleeding breast,
And steeps his eyelids in eternal rest:
Then cries, (and waves the steel that drops with gore)
" The tyrant dies; oppression is no more."


Now came an aged sire with trembling pace,
Sunk were his eyes and pale his ghastly face;
A ragged weed of dusky hue he wore,
And on his back a pond'rous coffer bore.
The queen with falt'ring speech he thus addrest:
" O, fill with gold thy true adorer's chest."


" Behold," said she, and wav'd her pow'rful hand,
" Where yon rich hills, in glitt'ring order stand:
There load thy coffer, with the golden store;
Then bear it full away, and ask no more."


With eager steps he took his hasty way,
Where the bright coin in heaps unnumber'd lay;
There hung enamour'd o'er the gleaming spoil
Scoop'd the gay dross, and bent beneath the toil.
But bitter was his anguish to behold
The coffer widen and its sides unfold:
And ev'ry time he heap'd the darling ore,
His greedy cheft grew larger than before;
Till spent with pain, and falling o'er his hoard,
With his sharp steel his man'ning breast he gor'd:
On the lov'd heap be cast his closing eye,
Contented on a golden couch to die.


A stripling, with the fair adventure pleas'd,
Step'd forward, and the massy coffer seiz'd:
But with surprise he saw the stores decay,
And all the long-sought treasures melt away;
In winding streams the liquid metal roll'd,
And through the palace ran a flood of gold.

Next to the shrine advanc'd a rev'rend sage,
Whose beard was hoary with the frost of age:
His few grey locks a sable fillet bound,
And his dark mantle flow'd along the ground:
Grave was his port, yet show'd a bold neglect,
And fill'd the young beholder with respect;
Time's envious hand had plough'd his wrinkled face,
Yet on those wrinkles sat superior grace;
Still full of fire appear'd his vivid eye,
Darted quick beams, and seem'd to pierce the sky.
At length with gentle voice and look serene,
He wav'd his hand, and thus address'd the queen:


" Twice forty winters tip my beard with snow,
And age's chilling gusts around me blow:
In early youth, by contemplation led,
With high pursuits my flatter'd thoughts were fed;
To nature first my labours were confin'd,
And all her charms were open'd to my mind,
Each flow'r that glisten'd in the morning dew,
And ev'ry shrub that in the forest grew:
From earth to heaven I cast my wond'ring eyes,
Saw suns unnumber'd sparkle in the skies,
Mark'd the just progress of each rolling sphere,
Describ'd the seasons, and reform'd the year.
At length sublimer studies I began,
And fix'd my level'd telescope on man;
Knew all his pow'rs, and all his passions trac'd,
What virtue rais'd him, and what vice debas'd;
But when I saw his knowledge so confin'd,
So vain his wishes, and so weak his mind,
His soul, a bright obscurity at best,
And rough with tempests his afflicted breast,
His life, a flow'r ere ev'ning sure to fade,
His highest joys, the shadow of a shade;
To thy fair court I took my weary way,
Bewail my folly, and heav'n's laws obey,

Confess my feeble mind for pray'rs unfit
And to my maker's will my soul submit :
Great empress of yon orb that rolls below,
On me the last best gift of heav'n bestow."

He spake : a sudden cloud his senses stole,
And thick'ning darkness swam o'er all his soul ;
His vital spark her earthly cell forsook,
And into air her fleeting progress took.

Now from the throng a deaf'ning sound was heard,
And all at once their various pray'rs prefer'd ;
The goddess, wearied with the noisy crowd,
Thrice wav'd her silver wand, and spake aloud :
" Our ears no more with vain petitions tire,
But take unheard whate'er you first desire."
She said : each wish'd, and what he wish'd obtain'd ;
And wild confusion in the palace reign'd.

But Maia, now grown senseless with delight,
Cast on an em'rald ring her roving sight ;
And, ere she could survey the rest with care,
Wish'd on her hand the precious gem to wear.

Sudden the palace vanish'd from her sight,
And the gay fabrick melted into night ;
But in its place she viewed with weeping eyes
Huge rocks around her, and sharp cliffs arise :
She sat deserted on the naked shore,
Saw the curl'd waves, and heard the tempest roar ;
Whilst on her finger shone the fatal ring,
A weak defence from hunger's pointed sting.
From sad remorse, from comfortless despair,
And all the ruthless company of care!
Frantick with grief her rosy cheek she tore,
And rent her locks, her darling charge no more :
But when the night his raven wing had spread,
And hung with sable ev'ry mountain's head,

Her tender limbs were numb'd with biting cold,
And round her feet the curling billows roll'd;
With trembling arms a rifted crag she grasp'd,
And the rough rock with hard embraces clasp'd.

While thus she stood, and made a piercing moan,
By chance her em'rald touch'd the rugged stone;
That moment gleam'd from heav'n a golden ray,
And taught the gloom to counterfeit the day:
A winged youth, for mortal eyes too fair,
Shot like a meteor through the dusky air;
His heav'nly charms o'ercame her dazzled sight
And drown'd her senses in a flood of light;
His sunny plumes descending he displayed,
And softly thus addressed the mournful maid:

" Say, thou that dost yon wondrous ring possess,
What cares disturb thee, or what wants oppress;
To faithful ears disclose thy secret grief,
And hope (so heav'n ordains) a quick relief."

The maid replied, " Ah, sacred genius, bear
A hopeless damsel from this land of care;
Waft me to softer climes and lovelier plains,
Where nature smiles, and spring eternal reigns."

She spoke; and swifter than the glance of thought
To a fair isle his sleeping charge he brought.

Now morning breath'd: the scented air was mild,
Each meadow blossom'd, and each valley smil'd;
On ev'ry shrub the pearly dewdrops hung,
On ev'ry branch a feather'd warbler sung;
The cheerful spring her flow'ry chaplets wove,
And incense-breathing gales perfum'd the grove.

The damsel wak'd; and, lost in glad surprize,
Cast round the gay expanse her op'ning eyes,

That shone with pleasure like a starry beam,
Or moonlight sparkling on a silver stream.
She thought some nymph must haunt that lovely
    scene,
Some woodland goddess, or some fairy queen;
At least she hop'd in some sequester'd vale
To hear the shepherd tell his am'rous tale:
Led by these flatt'ring hopes from glade to glade,
From lawn to lawn with hasty steps she stray'd;
But not a nymph by stream or fountain stood,
And not a fairy glided through the wood;
No damsel wanton'd o'er the dewy flow'rs,
No shepherd sung beneath the rosy bow'rs:
On ev'ry side she saw vast mountains rise,
That thrust their daring foreheads in the skies;
The rocks of polish'd alabaster seem'd,
And in the sun their lofty summits gleam'd.
She call'd aloud, but not a voice replied,
Save echo babbling from the mountain's side.

By this had night o'ercast the gloomy scene,
And twinkling stars emblaz'd the blue serene:
Yet on she wander'd, till with grief opprest
She fell; and, falling, smote her snowy breast
Now to the heav'ns her guilty head she rears,
And pours her bursting sorrow into tears;
Then plaintive speaks, "Ah! fond mistaken maid,
How was thy mind by gilded hopes betray'd?
Why didst thou wish for bow'rs and flow'ry hills,
For smiling meadows, and for purling rills;
Since on those hills no youth or damsel roves,
No shepherd haunts the solitary groves?
Ye meads that glow with intermingled dies,
Ye flow'ring palms that from yon hillocks rise,
Ye quiv'ring brooks that softly murmur by,
Ye panting gales that on the branches die,
Ah! why has nature through her gay domain
Display'd your beauties, yet display'd in vain?

In vain, ye flow'rs, you boast your vernal bloom,
And waste in barren air your fresh perfume.
Ah! leave, ye wanton birds, yon lonely spray;
Unheard you warble, and unseen you play:
Yet stay till fate has fix'd my early doom,
And strow with leaves a hapless damsel's tomb.
Some grot or grassy bank shall be my bier,
My maiden herse unwater'd with a tear."

Thus while she mourns, o'erwhelm'd in deep despair,
She rends her silken robes, and golden hair;
Her fatal ring, the cause of all her woes,
On a hard rock with mad'ning rage she throws;
The gem, rebounding from the stone, displays
Its verdant hue, and sheds refreshing rays:
Sudden descends the genius of the ring,
And drops celestial fragrance from his wing;
Then speaks, " Who calls me from the realms of day?
Ask, and I grant; command, and I obey."

She drank his melting words with ravish'd ears,
And stop'd the gushing current of her tears;
Then kiss'd his skirts, that like a ruby glow'd
And said, " O bear me to thy sire's abode."

Straight o'er her eyes a shady veil arose,
And all her soul was lull'd in still repose
By this with flow'rs the rosy-finger'd dawn
Had spread each dewy hill and verd'rous lawn;
She wak'd, and saw a new-built tomb that stood
In the dark bosom of the solemn wood,
While these sad sounds her trembling ears invade:
" Beneath yon marble sleeps thy father's shade."
She sigh'd, she wept; she struck her pensive breast,
And bade his urn in peaceful slumber rest.

And now in silence o'er the gloomy land
She saw advance a slowly-winding band;

Their cheeks were veil'd, their robes of mournful hue
Flow'd o'er the lawn, and swept the pearly dew:
O'er the fresh turf they sprinkled sweet perfume,
And strow'd with flow'rs the venerable tomb.
A graceful matron walk'd before the train,
And tun'd in notes of woe a plaintive strain:
When from her face her silken veil she drew,
The watchful maid her aged mother knew.
O'erpow'r'd with bursting joy she runs to meet
The mourning dame, and falls before her feet:
The matron with surprise her daughter rears,
Hangs on her neck, and mingles tears with tears.
Now o'er the tomb their hallow'd rites they pay,
And form with lamps an artificial day:
Erelong the damsel reach'd her native vale,
And told with joyful heart her moral tale;
Resign'd to heav'n, and lost to all beside,
She liv'd contented, and contented died.

## THE MAHABHARATA

20. What is that weapon, O sage, which is not made of steel, which is mild, which still cuts all hearts, and which I must use for correcting the tongues of my kinsmen?

Narada said :—

21. The giving of food to the best of your ability, forgiveness, sincerity, mildness, and honour to whom honour is due,—these make a weapon which is not made of steel.

22. With soft words alone turn away the anger of kinsmen about to utter cruel words, and please their hearts and minds and slanderous words.

23. None who is not a great man with purified soul and endued with accomplishments and having friends can bear a heavy burden. Take up this great weight and bear it on your shoulders.

24. All oxen can carry heavy loads on a level road. The stronger ones only among them can carry such loads on a difficult road.

25. Disunion will create destruction which will befall all the Bhojas and the Vrishnis! You, O Keshava, are the foremost of them. Do you act in such a way that the Bhojas and the Vrishnis may not meet with destruction.

26. Nothing but intelligence and forgiveness, control of the senses, and liberality, reside in a person of wisdom.

27. The advancement of one's own race is always praiseworthy and glorious and conducive to long life. Do you, O Krishna, act in such a way that destruction may not overtake your kinsmen.

28. There is nothing about policy and the art of war, O lord, which you do not know!

Vrihaspati said :—

3. Sweetness of speech, O Shakra, is the one thing by practising which a person is esteemed by all and becomes famous.

4. This is the one thing, O Shakra, which yields happiness to all. By practising it, one may always secure the love of all creatures.

5. The person who does not speak a word and whose face is always marked with frowns is hated of all. Want of sweet speeches makes him so.

6. That person who, on seeing others, speaks to them first with smiles, succeeds in winning over every one.

7. Even gifts, if not made with sweet speeches, do not please the recipients like rice without curry.

8. If even the wealth of men, O Shakra, be snatched away with sweet speeches, such sweetness of conduct can even propitiate the robbed.

9. A king, therefore, who is desirous of even inflicting punishment, should use sweet words. Sweetness of speech never fails, while at the same time it never pains any heart.

10. A person of good deeds and good, pleasant and sweet speeches, has no peer.

Yudhisthira said :—

1. "If any person, desirous of accomplishing acts of charity and sacrifices, fails to find (the necessary) wealth, and thirst of wealth gets the better of him, what course should he pursue to obtain happiness ? "

Bhisma said :—

2. He who makes no difference between two opposite agents viz., pleasure and pain, honour and insult, etc., who never troubles himself for the gratification of his desire for worldly possessions, who observes veracity of speech, who has freed himself from all kinds of attachment, and who has renounced his desire for action, is, O Bharata, a happy man.

3. The ancients say these are the five means by which perfect tranquillity or emancipation could be obtained. These are called Heaven. These are Religion. These form the highest happiness.

4. Regarding it is cited the old story of what Manki had sung, when freed from attachments. Hear it, O Yudhisthira.

5. Manki, desirous of wealth, found that he was doomed to an unending series of disappointments. With a little remnant of his property he purchased at last a couple of young bulls with a yoke for training them (to pastoral labour).

6–7. One day the two bulls, properly yoked, were taken out for training (in the fields). Shying at the sight of a camel which was lying down on the road, the animals suddenly ran towards the camel, and fell upon its neck. Enraged at finding the bulls fall upon its neck, the camel, possessed of great speed, got up and ran with full speed, bearing away the two helpless creatures dangling on either side of its neck.

8–9. Beholding his two bulls thus carried away by that strong camel, and seeing that they were on the point of death, Manki began to say,—If it is not ordained by destiny, wealth can never be obtained even by a clever man strenuously and confidently striving and skilfully doing all that is necessary towards the accomplishment of his object.

10. I had, all along, tried by all manner and means, and with great devotion, to acquire riches. But all this misfortune to my property is due to Destiny.

11. My bulls are carried away, rising and falling, as the camel is running in an uneven course. This event seems to be an accident like the one brought about by the crow to a ripe fruit while perching on a palmyra tree.

12. Alas, those dear bulls of mine are dangling on the camel's neck like a couple of gems! This is the result of Destiny alone. Exertion is of no avail in what is due to Chance.

13. Or if the existence of anything like Exertion (as a resulting factor) be admitted, a little more scrutiny would find that Destiny is at the bottom.

14. Therefore, he who is desirous of happiness, should renounce all attachment. He who is indifferent to worldly surroundings, has renounced all desires for acquiring wealth, can sleep happily.

15. Ho, it was well-said by Shuka while going to the great forest from his father's house, renouncing everything.

16. Amongst these two, viz., one who obtains the fruition of all his desires, and one who renounces all desires, the latter, who casts off everything, is superior to the first who obtains the fruition of all his desires.

17. No one could ever attain to the end of desire. Only he who is destitute of knowledge and judgment feels an avidity for protecting his body and life.

18. Renounce all desire for action. O my Soul which has become a prey of cupidity, adopt tranquillity by freeing

yourself from all worldly attachments. Repeatedly have you been cheated (by phantoms of hope). How is it that you do not still free yourself from attachments?

19. If I am not one who deserves to be crushed by you, if I am one with whom you should play in delight, then, O my wealth-coveting Soul, do not induce me towards cupidity.

20. You have now and again lost your hoarded wealth! O my wealth-coveting and foolish Soul, when will you succeed in getting rid of your desire for wealth?

21. Shame on my foolishness. I have become a toy of yours. It is thus that one becomes a slave of others.

22. No one born on Earth did ever attain to the end of desire and no one who will be born hereafter will succeed in attaining to it. Renouncing all acts, I have at last been roused from sleep. I am now awake.

23. Without doubt, O Desire, your heart is hard like that of an adamant, since though affected by a hundred reverses, you do not break into as many fragments.

24. I know you, O Desire, and all those things that are dear to you. Seeking what is dear to you, I shall feel happiness in my own Self.

25. O Desire, I know your origin. You originate from Will. I shall, therefore, avoid Will. You will then be rooted out.

26. The desire for wealth can never yield happiness. If acquired, the acquirer feels great anxiety. If lost after acquisition, it is felt like death. Again, acquisition itself is very uncertain.

27. Wealth cannot be secured by even the surrender of one's person. What can be more painful than this? When

acquired, one is never gratified with its quantity, but one continues to hanker after it.

28. Like the sweet water of the Ganges, riches only enhance one's hankering. It is my destruction. I am now awakened. Do you, O Desire, leave me.

29. May that desire which resides in this my body,—this compound of (five) elements,—go wherever it likes and live happily wherever it likes.

30. I do not like you all who are not of the Soul, for you bring on Desire and Cupidity! Forsaking all of you I shall seek refuge with the quality of Goodness.

31–32. Seeing all creatures in my own body and my own mind, and devoting my reason to Yoga, my life to the instructions of the wise, and soul to Brahma, I shall happily rove through the world, without attachment and without calamities of any kind, so that you may not be able to plunge me again into such sorrows.

33. If I continue to be unruffled by you, O desire, I shall necessarily be without a path (by which to effect my salvation). You, O desire, are always the parent of thirst, of sorrow, and of fatigue and toil.

34. I consider the sorrow that one feels at the loss of wealth is proportionately greater than what one feels under any other adverse circumstance. Relatives and friends forsake him who has lost his wealth.

35. With all sorts of humiliation numbering by thousands, there are many other faults in property which are even much more painful. On the other hand, the very small happiness that resides in wealth is mingled with pain and sorrow.

36. Robbers kill, in the sight of all, the person who has riches, or torment him with all sorts of severity, or put him into fright now and again.

37. At last, after a long time, I have realised that the desire for wealth is attended with sorrow. Whatever the object, O desire, upon which you set your heart, you force me to follow it! You are without judgment. You are a fool. You are difficult of being satisfied. You can never be contented. You burn like fire.

38. You do not enquire when following the object you pursue, whether it is easy or difficult of attainment. Like the nether region, you cannot be filled to the brim. You wish to cast me into grief. From this day, O desire, I am incapable of living with you.

39. I who was disappointed, at first, at the loss of my property, have now attained to the high state of perfect freedom from attachments. At this moment I no longer think of you and your train.

40. I had before this, felt great misery on your account. I do not (now) regard myself as devoid of intelligence. Having taken to Renunciation on account of the loss of my property, I now can rest, being freed from every kind of fever.

41. I cast you off, O Desire, with all the passions of my heart. You shall not again find any place in me nor shall you sport with me.

42. I shall forgive them who will slander or speak ill of me. I shall not harm even when I am injured. If anybody from aversion speaks disparagingly of me, without caring for those disagreeable words I shall greet him courteously. With a contented heart and with an easy mind, I shall always live upon what I may obtain for myself.

43. I shall not gratify those wishes of yours which are inimical to me. Indifference to worldly concerns, renunciation, contentment, tranquillity, veracity, self-control, forgiveness, and universal mercy, have now come to be my qualifications.

44. Therefore, let Desire, Cupidity, Thirst and Miserliness, bid me adieu. I have now taken to the path of Goodness.

45. Having renounced Desire and Cupidity, my happiness has now been great. I shall no longer surrender myself to the influence of Cupidity, nor shall I undergo the pangs of misery like a person of impure soul.

46. Inasmuch as one renounces his desires so sure is he to reap his deserts. Truly he who surrenders himself to Desire always undergoes the pangs of misery.

47. Whatever passions arising from Desire are cast off by a person, all come under the category of Passion. Sorrow and shamelessness, as also discontent, all owe their origin to Desire and Wealth.

48. As in the hot summer a person plunges himself into a cool lake, I have now merged myself into Brahma. I have renounced work. I have extricated myself from grief. Unalloyed happiness has now come to my share.

49. The happiness which results from the fruition of Desire or the serene happiness which one enjoys in heaven, is not equal to a sixteenth part of that which springs from renunciation of all kinds of thirst.

50. Laying axe at the root of desire, which with the body makes an aggregate of seven, and which is a bitter foe, I have made my way to the immortal city of Brahma and there shall I pass my days in happiness like a king.

51. Putting his faith upon such intelligence, Manki succeeded in freeing himself from attachments, by his self-renunciation and obtained the blissful region of Brahma.

52. Forsooth, on account of the loss of his two bulls, Manki attained to immortality. In fact, because he laid the axe at the very roots of desire, he succeeded, through that means to obtain for himself supreme happiness.

## THE MAHABHARATA

5. Nothing springs into existence without seed. Without seed, fruits do not grow. From seeds originate other seeds. Hence are fruits known to be sprung from seeds.

6. According to the good or bad seed that the husbandman sows in his field, he reaps good or bad fruits.

7. As, unsown with seed, the soil though tilled, becomes fruitless, so, without personal Exertion, Destiny is of no use.

8. One's own deeds are like the soil, and Destiny is compared to the seed. The harvest grows from the union of the soil and seed.

9–10. It is seen every day in the world that the doer reaps the fruit of his good and evil acts; that happiness results from good deeds, and pain is the outcome of evil ones; that acts, when done, always fructify; and that, if not done, no fruit arises.

11. A man of (good) acts gains merits with good fortune, while an idler loses his estate, and reaps evil like the infusion of alkaline matter injected into a wound.

12. By firm application, one acquires beauty, fortune, and all sorts of riches. Everything can be obtained by Exertion: but nothing can be gained through Destiny only, by a man who lacks personal Exertion.

13. One attains to heaven, and all the objects of enjoyment as also the fulfilment of his heart's desires, by well-applied personal Exertion.

14. All the luminaries in the sky, all the gods, the Nagas, and the Rakshasas, as also the Sun and the Moon and the

Winds, have acquired their high status by evolution from man's status, by dint of their own action.

15. Riches, friends, prosperity coming down from generation to generation, as also the sweets of life, are difficult of attainment by those who want Exertion.

16. The Brahmana acquires prosperity by holy living, the Kshatriya by prowess, the Vaishya by manly exertion, and the Shudra by service.

17. The stingy, the impotent, or the idler do not acquire riches and objects of enjoyment. Nor are these ever acquired by the man who is not active or manly or devoted to the exercise of religious austerities.

18. Even he, the worshipful Vishnu, who created the three worlds with the Daityas and all the gods, even He is engaged in austere penances in the heart of the deep.

19. If one's Karma bore no fruit, then all actions would become fruitless, and depending on Destiny men would become idlers.

21. The apprehension of good or evil in this world is not so great if Destiny be unfavourable as his apprehension of the same in the other world if Exertion be wanting while here.

22. Man's powers, if properly applied, only follow his Destiny, but Destiny alone cannot produce any good where Exertion is wanting.

23. When it is seen that even in the celestial regions, the position of the gods themselves is unstable, how would the gods maintain their own position or that of others without proper Karma.

24. The gods do not always approve of the good actions of others in this world, for fearing their own defeat, they try to thwart the acts of others.

25. There is a constant rivalry between the gods and the Rishis, and if they all have to go through their Karma, still it can never be said that there is no such thing as Destiny, for it is the latter that introduces all Karma.

26. How does Karma originate, if Destiny is the principal motive power of human action? By this means, many virtues are accumulated in the celestial regions.

27. One's own self is his friend and his enemy too, as also the witness of one's good and evil deeds.

28. Good and evil appear through Karma. Good and evil acts do not produce sufficient results.

29. Virtue is the refuge of the gods, and by virtue everything is acquired. Destiny thwarts not the man who has acquired virtue and righteousness.

42. If possessed by the wicked, all the good which is gained with difficulty in this world, is soon lost to them. Destiny does not help the man that is full of spiritual ignorance and avarice.

43. Even as a small fire, when fanned by the wind, becomes highly powerful, so does Destiny, when helped by individual Exertion, become greatly potent.

44. As by the diminution of oil in the lamp its light is put out, so does the influence of Destiny, by the abatement of one's acts.

45. Having obtained riches, and woman and all the enjoyments of this world, the man who is not hard-working

is unable to enjoy them long, but the great man, diligent in Exertion, can find riches buried deep in the Earth and watched over by the Fates.

46. The good man who is prodigal is sought by the gods for his good conduct, the celestial world being better than the world of men, but the house of the miser though full of riches is looked upon by the gods as the house of the dead.

47. The man who does not exert himself is never contented in this world, nor can Destiny change the course of a man who has gone wrong. There is no power inherent in Destiny. As the pupil follows the preceptor, so does one's action, guided by Destiny, follow his own personal exertion. Where one's own Exertion is displayed, there only Destiny shows its hand.

48. O Best of ascetics, I have thus described all the merits of personal Exertion, having always known in their true significance.

49. By the influence of Destiny and by showing personal Exertion, do men attain to heaven. The combined help of Destiny and Exertion, becomes fruitful.

## THE MAHABHARATA

1. Listen, O Janamejaya, to the nectarlike words that Vidura said to the son of Vichitravirya and by which he pleased that foremost of men.

Vidura said :—
2. Rise, O king! Why are you lying on the Earth. Cheer yourself up, O king, this is the final end of all living creatures.

3. Everything is liable to destruction ; everything that is high is sure to fall down. Union is sure to end in separation ; life is sure to end in death.

4. The Destroyer, O Bharata, takes both the hero and the coward. Why then, O foremost of Kshatriyas, should not Kshatriyas engage themselves in battle ?

5. He who never fights has been seen to die, while he who engages himself in battle has been seen to escape alive.

6. As regards living creatures, they did not exist at first. They exist in the intervening period. In the end they once more become non-existent. Why should then one grieve for the same ?

7. The man who grieves does not succeed in meeting with the dead. By grieving one does not himself die. While such is the course of the world, why do you indulge in grief ?

8. Death drags all creatures, even the gods. There is none dear or hateful to death, O Kuru chief.

9. As the wind tears off all the blades of grass, even so, O foremost of Bharata's race, Death rules over all creatures.

10. All creatures are like members of a caravan bound for the same country. When death will overtake all, it is immaterial whom he meets first.

11. O king, you should not grieve for those who have been killed in battle. If the scriptures are authoritative all of them must have obtained the highest end.

12. All of them were well read in the Vedas; all of them had practised vows. All of them have met with death after fighting with the enemy. What is there to be sorry in this?

13. They had been invisible before birth. Having come from that unknown region, they have again become invisible. They are not yours, nor are you theirs. Why should you grieve then for such disappearance?

14. If killed, one acquires heaven. By killing, fame is acquired. Both of these produce great merit. Battle, therefore, is not unproductive of good.

15. Forsooth, Indra will give them regions capable of granting every wish. These, O foremost of men, become the guests of Indra.

16. By celebrating sacrifices with profuse gifts, by ascetic penances and by learning, men cannot go so quickly to heaven as heroes killed in battle.

17. On the bodies of hostile heroes who were like the sacrificial fire, they poured libations of arrows. Highly energetic, they had in return to bear the arrowy libations poured upon them by their foes.

18. I tell you, O king, that for a Kshatriya in this world there is not a better way to heaven than battle.

19. They were all great Kshatriyas; brave as they were, they were ornaments of assemblies. They have attained highest of blessed regions. They are not persons for whom we should be sorry.

20. Solacing yourself, by your own self, cease to grieve, O best of men. You should not allow yourself to be overwhelmed with sorrow and to give up all action.

21. There are thousands of mothers and fathers and sons and wives in this world. Whose are they, and whose are we?

22. Thousands of causes spring up daily for sorrow and thousands for fear. These, however, affect the ignorant and not the wise.

23. There is none dear or hateful to Time, O Kuru chief. Time is indifferent to none. All are equally dragged by time.

24. Time makes all creatures grow, and it is Time that destroys all. When all else is asleep, Time is awake. Time is irresistible.

25. Youth, beauty, life, wealth, health, and friends, are all unstable. The wise will never seek any of these.

26. You should not grieve for what is universal. By indulging in grief a person may himself die, but grief itself by being indulged in, never becomes light.

27. If you feel any grief heavily, it should be overcome by not indulging in it. This is the only remedy for grief, viz., that one should not indulge in it.

28. By indulging in it, one cannot lessen it. On the other hand, it increases when being indulged in. When any evil

or bereavement of some dear one, comes on, only they that are of little intelligence allow their minds to be laden with grief.

29. This is neither Profit, nor Religion, nor Happiness, of which you are thinking.

30–31. The indulgence of grief is the sure means of one's losing one's objects. Through it, one deviates from the three great ends of life. They who are not contented are stupefied by the vicissitudes of fortune. The wise are, on the other hand, unaffected by such changes. One should destroy mental grief by wisdom, as physical grief should be destroyed by medicine. Wisdom has this power. They, however, that are foolish, can never acquire equanimity of mind.

32. Pristine actions closely follow a man, so much so that they lie by him when he lies down, stand by him when he stands, and run with him when he runs.

33. As a man acts well or ill, so he enjoys or suffers the fruit thereof.

34. In physical actions also one enjoys or suffers the fruits according to his acts.

35. One's own self is one's own friend, again one's own self is one's own enemy. One's own self is the witness of one's good and evil acts.

36. Good acts beget a state of happiness, and sinful deeds bring on woe. One always reaps the fruit of one's acts. One never enjoys or suffers happiness or misery that is not the outcome of one's own acts.

37. Intelligent persons like you, O king, never commit sinful deeds, that are disapproved by knowledge and that strike at the very root of virtue and happiness.

## CHAPTER III

Dhritarashtra said :—

1. O you of great wisdom, my grief has been removed by your excellent words. I wish you, however, to speak again.

2. How, indeed, do the wise free themselves from mental grief begotten by evil deeds and the bereavement of dear objects ?

Vidura said :—

3. He that is wise enjoys peace by subduing both grief and joy by means by which one may escape from grief and joy.

4. Everything we are anxious for, O foremost of men, is ephemeral. The world is like a weak plantain tree.

5–6. Since the wise and the ignorant, the rich and the poor, all, shorn of their anxieties, sleep on the crematorium, with bodies devoid of flesh and full of naked bones, and sinews, whom amongst them will the survivors regard as possessed of distinguishing marks by which the attributes of birth and beauty may be determined ? Since every thing is equal in death why should men, whose understandings are always deceived, covet one another's rank and position ?

7. The learned say that the bodies of men are like houses, which are destroyed in time. There is one being, however, that is eternal.

8. As a person casting off an old cloth puts on a fresh one, so is the case with the bodies of all embodied beings.

9. O son of Vichitravirja, creatures reap happiness or misery, as the fruit of their own acts.

10. By their acts they secure heaven, O Bharata, or happiness or misery. Whether competent or otherwise, they have to bear their burdens which are the result of their own acts.

11–13. As amongst earthen pots some break while still on the potter's wheel, some while partially shaped, some as soon as shaped, some after removal from the wheel, some while in course of being removed, some after removal, some while wet, some while dry, some while being burnt, some while being removed from the kiln, some after removal therefrom, and some while being used, so is the case with the bodies of embodied creatures.

14–15. Some are destroyed while in embryo, some after coming out of the womb, some on the day after, some after a fortnight or a month, some after a year or two, some in youth, some in middle age, and some when old.

16. Creatures are born or destroyed according to their pristine acts. When such is the course of the world, why do you grieve?

17–18. As men, while swimming, sometimes dive and sometimes emerge, so, O king, creatures sink and emerge in life's stream. They that are of limited understanding suffer or meet with death as the result of their own acts.

19. They, however, that are wise, virtuous and desirous of doing good to all living creatures, who are acquainted with the real nature of things in this world, attain at last to the highest end.

# THE RAMAYAN
## OCEAN THREATENED

*H*IS hands in reverence Ráma raised
And southward o'er the ocean gazed;
Then on the sacred grass that made
His lowly couch his limbs he laid.
His head on that strong arm reclined
Which Sítá, best of womankind,
Had loved in happier days to hold
With soft arms decked with pearl and gold.
Then rising from his bed of grass,
" This day," he cried, " the host shall pass
Triumphant to the southern shore,
Or Ocean's self shall be no more."
Thus vowing in his constant breast
Again he turned him to his rest,
And there, his eyes in slumber closed,
Silent beside the sea reposed.
Thrice rose the Day-God, thrice he set,
The lord of Ocean came not yet.
Thrice came the night, but Raghu's son
No answer by his service won.
To Lakshman thus the hero cried,
His eyes aflame with wrath and pride:
" In vain the softer gifts that grace
The good are offered to the base.
Long-suffering, patience, gentle speech
Their thankless hearts can never reach.
The world to him its honour pays
Whose ready tongue himself can praise,
Who scorns the true, and hates the right,
Whose hand is ever raised to smite.
Each milder art is tried in vain:
It wins no glory, but disdain.
And victory owns no softer charm
Than might which nerves a warrior's arm.
My humble suit is still denied

By Ocean's overweening pride.
This day the monsters of the deep
In throes of death shall wildly leap.
My shafts shall rend the serpents curled
In caverns of the watery world,
Disclose each sunless depth and bare
The tangled pearl and coral there.
Away with mercy! at a time
Like this compassion is a crime.
Welcome, the battle and the foe!
My bow! my arrows and my bow!
This day the Vánars' feet shall tread
The conquered Sea's exhausted bed,
And he who never feared before
Shall tremble to his farthest shore."

Red flashed his eyes with angry glow:
He stood and grasped his mighty bow,
Terrific as the fire of doom
Whose quenchless flames the world consume.
His clanging cord the archer drew,
And swift the fiery arrows flew
Fierce as the flashing levin sent
By him who rules the firmament.
Down through the startled waters sped
Each missile with its flaming head.
The foamy billows rose and sank,
And dashed upon the trembling bank
Sea monsters of tremendous form,
With crash and roar of thunder storm.
Still the wild waters rose and fell
Crowned with white foam and pearl and shell.
Each serpent, startled from his rest,
Raised his fierce eyes and glowing crest,
And prisoned Dánavs' where they dwelt
In depths below the terror felt.
Again upon his string he laid
A flaming shaft, but Lakshman stayed

His arm, with gentle reasoning tried
To soothe his angry mood, and cried:
" Brother reflect: the wise control
The rising passions of the soul.
Let Ocean grant, without thy threat,
The boon on which thy heart is set.
That gracious lord will ne'er refuse
When Ráma son of Raghu sues."
He ceased: and voices from the air
Fell clear and loud, Spare Ráma, spare.

# THE OMENS

$\mathcal{T}$HEN Ráma, peerless in the skill
   That marks each sign of good and ill,
Strained his dear brother to his breast,
And thus with prudent words addressed:
"Now, Lakshman, by the water's side
In fruitful groves the host divide,
That warriors of each woodland race
May keep their own appointed place.
Dire is the danger: loss of friends,
Of Vánars and of bears, impends.
Disdained with dust the breezes blow,
And earth is shaken from below.
The tall hills rock from foot to crown,
And stately trees come toppling down,
In threatening shape, with voice of fear,
The clouds like cannibals appear,
And rain in fitful torrents, red
With sanguinary drops, is shed.
Long streaks of lurid light invest
The evening skies from east to west,
And from the sun at times a ball
Of angry fire is seen to fall.
From every glen and brake is heard
The boding voice of beast and bird:
From den and lair night-prowlers run
And shriek against the falling sun.
Up springs the moon, but hot and red
Kills the sad night with woe and dread;
No gentle lustre, but the gloom
That heralds universal doom.
A cloud of dust and vapour mars
The beauty of the evening stars,
And wild and fearful is the sky
As though the wreck of worlds were nigh.
Around our heads in boding flight
Wheel hawk and vulture, crow and kite;

And every bird of happy note
Shrieks terror from his altered throat.
Sword, spear and shaft shall strew the plain
Dyed red with torrents of the slain.
To-day the Vánar troops shall close
Around the city of our foes."

## THE NIGHT

THE Lord of Light had sunk and set:
  Night came; the foeman struggled yet
And fiercer for the gloom of night
Grew the wild fury of the fight.
Scarce could each warrior's eager eye
The foeman from the friend descry.
" Rákashas or Vánar? say; " cried each,
And foe knew foeman by his speech.
" Why wilt thou fly? O warrior, stay:
Turn on the foe, and rend and slay: "
Such were the cries, such words of fear
Smote through the gloom each listening ear.
Each swarthy rover of the night
Whose golden armour flashed with light,
Showed like a towering hill embraced
By burning woods about his waist.
The giants at the Vánars flew,
And ravening ate the foes they slew:
With mortal bite like serpent's fang,
The Vánars at the giants sprang
And car and steeds and they who bore
The pennons fell bedewed with gore
No serried band, no firm array
The fury of their charge could stay.
Down went the horse and rider, down
Went giant lords of high renown.
Though midnight's shade was dense and dark,
With skill that swerved not from the mark
Their bows the sins of Raghu drew,
And each keen shaft a chieftain slew.
Uprose the blinding dust from meads
Ploughed by the cars and tramping steeds,
And where the warriors fell the flood
Was dark and terrible with blood.
Six giants singled Ráma out,
And charged him with a furious shout

Loud as the roaring of the sea
When every wind is raging free.
Six times he shot: six heads were cleft;
Six giants dead on earth were left.
Nor ceased he yet: his bow he strained,
And from the sounding weapon rained
A storm of shafts whose fiery glare
Filled all the region of the air;
And chieftains dropped before his aim
Like moths that perish in the flame.
Earth glistened where the arrows fell,
As shines in autumn nights a dell
Which fireflies, flashing through the gloom,
With momentary light illume.

But Indrajit, when Báli's son
The victory o'er the foe had won,
Saw with a fury-kindled eye
His mangled steeds and driver die;
Then, lost in air, he fled the fight,
And vanished from the victor's sight.
The Gods and saints glad voices raised,
And Angad for his virtue praised;
And Raghu's sons bestowed the meed
Of honour due to valorous deed.

Compelled his shattered car to quit,
Rage filled the soul of Indrajit,
Who brooked not, strong by Brahmá's grace,
Defeat from one of Vánar race.
In magic mist concealed from view
His bow the treacherous warrior drew,
And Raghu's sons were first to feel
The tempest of his winged steel.
Then when his arrows failed to kill
The princes who defied him still,
He bound them with the serpent noose,
The magic bond which none might loose.

ϡϡϡϡϡϡϡϡϡϡϡϡϡϡϡϡϡϡϡϡϡϡ

## THE VÁNAR'S ALARM

⟨*T*⟩HE son of Raghu near the wall
   Saw, proudly towering over all,
The mighty giant stride along
Attended by the warrior throng;
Heard Kumbhakarna's heavy feet
Awake the echoes of the street;
And, with the lust of battle fired,
Turned to Vibhíshan and inquired:
"Vibhíshan, tell that chieftain's name
Who rears so high his mountain frame;
With glittering helm and lion eyes,
Preëminent in might and size
Above the rest of giant birth,
He towers the standard of the earth;
And all the Vánars when they see
The mighty warrior turn and flee."

"In him," Vibhíshan answered, " know
Visravas' son, the Immortals' foe,
Fierce Kumbhakarna, mightier far
Than Gods and fiends and giants are.
He conquered Yama in the fight,
And Indra trembling owned his might.
His arm the Gods and fiends subdued,
Gandharvas and the serpent brood.
The rest of his gigantic race
Are wondrous strong by God-Given grace;
But nature at its birth to him
Gave matchless power and strength of limb.
Scarce was he born, fierce monster, when
He killed and ate a thousand men.
The trembling race of men, appalled,
On Indra for protection called;
And he, to save the suffering world,
His bolt at Kumbhakarna hurled.
So awful was the monster's yell

That fear on all the nations fell.
He, rushing on with furious roar,
A tusk from huge Airavat tore,
And dealt the God so dire a blow
That Indra reeling left his foe,
And with the Gods and mortals fled
To Brahma's throne dispirited.
' O Brahma,' thus the suppliants cried,
' Some refuge for this woe provide
If thus his maw the giant sate
Soon will the world be desolate.'
The Self-existent calmed their woe,
And spake in anger to their foe :
' As thou was born, Paulastya's son,
That worlds might weep by thee undone,
Thou like the dead henceforth shalt be :
Such is the curse I lay on thee.'
Senseless he lay, nor spoke nor stirred ;
Such was the power of Brahma's word.
But Ravan, troubled for his sake,
Thus to the Self-existent spake :
' Who lops the tree his care has reared
When golden fruit has first appeared ?
Not thus, O Brahma, deal with one
Descended from thin own dear son.'
Still thou, O Lord, thy word must keep :
He may not die, but let him sleep.
Yet fix a time for him to break
The chains of slumber and awake."
He ceased : and Brahma made reply :
" Six months in slumber shall he lie,
And then arising for a day
Shall cast the numbing bonds away.
Now Ravan in his doubt and dread
Has roused the monster from his bed,
Who comes in this the hour of need
On slaughtered Vánar's flesh to feed.
Each Vánar, when his awe-strick eyes

Behold the monstrous chieftain, flies
With hopeful words their minds deceive,
And let our trembling hosts believe
They see no giant, but, displayed,
A lifeless engine, deftly made."

Then Rama called to Nila : " Haste
Let troops near every gate be placed,
And, armed with fragments of the rock
And trees, each lane and alley block."

Thus Rama spoke : the chief obeyed,
And swift the Vánars stood arrayed,
As when black clouds their battle form,
The summit of a hill to storm.

## THE MAGIC CAR

THEN slept the tamer of his foes
And spent the night in calm repose.
Vibhishan came when morning broke,
And hailed the royal chief and spoke:
"Here wait thee precious oils and scents,
And rich attire and ornaments.
The brimming urns are newly filled,
And women in their duty skilled,
With lotus-eyes, thy call attend,
Assistance at thy bath to lend."
"Let others," Rama cried, "desire
These precious scents, this rich attire.
I heed not such delights as these,
For faithful Bharat, ill at ease,
Watching for me is keeping now
Far far away his rigorous vow.
By Bharat's side I long to stand,
I long to see my fatherland.
Far is Ayodhya; long, alas,
The dreary road and hard to pass."

"One day," Vibhishan cried, "one day
Shall bear thee o'er that length of way.
Is not the wondrous chariot mine,
Named Pushpak, wrought by hands divine,
The prize which Ravan seized of old
Victorious o'er the God of Gold!
This chariot, kept with utmost care,
Will waft thee through the fields of air,
And thou shalt light unwearied down
In fair Ayodhya's royal town.
But yet if aught that I have done
Has pleased thee well, O Raghu's son;
If still tho carest for thy friend,
Some little time in Lanka spend;
There after toil of battle rest

Within my halls an honoured guest."
Again the son of Raghu spake:
" Thy life was perilled for my sake.
Thy counsel gave me priceless aid:
All honours have been richly paid.
Scarce can my love refuse, O best
Of giant kind, thy last request.
But still I yearn once more to see
My home and all most dear to me;
Nor can I brook one hour's delay:
Forgive me, speed me on my way."

He ceased: the magic car was brought,
Of yore by Visvakarma wrought.
In sunlight sheen it flashed and blazed;
And Raghu's sons in wonder gazed.

## THE DEPARTURE

*T*HE giant lord the chariot viewed,
    And humbly thus his speech renewed:
" Behold, O King, the car prepared:
Now be' thy further will declared."
He ceased: and Rama spake once more:
" These hosts who thronged to Lanka's shore
Their faith and might have nobly shown,
And set thee on the giant's throne.
Let pearls and gems and gold repay
The feats of many a desperate day,
That all may go triumphant hence
Proud of their noble recompense."

    Vibhishan, ready at his call,
With gold and gems enriched them all.
Then Rama clomb the glorious car
That shone like day's resplendent star
There in his lap he held his dame
Vailing her eyes in modest shame.
Beside him Lakshman took his stand,
Whose mighty bow still armed his hand.
" O King Vibhishan," Rama cried,
" O Vanar chiefs, so long allied,
My comrades till the foemen fell,
List, for I speak a long farewell.
The task in doubt and fear begun,
With your good aid is nobly done.
Leave Lanka's shore, your steps retrace,
Brave warriors of the Vanar race.
Thou, King Sugriva, true, through all,
To friendship's bond and duty's call,
Seek far Kishkindha with thy train
And o'er thy realm in glory reign.
Farewell, Vibhishan, Lanka's throne
Won by our arms is now thine own.
Thou, mighty lord, has nought to dread

From heavenly Gods by Indra led.
My last farewell, O King receive
For Lanka's isle this hour I leave."

Loud rose their cry in answer : " We
O Raghu's son, would go with thee.
With thee delighted would we stray
Where sweet Ayodhya's groves are gay.
Then in the joyous synod view
King-making balm thy brows bedew ;
Our homage to Kausalya pay,
And hasten on our homeward way."

Their prayer the son of Raghu heard,
And spoke, his heart with rapture stirred :
" Sugriva, O my faithful friend,
Vibhishan and ye chiefs, ascend
A joy beyond all joys the best
Will fill my overflowing breast,
If girt by you, O noble band,
I seek again my native land."
With Vanar lords in danger tried
Sugriva sprang to Rama's side,
And girt by chiefs of giant kind
Vibhishan's step was close behind.
Swift through the air, as Rama chose,
The wondrous car from earth arose,
And decked with swans and silver wings
Bore through the clouds its freight of kings.

## THE RETURN

THEN Rama, speeding through the skies,
   Bent on the earth his eager eyes;
"Look Sita, see, divinely planned
And built by Visvakarma's hand,
Lanka the lovely city rest
Enthroned on Mount Trikuta's crest.
Behold those fields, ensanguined yet,
Where Vanar hosts and giants met.
There, vainly screened by charm and spell,
The robber Ravan fought and fell.
There knelt Mandodari and shed
Her tears in floods for Ravan dead,
And every dame who loved him sent
From her sad heart her wild lament.
There gleams the margin of the deep,
Where, worn with toil, we sank to sleep.
Look, love, the unconquered sea behold,
King Varun's home ordained of old,
Whose boundless waters roar and swell
Rich with their store of pearl and shell.
O see, the morning sun is bright
On fair Hiranyanabha's height,
Who rose from Ocean's sheltering breast
That Hanuman might stay and rest
There stretches, famed for evermore,
The wondrous bridge from shore to shore.
The worlds, to life's remotest day,
Due reverence to the work shall pay,
Which holier for the lapse of time
Shall give release from sin and crime.
Now thither tend, dear love, thine eyes
Where green with groves Kishkindha lies,
The seat of King Sugriva's reign,
Where Bali by this hand was slain.
There Rishyamuka's hill behold
Bright gleaming with embedded gold.

There too my wandering foot I set,
There King Sugriva first I met,
And, where yon trees their branches wave,
My promise of assistance gave.
There, flushed with lilies, Pampa shines
With banks which greenest foliage lines,
Where melancholy steps I bent
And mourned thee with a mad lament
There fierce Kabandha, spreading wide
His giant arms, in battle died.
Turn, Sita, turn thine eyes and see
In Janasthan that glorious tree:
There Ravan, lord of giants, slew
Our friend Jatayus brave and true,
Thy champion in the hopeless strife,
Who gave for thee his noble life.
Now mark that glade amid the trees
Where once we lived as devotees.
See, see our leafy cot between
Those waving boughs of densest green
Where Ravan seized his prize and stole
My love the darling of my soul.
O, look again : beneath thee gleams
Godavari the best of streams,
Whose lucid waters sweetly glide
By lilies that adorn her side.
There dwelt Agastya, holy sage,
In plantain-sheltered hermitage.
See Sarabhanga's humble shed
Which sovereign Indra visited.
See where the gentle hermits dwell
Neath Atri's rule who loved us well ;
Where once thine eyes were blest to see
His sainted dame who talked with thee.
Now rest thine eyes with new delight
On Chitrakuta's woody height,
See Jumna flashing in the sun
Through groves of brilliant foliage run.

Screened by the shade of spreading boughs
There Bharadvaja keeps his vows.
There Ganga, river of the skies,
Rolls the sweet wave that purifies.
There Springavera's towers ascend
Where Guha reigns, mine ancient friend.
I see, I see thy glittering spires,
Ayodhya, city of my sires.
Bow down, bow down thy head, my sweet,
Our home, our long-lost home to greet."

## THE CONSECRATION

THEN, reverent hand to hand applied,
  Thus Bharat to his brother cried:
" Thy realm, O King, is now restored.
Uninjured to the rightful lord.
This feeble arm, with toil and pain
The weighty charge could scarce sustain,
And the great burthen well nigh broke
The neck untrained to bear the yoke.
The royal swan outspeeds the crow:
The steed is swift, the mule is slow,
Nor can my feeble feet be led
O'er the rough ways where thine should
    tread.
Now grant what all thy subjects ask:
Begin, O King, thy royal task.
Now let our longing eyes behold,
The glorious rite ordained of old,
And on the new-found monarch's head,
Let consecrating drops be shed."

  He ceased: victorious Rama bent
His head in token of assent.
He sat, and tonsors trimmed with care
His tangles of neglected hair.
Then, duly bathed, the hero shone
With all his splendid raiment on.
And Sita with the matron's aid
Her limbs in shining robes arrayed.
Sumantra then, the charioteer,
Drew, ordered by Satrughna, near
And stayed within the hermit grove
The chariot and the steeds he drove.
Therein Sugriva's consorts, graced
With gems, and Rama's queen were placed
All fain Ayodhya to behold;
And swift away the chariot rolled.

Like Indra Lord of Thousand Eyes,
Drawn by fleet lions through the skies,
Thus radiant in his glory showed
King Rama as he homeward rode,
In power and might unparalleled.
The reins the hand of Bharat held :
Above the peerless victor's head
The snow-white shade Satrughna spread,
And Lakshman's ever-ready hand
His forehead with a chourie fanned.
Vibhishan close to Lakshman's side
Sharing his task a chourie plied,
Sugriva on Satrunjay came,
An elephant of hugest frame ;
Nine thousand others bore, behind,
The chieftains of the Vanar kind
All gay, in forms of human mould,
With rich attire and gems and gold,
Thus borne along in royal state
King Rama reached Ayodhya's gate
With merry noise of shells and drums
And joyful shouts, He comes, he comes,
A Brahman host with solemn tread,
And kine the long procession led,
And happy maids in ordered bands
Threw grain and gold with liberal hands,
Neath gorgeous flags that waved in rows
On towers and roofs and porticoes,
Mid merry crowds who sang and cheered
The palace of the king they neared.
Then Raghu's son to Bharat, best
Of duty's slaves, these words addressed :
" Pass onward to the monarch's hall,
The high-souled Vanars with thee call,
And let the chieftains, as is meet,
The widows of our father greet
And to the Vanar king assign
Those chambers, best of all, which shine

"With lazulite and pearl inlaid,
And pleasant grounds with flowers and
    shade."

   He ceased: and Bharat bent his head;
Sugriva by the hand he led
And passed within the palace where
Stood couches which Satrughna's care
With robes and hangings richly dyed,
And burning lamps, had been supplied.
Then Bharat spake: "I pray thee, friend,
Thy speedy messengers to send,
Each sacred requisite to bring
That we may consecrate our king."
Sugriva raised four urns of gold,
The water for the rite to hold,
And bade four swiftest Vanars flee
And fill them from each distant sea.
Then east and west and south and north
The Vanar envoys hastened forth.
Each in swift flight an ocean sought
And back through air his treasure brought,
And full five hundred floods beside
Pure water for the king supplied.
Then girt by many a Brahman sage,
Vasishtha, chief for reverend age,
High on a throne with jewels graced
King Rama and his Sita placed.
There by Jabali, far revered,
Vijay and Kasyap's son appeared;
By Gautam's side Katyayan stood,
And Vamadeva wise and good,
Whose holy hands in order shed
The pure sweet drops on Rama's head.
Then priests and maids and warriors, all
Approaching at Vasishtha's call,
With sacred drops bedewed their king,
The centre of a joyous ring.

The guardians of the worlds, on high,
And all the children of the sky
From herbs wherewith their hands were filled
Rare juices on his brow distilled.
His brows were bound with glistering gold
Which Manu's self had worn of old,
Bright with the flash of many a gem,
His sire's ancestral diadem.
Satrughna lent his willing aid
And o'er him held the regal shade :
The monarchs whom his arm had saved
The chouries round his forehead waved.
A golden chain, that flashed and glowed
With gems, the God of Wind bestowed :
Mahendra gave a glorious string
Of fairest pearls to deck the king.
The skies with acclamation rang,
The gay nymphs danced, the minstrels sang.
On that blest day the joyful plain
Was clothed anew with golden grain.
The trees the witching influence knew,
And bent with fruits of loveliest hue,
And Rama's consecration lent
New sweetness to each flowret's scent.
The monarch, joy of Raghu's line,
Gave largess to the Brahmans, kine
And steeds unnumbered, wealth untold
Of robes and pearls and gems and gold.
A jewelled chain, whose lustre passed
The glory of the sun, he cast
About his friend Sugriva's neck
And, Angad Bali's son to deck,
He gave a pair of armlets bright
With diamond and lazulite.
A string of pearls of matchless hue
Which gleams like tender moonlight threw,
Adorned with gems of brightest sheen,
He gave to grace his darling queen.

The offering from his hand received
A moment on her bosom heaved;
Then from her neck the chain she drew,
A glance on all the Vanars threw,
And wistful eyes on Rama bent
As still she held the ornament.
Her wish he knew, and made reply
To that mute question of her eye:
" Yea, love; the chain on him bestow
Whose wisdom, truth and might we know,
The firm ally, the faithful friend
Through toil and peril to the end."

Then on Hanuman's bosom hung
The chain which Sita's hand had flung:
So may a cloud, when winds are still,
With moon-lit silver gird a hill.

To every Vanar Rama gave
Rich treasures from the mine and wave:
And with their honours well content
Homeward their steps the chieftains bent.
Ten thousand years Ayodhya, blest
With Rama's rule, had peace and rest.
No widow mourned her murdered mate,
No house was ever desolate.
The happy land no murrain knew,
The flocks and herds increased and grew.
The earth her kindly fruits supplied,
No harvest failed, no children died.
Unknown were want, disease and crime:
So calm, so happy was the time.

## THE COWS CONVEYED
## THEIR THIEF BETRAYED

### FROM TAMIL WISDOM

THUS one who many beasts possessed
His neighbour who'd but ten address'd,—
" Your cows with mine, in field and stall,
May mix, if you will tend them all
Whenever I'm from home."

One day,

When business had call'd him away,
His neighbour left in charge was glad
To carry out a plan he had.
Three heifers from the herd he led,
And left three sorry calves instead.

A murrain pass'd the country through,
And all the farmer's cattle slew,
But spared the stolen cows full-grown,
A calf each suckling of its own.

The owner of the emptied stall
For cup of milk was fain to call.

'Twas brought from one of the young kine.
" The cow you have just milk'd is mine,"
When he had tasted, he averr'd,
To Raman hasted, and was heard.

The judge inquired, with dark'ning brow,
" Why did you steal your neighbour's cow ? "
He said, " 'Tis false ; he'd better bid
His witnesses, to prove I did."
" True," Raman answer'd, " show me now
How you can tell it is your cow."
Rejoin'd he with a tongue not slow,
" The taste of my cow's milk I know."
The judge replied, " The case to weigh
Will take a fortnight and a day :
Both go, and wait."

                    Three plots of ground
With vegetables set he found;
Applied, to make his judgment sure,
To each a different manure;
And when the plants were ripe at last,
The herdsmen bade to a repast.
From every bed a share he drew,
Then all the three together threw;
And with the mass three sorts of curd,
The sheep's, cow's, buffalo's, were stirr'd.

   The dish was served in fashion neat,
And each desired to take and eat.
It was not long before the thief
With seeming relish cleared his leaf.
Ask'd if he had been satisfied,
" 'Twas admirable!" he replied.
The other stopped to taste and taste,
And to the end would make no haste.
Ask'd his opinion, thus 'twas shown,—
" I tasted vegetables grown
in three manures, nor failed to find
Three several sorts of curd combined."

   In wisdom knowing now the case,
The judge look'd in the culprit's face,
And said, " At once the truth reveal,
If punishment you would not feel."
" Three heifers," he confess'd, " I led
Away, and put three calves instead."

   The clever farmer gain'd his cause,
And left the court mid high applause.
Deny the proverb no one can,
" There's nothing hard to a wise man."

## THE CHIT IS TORN
## THE DEBT FORSWORN

*A* CITIZEN for money lent
A note of promise did present.
The lender, when some days had flown,
Demanded payment of the loan.
" I shall," the gentleman replied,
" Be on the hill the town outside
to-morrow; bring the note I sign'd,
And all with interest you'll find."

He went: the note the debtor took.
Examined it with searching look,—
A fire with fuel fresh supplied
Was burning ready at his side,—
Then tore, and cast it in the flame,
And said, " Be off, you have no claim."

The merchant sought the judge's face,
and sorrowfully told his case.
The summon'd rogue heard the demand,
" Why did you tear the note of hand ? "
" No note have I destroy'd," said he,
" This fellow nothing lent to me."
Its size the judge inquired aside.
" A span," the creditor replied.
" Say two, when I in public ask,"
Said Raman, and resumed his task.

Then from the bench, on his return,
He with judicial aspect stern
Inform'd the lender 't must be learnt
How long the bond was that was burnt.
He solemnly a cubit named.
The citizen aroused, exclaim'd,

" He lies, your lordship, in his throat,
Calling a span a cubit-note;

If here such glaring lies he'll dare
How many won't he tell elsewhere?"
"Ah," said the judge, "my clever man,
How could you know it was a span,
If not by your own fingers penn'd,
And by you given to your friend?"

Then not alone the perjurer's due,
As law imposed, th' offender knew;
But all for which the note he'd sign'd
With heavy interest resign'd.
He show'd how well the saying fits,
"A man in haste outruns his wits."

## MARIYATHAY-RAMAN

### I

#### ONE OF FOUR THIEVES
#### THE REST DECEIVES

Four lodgers with an ancient dame
Received contentedly what came,
Were gainers by what others lost,
And boarded at the public cost.
Now coins and jewels music yield,
Within a brazen vessel seal'd;
But they must keep the common prey
To charm them on a safer day.
"Ho, bury this beneath the floor,
Till call'd for, moth, by all four,"
They said, and still their lodgings kept,
And ate and drank, and watch'd and slept.

Once on a day, as o'er the way
In a verandah's shade they lay,
And of the common good conversed,
The faithful four were plagued with thirst.
"Who'll go to the old dame, and say
That we must have a pot of whey?"
Was ask'd; and, flying like a shot,
One said to her, "Produce the Pot."
Pledged not to part with it at all
Without an order from them all,
Into the street she trusty went,
And ask'd if for the pot they'd sent.
"Yes, give it him, and don't be slow."
So, turning back, an iron crow
She lent her lodger, and reveal'd
The place where she'd the jar conceal'd.
"With this you'll turn it up with ease,"
Said she; and he was on his knees.
The metal in his hands he feels,
And then the metal in his heels;

Through the back door he bears the prize;
And like the thief of thieves he flies.

Minutes twice twelve the thirsty three
Had waited, wondering not to see
Their partner with a pot supplied,
When all got up, and went inside.
The chest perceived, the dame they cursed;
And vengeance now was all their thirst.
They hail'd her to the judgment-bar,
And swore she'd stolen their brazen jar.
The Lord Chief Justice weigh'd the case,
Look'd the poor woman in the face,
And said he could not let it pass,
She must restore the pot of brass.
" O dear! what shall I do? " she cries,
And tears are streaming down her eyes.

As bright a youth as e'er you'll meet
Was in the middle of the street,
With playmates busy at the game
Of pitch and toss: he ask'd the dame,
" Good grandmother, why all these tears? "
She with her story fill'd his ears.
Then, turning to his play anew,
As from his hands the nuts he threw,
Exclaimed the grieved precocious soul,
" May these as surely find the hole
As earth his mouth shall quickly choke
Who this unrighteous sentence spoke! "

Some busybodies to the throne
Made Raman's daring comment known.
The boy was to the monarch led,
And thus the awful Cholan said,
" Who thinks the sentence so unjust,
Himself the case may try, and must."
The child of Menu, unappall'd,
The prisoner and the plaintiffs call'd,

The matter sifted, set her free,
And thus addressed the baffled three :
" She will, as pledged, the jar restore,
When told to do so by all four."

Grief goes the way that treasures go,
They say : the lady found it so.
The king with joy the tidings heard.
The title of " The Just " conferr'd
On Raman, made the bench his own.
Sent gifts of honour from the throne,
With special countenance caress'd,
And held him a familiar guest.

## CONDAY-VENTHAN

SIMPLICITY is woman's jewel bright.
  The earth bears longest those who gently move.
All kinds of evil banish out of sight.
The ploughman's honest meal is food indeed.
  With guests your meat, however costly, share.
Where rain is wanted, there is every need.
  The welcome showers succeed the lightning's glare.
The ship without a pilot makes no head.
  At eve, the fruit of morning's acts you reap.
There's nectar found in what the ancients said.
  Who softly lie, enjoy the sweetest sleep.
What wealth the plough produces will remain.
  In silence wisdom has its end and proof.
Their efforts, who disdain advice, are vain.
  From black-eyed women go, and keep aloof.
Be all excess e'en by the king eschew'd.
  No showers descending, fee-less Brahmans smart.
Good manners hospitality include.
  A hero's friendship pierces like a dart.
The boy who scorns to beg deserves respect.
  The strength of wealth in perseverance lies.
The incorrupt deceitful thoughts reject.
  Let but the king be angry, succour flies.
Go, worship God in every fane on earth.
  Choose places fit wherein to close your eyes.
The lagging student gains nor lore nor worth.

## MUTHURAY

Who stately with floral gifts attend,
  Before the trunk-faced red-one's footstool bend,
  And pious homage reverently pay,
Shall from the goddess lotus-throned acquire
Wit, eloquence, and all that they desire,
  And never sink to bodily decay.


If suffering worth to acts of kindness move,
Dismiss the fear your bounty may not prove
  A source at last of profit and delight;
The water furnish'd to its early root,
In sweeter draughts from future plenteous fruit
  The cocoa's crown will gratefully requite.


The valued favours the deserving gain
Like sculptures in eternal rock remain;
  Of virtue's tribute charity is sure:
But vain is kindness to the worthless shown,
Who debts and duties evermore disown;
  On water written words as well ensure.


When senseless grief the live-long day englooms,
In vain attractively the garden blooms;
  In vain the spouseless maid her beauty wears:
So youth when needy is a tiresome stage,
And wealth but misery in helpless age,
  A bitter mockery of peevish cares.


To love, though loved, the callous base ne'er learn;
But love for love the good and wise return;
  Their greatness through calamities remains;
A purer whiteness as the sea-shell shows,
When fiercely the containing furnace glows;
  As seething milk its flavour still retains.

Although in foliage richly dress'd they rise,
In figure faultless, and mature in size,
　　As trees no fruit except in season bear,
In any project sooner to succeed,
And gain the end before the time decreed,
　　Nor wealth avails, nor toil, nor wakeful care.

### SELF-CONTROL

SELF-RULE to the immortals tends:
Its want in densest darkness ends.
A treasure to be kept with care,
No gains with self-restraint compare.
Who self-control true knowledge deem,
And practise it, command esteem.
Adhering to their proper state,
They rise above the mountain great.
Though good for all, the wealthy gain
In humbleness the richest vein.
One birth keep in the senses five,
Like tortoise, through the seven to thrive.
If nothing else, the tongue restrain:
Unruly talkers suffer pain.
One sinful word, its power so strong,
Turns good to bad, and right to wrong.
A burn will heal, but festering stays
The wound a burning tongue conveys.
Virtue will watch their steps to bless
Who anger and desire suppress.

## FAME

THEY live with praise who freely give,
    And profit most of all that live.
His lasting praise no voice but shows,
One alms who on the poor bestows.
'Gainst ruin proof there's nothing known
Save fame, that towering stands alone.
From praising gods the god-world turns
To praise the man who praises earns.
The famous flourish in decay,
And none in dying live but they.
If praise may not this life adorn,
'Twere better never to be born.
How without pain can they remain
Who, praised by none, their censors pain?
All own it shame to end our days,
And leave no progeny of praise.
The ground will lose its fertile name,
That bears a body void of fame.
They live who live above disgrace:
They're not alive whose life is base.

## INDIAN EPIGRAMS

### BHARTRIHARI

#### VII

THE silvery laughter; eyes that sparkle bold,
    Or droop in virgin rue;
The prattling words of wonder uncontrolled
When world and life are new;

The startled flight and dallying slow return,
And all their girlish sport;—
Ah me, that they time's ruinous truth must learn,
Their flowering be so short!

#### X

My love within a forest walked alone,
All in a moonlit dale;
And here awhile she rested, weary grown,
And from her shoulders threw the wimpled veil
To court the little gale.

I peering through the thicket saw it all,
The yellow moonbeams fall,
I saw them mirrored from her bosom fly
Back to the moon on high.

#### XI

O fair Acoka-tree, with love's own red
Thy boughs are all aflame;
Whither, I pray thee, hath my wanton fled?
This way I know she came.

In vain thy nodding in the wind, thy sigh
Of ignorance assumed;
I know because my flower-love wandered by
For joy thy branches bloomed.

I know thee : ever with thy buds unblown,
Till touched by maiden's foot;
And thou so fair—one fairest maid alone
Hath trod upon thy root.

### XX

Harder than faces in a glass designed,
A woman's heart to bind;
Like mountain paths up cragged heights that twist,
Her ways are lightly missed.

Like early dew-drops quivering on a leaf,
Her thoughts are idly brief;
And errors round her grow, as on a vine
The poison-tendrils twine.

### XXXI

Oil from the sand a man may strain,
If chance he squeeze with might and main;
The pilgrim at the magic well
Of the mirage his desert thirst may quell.

So travelling far a man by luck
May find a hare horned like a buck;—
But who by art may straighten out
The crooked counsels of a stubborn lout?

### XXXIV

I saw an ass who bore a load
Of sandal wood along the road,
And almost with the burden bent,
Yet never guessed the sandal scent;
So pedants bear a ponderous mass
Of books they comprehend not,—like the ass.

### XL

This have I done, and that will do,
And this half-done must carry through :—
So busied, bustling, full of care,
Poor fools, Death pounces on us unaware.

To-day is thine, fulfil its work,
Let no loose hour her duty shirk;
Still ere thy task is done, comes Death,
The Finisher,—he ends it with thy breath.


### XLV

O'er perilous mountain roads with pain
I've journeyed, yet acquired no gain;
The pride of birth I have forsworn
And toiled in service, yet no profit borne.


In strange homes where I blushed to go
My food I've taken, like the crow,
And eaten shame.—Oh lust of gold!
Oh Greed! that younger grow'st as I wax old!


### XLIX

I see a dog—no stone to shy at him;
Yonder a stone—no dog's in view:
There is your dog, here stones to try at him—
The king's dog! what's a man to do?


### LIV

The harvest ripens as the seed was sown,
And he that scattered reaps alone;—
So from each deed there falls a germ
That shall in coming lives its source affirm.


UNSEEN they call it, for it lurks
The hidden spring of present works;
UNKNOWN BEFORE, even as the fruit
Was undiscovered in the vital root.


And he that now impure hath been
Impure shall be, the clean be clean;
We wrestle in our present state
With bonds ourselves we forged,—and call it Fate.

### LXV

Seated within this body's car
The silent Self is driven afar;
And the five senses at the pole
Like steeds are tugging restive of control.

And if the driver lose his way,
Or the reins sunder, who can say
In what blind paths, what pits of fear
Will plunge the chargers in their mad career?

Drive well, O Mind, use all thy art,
Thou charioteer!—O feeling Heart,
Be thou a bridle firm and strong!
For the Lord rideth and the way is long.

### LXIX

A hundred years we barely keep,
Yet half of this is lost in sleep;
And half our waking time we spend
In the child's folly and the old man's end.

And of the hours remaining, fears
And gaunt disease and parting tears
Are all the prize :—fie on the slave
Who life more values than a bubbling wave!

### LXXI

Fallen our father, fallen who bore
For us the pangs—they went before :
And some with our years grew, but they,
They too now tread on memory's dusty way.

And we ourselves from morn to morn
Now shiver like old trees forlorn
Upon a sandy shore, and all
Our care the lapping waves that haste our fall.

## HYMN OF CREATION

" Of the four Vedas which constitute the earliest stage of Indian literature, the Rigveda is by far the most ancient and important," says Professor Macdonell, from whose English translation of the " Hymns from the Rigveda " the following is taken. The exact date of this piece of hoary religious literature of the Hindus is not determinable, although it cannot be later than the thirteenth century B.C. The hymns contained in this work were almost exclusively composed by a hereditary priesthood.

*N*ON-BEING then existed not nor being :
There was no air, nor sky that is beyond it.
What was concealed ? Wherein ? In whose protection ?
And was there deep unfathomable water ?

Death then existed not nor life immortal ;
Of neither night nor day was any token.
By its inherent force the One breathed windless :
No other thing than that beyond existed.

Darkness there was at first by darkness hidden ;
Without distinctive marks, this all was water.
That which, becoming, by the void was covered,
That One by force of heat came into being.
Desire entered the One in the beginning :
It was the earliest seed, of thought the product.
The sages searching in their hearts with wisdom,
Found out the bond of being in non-being.

Their ray extended light across the darkness :
But was the One above or was it under ?
Creative force was there, and fertile power :
Below was energy, above was impulse.

Who knows for certain? Who shall here declare it?
Whence was it born, and whence came this creation?
The gods were born after this world's creation:
Then who can know from whence it has arisen?

None knoweth whence creation has arisen;
And whether he has or has not produced it;
He who surveys it in the highest heaven,
He only knows, or haply he may know not.

## SURYA

THE gods' refulgent countenance has risen,
  The eye of Mitra, Varuna and Agni.
He has pervaded air, and earth, and heaven :
The soul of all that moves and stands is Surya.

The Sun pursues the Dawn, the gleaming goddess,
As a young man a maiden, to the region
Where god-devoted men lay on the harness
Of brilliant offerings for the brilliant godhead.

The brilliant steeds, bay coursers of the sun-god,
Refulgent, dappled, meet for joyful praises,
Wafting our worship, heaven's ridge have mounted,
And in one day round earth and sky they travel.

This is the Sun's divinity, his greatness :
In midst of action he withdraws the daylight.
When from their stand he has withdrawn his coursers,
Then straightway night for him spreads out her
    garment.

This form the Sun takes in the lap of heaven,
That Varuna and Mitra may regard him.
One glow of his appears unending, splendid ;
His bay steeds roll the other up, the black one.

To-day, O gods, do ye at Surya's rising
Release us from distress and from dishonour :
This boon may Varuna and Mitra grant us,
And Aditi and Sindhu, Earth and Heaven.

## IN PRAISE OF A WEDDED LIFE

THE love dwelling in a wife's eye is not like
The affectionate care of a father upon his babe;
Nor that of a mother to her cradle-child!
Not, indeed, likened either to lustrous gaze of an un-
wedded maid:
Hers is a glorious light, darting——
darting, too;
through the Windows of her heart;
Towards one, to whom she hath given; her
Youth, her love, her soul, and all that is dear
to Life——
So guard thee well; for thou
Hast bought a precious thing: THE HEART OF A WOMAN!

*(Amir.)*


## THE WITHERED ROSE

SWEET object of the Zephyr's Kiss,
Come, rose, come courted to my bower;
Mine eyes' delight! thou garden's bliss!
Come and abash yon flaunting flower.

Why call us to revokeless doom?
With grief the opening buds reply.
Not suffered to extend our bloom;
Scarce born, alas! before we die.

Man having passed appointed years,
Ours are but days—the scene must close!
And when Fate's messenger appears,
What is he but a Withered Rose?

*(Anon.)*

## TO SLEEP

COME, gentle Sleep! Image of Death approach,
 And kindly hover o'er my lonesome couch:
How sweet in sleep to rest the weary eyes,
 Live without life, and with dying die!

Oh, gentle Sleep! Tho' thou 'rt like Death,
 I woo thee to my bed:
Come, wish'd-for rest!—thy balmy breath,
 Thro' all my members shed!
For oh! How sweet such death and life:
 To die with death's fatal knife—
And live when life is fled.

       (*Anon.*)

# THE MEANING OF PRAYER

## By Sir Muhammad Iqbal

RELIGION is not satisfied with mere conception; it seeks a more intimate knowledge of and association with the object of its pursuit. The agency through which this association is achieved is the act of worship or prayer ending in spiritual illumination. The act of worship, however, affects different varieties of consciousness differently. In the case of the prophetic consciousness it is in the main creative, i.e., it tends to create a fresh ethical world wherein the Prophet, so to speak, applies the pragmatic test to his revelations. In the case of the mystic consciousness it is in the main cognitive. It is from this cognitive point of view that I will try to discover the meaning of prayer. And this point of view is perfectly justifiable in view of the ultimate motive of prayer. I would draw your attention to the following passage from the great American psychologist, Professor William James :

"It seems probable that in spite of all that science may do to the contrary, men will continue to pray to the end of time unless their mental nature changes in a manner which nothing we know should lead us to expect. The impulse to pray is a necessary consequence of the fact that whilst the innermost of the empirical selves of a man is a self of the social sort it yet can find its only adequate socius (its great companion) in an ideal world. . . . Most men, either continually or occasionally, carry a reference to it in their breasts. The humblest outcast on this earth can feel himself to be real and valid by means of this higher recognition. And, on the other hand, for most of us, a world with no such inner refuge when the outer social self failed and dropped from us would be the abyss of horror. I say 'for most of us,' because it is probable that men differ a good deal in the degree in which they are haunted by this sense of an ideal spectator. It is a much more essential part of the consciousness of some men than of others. Those who have the most of it are possibly the most religious men. But I am sure that even those who say they are altogether without it decline themselves, and really have it in some degree."

Thus you will see that, psychologically speaking, prayer is instinctive in its origin. The act of prayer as aiming at knowledge resembles reflection. Yet prayer at its highest is much more than abstract reflection. Like reflection it too is a process of assimilation but the assimilative process in the case of prayer draws itself closely together and thereby acquires a power unknown to pure thought. In thought the mind observes and follows the working of Reality; in the act of prayer it gives up its career as a seeker of slow-footed universality and rises higher than thought to capture Reality itself with a view to become a conscious participator in its life. There is nothing mystical about it. Prayer as a means of spiritual illumination is a normal vital act by which the little island of our personality suddenly discovers its situation in a larger whole of life. Do not think I am talking of auto-suggestion. Auto-suggestion has nothing to do with the opening up of the sources of life that lie in the depths of the human ego. Unlike spiritual illumination which brings fresh power by shaping human personality, it leaves no permanent life effects behind. Nor am I speaking of some occult and special way of knowledge. All that I mean is to fix your attention on a real human experience which has a history behind it and a future before it. Mysticism has, no doubt, revealed fresh regions of the self by making a special study of this experience. Its literature is illuminating; yet its set phraseology shaped by the thought-forms of a worn-out metaphysics has rather deadening effect on the modern mind. The quest after a nameless nothing, as disclosed in Neo-Platonic mysticism—be it Christian or Muslim—cannot satisfy the modern mind which, with its habits of concrete thinking, demands a concrete living experience of God. And the history of the race shows that the attitude of the mind embodied in the act of worship is a condition for such an experience. In fact, prayer must be regarded as a necessary complement to the intellectual activity of the observer of Nature. The scientific observation of Nature keeps us in close contact with the behaviour of Reality, and thus sharpens our inner perception for a deeper vision of it. The truth is that all search for knowledge is essentially a form of prayer. The scientific observer of Nature is a kind of mystic seeker in the act of prayer. Although at present he follows only the footprints of the musk-deer, and thus modesty limits the method of his quest, his thirst for knowledge is eventually sure to lead him to the point where the scent of the musk-gland is a better guide than the footprints of the deer. This alone will add to his power over Nature and give him that vision of the total-infinite which philosophy seeks but cannot find. Vision without power does bring moral elevation but cannot give a lasting culture. Power without vision tends to become destructive and inhuman. Both must combine for the spiritual expansion of humanity.

The real object of prayer, however, is better achieved when the act of prayer becomes congregational. The spirit of all true prayer is social. Even the hermit abandons the society of men in the hope of finding, in a solitary abode, the fellowship of God. A congregation is an association of men who, animated by the same aspiration, concentrate themselves on a single object and open up their inner selves to the working of a single impulse. It is a psychological truth that association multiplies the normal man's power of perception, deepens his emotion, and dynamizes his will to a degree unknown to him in the privacy of his individuality. Indeed regarded as a psychological phenomenon prayer is still a mystery; for psychology has not yet discovered the laws relating to the enhancement of human sensibility in a state of association. With Islam, however, this socialization of spiritual illumination through associative prayer to the annual ceremony round the central mosque of Mecca, you can easily see how the Islamic institution of worship gradually enlarges the sphere of human association.

Prayer, whether individual or associative, is an expression of man's inner yearning for a response in the awful silence of universe. It is a unique process of discovery whereby the searching ego affirms itself in the very moment of self-negation, and thus discovers its own worth and justification as a dynamic factor in the life of the universe. True to the psychology of mental attitude in prayer, the form of worship in Islam symbolizes both affirmation and negation. Yet, in view of the fact borne out by the experience of the race that prayer, as an inner act, has found expression in a variety of forms, the Quran says:

" To every people have We appointed ways of worship which they observe. Therefore let them not dispute this matter with thee but bid them to thy Lord thou art on the right way; but if they debate with thee then say: God best knoweth what ye do! He will judge between you on the Day of Resurrection, to the matters wherein ye differ." (22 : 66–9)

The form of prayer ought not to become a matter of dispute. Which side you turn your face is certainly not essential to the spirit of prayer. The Quran is perfectly clear on this point: " The East and West is God's! therefore whichever way ye turn, there is the face of God." (2 : 109)

" There is no piety in turning your faces towards the East or the West but he is pious who believeth in God, and the Last Day, and the angels, and the scriptures, and the prophets; who for the love of God disperseth his wealth to his kindred, and to the orphans, and the needy, and the wayfarer, and those who ask, and for ransoming;

who observeth prayer, and payeth legal alms, and who is of those who are faithful to their engagements when they have engaged in them; and patient under ills and hardships, in time of trouble: those are they who are just, and those are they who fear the Lord." (2 : 172)

Yet we cannot ignore the important consideration that the posture of the body is a real factor in determining the attitude of the mind. The choice of one particular direction in Islamic worship is meant to secure the unity of feeling in the congregation, and its form in general creates and fosters the sense of social equality inasmuch as it tends to destroy the feeling of rank or race superiority in the worshippers. From the unity of the all-inclusive Ego who creates and sustains all egos follows the essential unity of all mankind. The division of mankind into races, nations and tribes according to the Quran, is for purposes of identification only. The Islamic form of association in prayer, therefore, besides its cognitive value is further indicative of the aspiration to realize this essential unity of all mankind as a fact in life by demolishing all barriers which stand between man and man.

# THE LOVE SONGS OF ASIA

## By Francis H. Skrine

" *W*HEN I call thy long black tresses to mind, happiness fills my eyes with tears, which glitter like diamonds as they roll down my cheeks. I do not know why it is so, but in watching them fall, I bethink me of a certain dark night, of rain drops pattering on our casement, and fireflies scintillating on the trees outside.

" All my friends smile when they see how greatly my features are changed. Let them smile! Perchance they would envy me if they knew that it is the intensity of my love for thee which has changed my face into a bed of saffron. When thy soft arms encircle my neck, thy curling tresses are bespangled with beads of perspiration, which flash like falling stars against the midnight sky."

" The Fifth Element" is by a poet of our own day named Mir Mohammad Rahshan Kayyil, born in Kashmir, 1852 :

" After creating earth, water, fire and air, Allah resolved to create a fifth element : He fashioned Woman. More swiftly than the wind do a lover's thoughts fly towards the object of his desire, were she at the other end of the world. My Kharo's body enshrines all Earth's treasures. Her lips are flowers, her breasts are swelling fruit, her face is daylight, her locks the night. Rubies and pearls shine in her pretty mouth ; diamonds glitter in her eyes. Fathomless as the ocean is the delight of her caresses. Like all who have seen Kharo, Rahshan Kayyil bears in his bosom this Fifth Element."

### THE LADY OF MOONLIGHT

" That night into the garden came she, the flower-limbed Lady of Moonlight, clad in a white robe interwoven with gold and silver thread which seemed to catch fire from the moonbeams. There stood she, in a blaze which eclipsed the moon itself. On that night by happy chance she and I were alone. It was a night of love, kisses, and wine-cups, of rippling laughter, and the old, old music of speech. Just then the cock crew, day dawned, flowers awoke, the wind blew, and she stole from my side : God knows, wither she went, leaving me done, with all my desires dead within me."

### THE ARAB GIRL'S LAMENT

" The sun is setting, O Mohammad Ben Sulluk, and darkness descends on the desert, even as her mourning veil conceals the widow's forehead. The warrior unsaddles his horse with lissom limbs, tired servants lie stretched beside the tents, flocks return from the pasturage ; a vapour rises from the desert like the canopy of smoke above an encampment. Dost hear the Muezzin's voice calling the faithful to prayer ? Prostrate thyself, bathe thy exhausted limbs, and turn towards Mecca.

" The shades of evening deepen and I, O my Spouse, my loved one, am watching for thy approach as the tigress watches for her absent cub. My soul is gnawed by anxiety, it is like the bones of travellers which whiten the caravan's track. My tears are falling as almond-blossom fall before the sirrocco's blast. Come to me, O Mohammad, for I am filled with a longing like the hyena's which prowls round a graveyard, eager to devour the flesh of the buried dead. But thou hearest not, thou turnest thy head away like the lion which passes a sleeping man with proud disdain. For thy heart is no longer in my keeping, thine eyes are riveted on the eyes of an infidel girl, blue as the turquoises set in thy warsteed's bit, thy hands tremble with desire to stroke her tresses, yellow as ripe maize.

Yes; thou lovest an infidel maiden, O Mohammad! She has weaned thee from me; she has taken my very life away. I used to dye my nails with henna, and darken my eyes with kohal to please thee. Thy new love knows them not; her skin is white as a Chieftain's burnus; and clammy like the snake that coils itself round a charmer's arm. And my breast swells as a mountain torrent in spring-time; I feel my hatred spreading as the shades at nightfall. For I hate that infidel, who is no daughter of the Prophet, and contemns the God we worship. May she suffer what I am suffering! May her husband forsake her; may her sons be pierced with arrows through their cowardly backs! I long to satisfy my love for thee and my loathing for her. She must give me back the man I love. O Mohammad, that I could drink her heart's blood on thy lips!"

# INDIAN DOHRAS, OR THE INDIAN
# PEASANT POETRY

'TIS Sawun; mark—the river flows
    With rippling eddies to the sea;
The slender jasmine closer grows,
    And clings about its wedded tree.


The lightning wantons with the rain,
    And brighter seems to gleam around;
The peacock woos in jocund strain,
    While laughing earth returns the sound.


'Tis Sawun, love!—'twixt man and wife
    Let no sad parting moment be;
Who journies now? what gain or strife
    In Sawun tears my love from me.


A husband, preparing to go a journey, is dissuaded
from it by his wife; who tells him that it is now the month
of Sawun, when all the works of Nature rejoice, and
indulge in connubial joys. The Hindoo poets not only
feign the various and beautiful creepers that adorn their
groves to be wedded to the more robust trees, but with
the latitude of Orientalists, assign the sea as a husband
to the rivers; and the lightning, which in Sawun, when
the rainy season has completely set in, is very frequent,
as a consort to the rain. That month falls about the middle
of July, and in the reanimation of vegetable life, almost
suspended by the preceding heats, presents to the delighted
senses all the natural phenomena of the spring of Europe.


The lively drum is heard around;
The tambourine and cymbals sound:
I in the flames of absence burn,
And languish for my love's return.

The women all around me sing,
And own th' inspiring joys of spring:
While I, from darts of ruthless love,
Never-ending torments prove.

The amorous Kokil strains his throat,
And pours his plaintive pleasing note;
My breast responsive heaves with grief,
Hopeless and reckless of relief.

When he again shall glad my hours,
Then, girl, I'll take thy blooming flowers;
But now my love is far away,
Where should I place thy Busunt gay?

The pangs of absence are sung in this little poem by a woman, who observes the general joy diffused around her, upon the approach of the Busunt or Spring.

If other voice than his was near,
It seemed a worm within my ear:
He went.—I heard the dreadful sound;
Yet both my ears unhurt I found.

Hid by my veil, my eyes have burned;—
Yet weeks past on;—nor he returned.
Then, heart, no more on love rely;
Beat on, and Death himself defy.

A young girl so intoxicated with a first passion as to suppose that she could not survive a separation from her lover, finds, after he had quitted the village for some weeks, that her ears still served her to hear with, though they no longer received the soft sounds of his voice; and her eyes for all the purposes of vision, though no more impressed with the image of her beloved. In the above stanzas she expresses her astonishment at all this, and very wisely determines never again to involve herself in so fleeting and troublesome a passion.

Is it, sweet maid, the breathing flute
That tells to Love some plaintive suit;
While o'er the cup of Indra's bed
Passes a shade of deeper red?

Art thou some Diuta's mistress bright;
Or the fair sister of Delight?
Or Wit's gay parent art thou born,—
Such winning words thy lips adorn?

No;—thou art Music's melting queen;
Or Love's enchanting bride I ween:
And Muttra's shepherd owns thy flame;
And Kokils stay their notes for shame.

O fairest of the Muttra maids!
While thy soft voice my soul pervades,
Seems on thy rosy lips to die
The Beena's heavenly minstrelsy.

A soft voice has in all ages and by all nations been
deemed an irresistible charm, and a proper subject for
poetic praise : in the above stanzas of Kesheo Das, Krishna
is supposed to celebrate, and certainly not inelegantly, the
voice of his beloved Rhada.

## TO BURKA

*B*RIGHT Indra's bow appears; the genial rains
      From the full clouds descend, and drench the
   plains.
Quick lightnings flash along the turbid sky,
Pierce the fresh moisten'd earth, and parch it dry.
O'er the pale moon a showery veil is thrown;
The frequent floods the lily's leaflet drown;
Like curling dust the distant showers appear,
And the swan flies before the watery year.
Dark with her varying clouds, and peacocks gay,
See Burka comes, and steals our hearts away.

> Mark,—her slender form bend low,
> As the zephyrs lightly blow!
> Mark,—her robe, like blossoms rare,
> Scatter fragrance on the air!
> See, her face as soft moon beaming;
> From her smiles ambrosia streaming;
> And on brows, more white than snow,
> See, the raven tresses glow!
> Lotus-like her dewy feet
> Treasures yield of nectar'd sweet:
> Light as on her footsteps pass,
> Blushes all the bending grass;
> And rings of jewels, Beauty's powers,
> Freshen into living flowers:
> While brighter tints, and rosier hues,
> All the smiling earth suffuse.

Her forehead some fair moon; her brows a bow;
Love's pointed darts, her piercing eyebeams glow:
Her breath adds fragrance to the morning air;
Her well-turned neck as polished ivory fair:
Her teeth pomegranate seeds,—her smiles soft light-
   nings are.
Her feet, light leaves of lotus on the lake,

When with the passing breeze they gently shake;
Her movements graceful as the Swan, that laves
His snowy plumage in the rippling waves,
Such, godlike youth, I've seen; a maid so fair;
Than gold more bright, more sweet than flower-fed air!

In the above little poem, an old woman is supposed
to describe to Kunya the charms of a nymph who, like
all her companions, was a candidate for his notice. The
poet has indulged his fancy in particularizing her several
attractions. The simile of the lotus is not less just; whose
velvet leaf always floats on the surface of the water, seeming
scarcely to rest upon it.

To view the waning moon at evening hour,
Fasting, a lovely maid ascends her bower;
Herself a full-orbed moon!—though brighter gleamed
The rays of beauty that around her beamed.
The women, wondering, from their Pooja ceased;
And thus with taunts addressed the wondering Priest:
"To you is heavenly science given!—then say,
Is't the full moon, or only Chout to-day?"

On the fourth of the month Katik, the Hindu women
fast till the moon rises; when they offer up *Pooja*, or
sacrificial rites; praying at the same time that their hus-
bands may now grow prematurely old. The day is called
"Kurwa chout,"; *chout* signifying fourth, and *kurwa* being
the name of certain little earthen vessels which the women
stain with a mixture of rice and turmeric called *aipun*,
and filling them with water and grass, place them before
figures drawn upon the wall, called *Ahoi;* where they
are left till the festival of the Diwalee, which occurs nine
days afterwards. The Hindu months commence on the
day subsequent to the full moon (Poorun masee); and
the foregoing lines describe a beautiful young woman
ascending her balcony to await the rising of the planet
on the evening of the Kurwa-Chout.

Though hair as black as glossy raven,
On me's bestowed by bounteous Heaven;
The gift I find a source of pain;
Yet who of Heaven may dare complain?
They sneer, and scoff, and taunting swear
I'm proud, because my face is fair:
And how should such a child as I
Restrain their cruel raillery?

My mother, if I stir, will chide;
My sister watches by my side;
And then my brother scolds me so,
My cheeks with constant blushes glow:
Ah then, kind Heaven! restore to me
The happy days of infancy;
And take this boasted youth again,
Productive but of care and pain!

A merry group at evening hour
Kunya spied in shady bower,
Lovely as pearls on lady's breast;
And Rhada shone above the rest.
Sweetly to their chiming bells,
On the glad ear the chorus swells;
And, as so true they strike the ground,
Each heart grows lighter at the sound.

Th' enraptured youth no more concealed,
At once his radiant form revealed:
And how shall I by words convey
Their consternation and dismay!
Their cheeks, till then unknown to shame,
Now redden with the mantling flame;
And their sweet eyes, of lotus hue,
Bend just like lilies filled with dew.

## TO KRISHNA

For thy dark form and look divine,
　The god of love upon thy shrine
　　A million times I'd lay;
And give the riving flame of night
In millions, for those smiles of light,
　　Around thy lips that play.

O let a million moons redeem
The glorious sun, whose cheering beam
　　Illumes thy awful face!
And let me for thy nature bland
A million suns, with pious hand,
　　Upon thy altar place!

The trembling lilies of the lake
In blooming millions let me take,
　　Meet offering for thine eyes!
Come then—descend into my soul;—
There dwell and reign without control,
　　Bright regent of the skies!

Why should I Baids or Shasturs name,
The venerable leaves, that claim
　　Our pious care and love;—
The three vast worlds unawed I'd take,
Nor shrink to offer for thy sake,
　　Sweet gardener of the grove!

Pleasure and pain pass away; and wealth and poverty
depart from us. O, therefore, learn wisdom.

The land remains not, nor the landholder; the princes
of the land remain not: yet be thou fixed, O my soul.

If love or hatred, avarice, passion, or pride, have
influenced thee; now, O my heart, receive the rigid lessons
of virtue:

They admonish thee night and day to cry, Rhada
Krishn! Rhada Krishn! Rhada Krishn'

On an enemy, a prisoner, a trader, a gamester, a thief,
   or a liar,
An adulterer, a diseased man, a debtor, or a whoremaster,
   (On the whoremaster especially) place no reliance.
Let them swear an hundred oaths; but believe not one.
The poet Gidhur has said, if any enemy enters your house,
Though he vows eternal friendship, he is still an enemy.


It becometh not a gentleman to desert his patron;
The tiger to skulk from the elephant;
Wisdom to dwell in darkness;
A warrior to shun the combat;
An adviser to speak words of detriment;
A Pundit to forget his learning;
A man of noble birth to associate with the vile;
Nor a wise man to consort with harlots.


   Shame to him who solicits without worth,
   Shame to him who beholds worth, and is not
      pleased;
   Shame to him who is pleased, yet bestows not,
   Shame to him who bestows with reluctance;
   Shame to the gift that is without sincerity,
   Shame to the sincerity that is without conscience;
   Shame to the conscience untempered with mercy,
   Shame to mercy when extended to a foe;
   Shame to the foe who cannot dive into the heart,
   Shame to the heart, where the mind is without
      honour;
   Shame to the honour that is devoid of wisdom,
   Shame to wisdom which is without the fear of God.
      Your anger cease, and know me still
      The humble bearer of his will.
   You, who have seen and shared his pleasant ways,
      On me your rage and scorn unjustly pour:
   Truly I state, what he in pity says:
      Nor dare say less, nor add one sentence more.

Lord of three worlds, a present Godhead named,
  What single tongue to speak his praise may dare!
Wanton you've known him still as colt untamed;
  And sportive as the bee in summer air.

With him the days of infancy rolled by;—
  And is he now a traitor deemed by you!
You're doubtless wise;—and poor of wit am I—
  Speak what you will; I'm bound to call it true.

Yet still my heart would heal this mortal hate;
  If I speak false; may wealth, may honour fly!—
Softened, they own 'tis hard the bolts of Fate
  To shun; and sighing, yield to Destiny.

  Why on my neck with fondness hang?—
  I am not she, who all night long
    Upon thy panting bosom lies;
  Who can thy wasted flesh imbue,
  With Chumpa's dye, of yellow hue,
    With Goolilala tinge thine eyes.

  Go thou perverse; nor foolish, say,
  That heart can own another's sway,
    Which once for thee has fondly beat;
  With neem-leaves who would heat his lip,
  That e'er had known the bliss to sip
    The cooling grapes delicious treat?

  In vain I court the noon-tide rays,
  In vain I wrap my cloak of baize;—
  Fierce winter reigns; nor will give place,
  But to a warm and fond embrace.

  Yes, genial warmth has fled the earth,
  And yields to chilling winter's wrath:
  But, banished, finds a place of rest,
  Impregnable,—in Woman's breast.

Say, lovely moon,—say, deer-eyed maid
   Whose locks like lilies wave in air,
While this green Kewra scorns to fade,
   Say, why neglect a form so fair?

O, would the Kewra's leaves were sere!
   In ashes would the village lay!
For he, whose false hands placed it here,
   From love and me stays far away!

And why should the Kewra's leaves be sere?
   Or, tell me, why the village burned?—
For he, whose true hands placed it here,
   Behold, in beggar's garb returned.

Was paper then more dear than gold?—
   Or ink more scarce than rubies bright?
Were slender reeds for thousands sold;
   One line of love you could not write?

I strove;—but only strove, to sigh;—
   When memory placed thee in my sight,
My fingers failed, my heart beat high,—
   I strove in vain;—I could not write.

A man, soon after his marriage with a beautiful young girl, is obliged to travel into some distant country. Upon taking leave of his bride, he plants a Kewra (supposed to be the spikenard), in the garden, and bids her observe it well; for that, so long as it continued to flourish, all would be right with him; but should she on the contrary behold it wither and die away, she might be assured that some fatal accident had happened to himself. After several years' absence, the man returns to his own country; and resolves to appear before his wife in the character of a Jogee, or Hindu mendicant; and thus to ascertain how she had employed herself during his long absence. He finds her listless and sad; her person and dress neglected;

and her sole employment, watching and weeping over the still flourishing Kewra plant. The above dialogue then takes place between them.

> The terrace now she gains;—and now
>     Unwearied seeks again the ground:
> Like juggler's ball tossed to and fro,
>     And fast in Love's soft fetters bound.

> A cord, of eager glances spun,
>     They mount; what will not lovers dare!
> From roof to roof on eye-beams run,
>     And dart like vaulters through the air.

In these stanzas, a girl is described as anxiously expecting the appearance of her lover, upon the terraces of their respective houses: and in a metaphor, allowable perhaps only to an Asiatic poet, their transport upon seeing each other is depicted.

> Wife, why thus sadly gaze around,
> And why thus heave such sighs profound,
>     And whence these strange alarms?
> Husband, because thy locks are grey,
> And all thy youth hath passed away,
>     In wicked syren's arms.

> Disclose that lovely face, sweet maid,
>     And glad the eyes of all around.
> No;—for the lily's bloom will fade;
>     And taunts the vanquished moon confound.

> From my Love's hair some loosened tresses hung,
>     And angry round her ring of jewels grew:
> Just like, at early dawn, a snake's soft young,
>     Curling with eager folds to sip the dew.

In this stanza, the poet merely means to say that a lock of his mistress' hair was blown by the wind and entangled in her ear-ring. The constant strife between the natural and artificial ornament is a favourite fiction of the Hindu poets.

How that dark little spot on thy chin
 Enhances thy beauty and power!
'Tis a rose, and a poor bee within,
 Deceived, lies entranced in the flower.

My eyes as sly robbers I use,
 To ensnare silly hearts passing by;
And when bound by a smile for a noose,
 In that dimple I plunge them,—to die.

A fatal dart upon her brow she placed,
 And once upon her lover turned to gaze;
Then slow retired, and peeping as she paced,
 Gleamed like the flashing of a sudden blaze.

Wear not rings and chains of gold,
 And deem the words of friendship true;
Like rust upon a polished mould
 Of steel they seem, when worn by you.

These jewels on my neck are tied,
 And crimson dyes my feet adorn,
Not to increase my beauty's pride,
 But mark a matron's honoured form.

A handsome woman, richly adorned with jewels and other ornaments, is addressed in the street by a man, who pays her the compliment contained in the first of the above stanzas; in the second she replies, and delicately reproves his presumption. It will be recollected that among the Hindus married women only are permitted to wear such ornaments.

Eager my lover tow'rds me ran;
His hand an army, and his plan,
    The careless city to surprise:
But my eyes form a fortress good,
And eye-lashes a fencing wood,
    Where modesty securely lies.


Enter quick, O fly the place!—
Veil, O veil, thy fairer face!—
See, yon planet's fate delayed,
See, the monster's grasp is stayed!—
Thou, whose face no spot defiles,
Dread his force, and dread his wiles;
Soon a meaner prey he'll free,
And quit a moon less pure, for thee.


The popular superstition of the Hindus respecting an
eclipse of the moon is that it is caused by a giant, who
attacks and devours the planet; in revenge for her having,
in conjunction with the sun, discovered him when, in the
disguise of a Deota, or good spirit, he endeavoured to
secure a portion of the Umvit or water of life. It is
necessary to premise so much, that the English reader may
comprehend the foregoing lines, which are supposed to
be addressed to a beautiful woman looking at an eclipse
of the moon from her terrace.


The spring returns with all its joyous train,
Yet he so fondly lov'd, stays far away:
My fluttering soul will quit its present clay,
In some avenging form to live again.


A fowler's, to ensnare the murmuring dove,
Or monster's fell, to quench the moon's pale light;
Or his fierce eye, the Lord of wondrous night,
Whose lightning glance consum'd the god of love.

The transmigration of souls is one of the doctrines of
the Hindu religion. In the preceding stanzas, a young
bride laments the protracted absence of her husband, and
wishes that after death she may revive in some form to
avenge herself on the objects which now increase her
misery, by exciting the tenderest emotions : the ring dove,
the full moon, and the God of love himself.

> O say, within that coral cell
> What mighty magic power can dwell ;
> That cheats my hopes, my sight misleads,
> And makes my pearls seem coral beads!
> In those black eyes now fury burns ;—
> To crabs' eyes all my coral turns!
> But see, she smiles ;—my fears were vain ;
> My worthless beads are pearls again.

The daughter of a certain Raja, young and beautiful,
fell suddenly into a deep melancholy. No art was left
untried to effect a cure ; plays and pantomimes were
acted before her ; the most ridiculous mimics and buffoons
were sent for, and exhibited in her presence : but all in
vain ; the young Ranee could by no means be induced to
smile. At length a facetious Brahman undertook to cure
her ; and, in the character of a jeweller, offered some
fine pearls for sale. The above lines contain the Brahman's
speech, with its effect : the first hyperbole failed ; but in
the next attempt he was more successful.

## AHALYA

(Ahalya, sinning against the purity of married love, incurred her husband's curse, turning into a stone to be restored to her humanity by the touch of Ramchandra.)

STRUCK with the curse in midwave of your tumultuous passion, your life stilled into a stone, clean, cool and impassive.

You took your sacred bath of dust, plunging deep into the primitive peace of the earth.

You lay down in the dumb immense where faded days drop, like dead flowers with seeds, to sprout again into new dawns.

You felt the thrill of the sun's kiss with the roots of grass and trees that are like infant's fingers clasping at mother's breast.

In the night, when the tired children of dust came back to the dust, their rhythmic breath touched you with the large and placid motherliness of the earth.

Wild weeds twined round you their bonds of flowering intimacy;

You were lapped by the sea of life whose ripples are the leaves' flutter, bees' flight, grasshoppers' dance and tremor of moths' wings.

For ages you kept your ear to the ground, counting the footsteps of the unseen comer, at whose touch silence flames into music.

Woman, the sin has stripped you naked, the curse has washed you pure, you have risen into a perfect life.

The dew of that unfathomed night trembles on your eyelids, the mosses of ever-green years cling to your hair.

You have the wonder of new birth and the wonder of old time in your awakening.

You are young as the newborn flowers and old as the hills.

## THE MAIDEN'S SMILE

TRANSLATED BY SIR RABINDRANATH TAGORE FROM A
BENGALI POEM BY DEVENDRANATH SEN.

METHINKS, my love, in the dim daybreak of life, before
you came to this shore
You stood by some river-source of run-away dreams
filling your blood with its liquid notes.
Or, perhaps, your path was through the shade of the
garden of gods where the merry multitude of jasmines,
lilies and white oleanders fell in your arms in heaps
and entering your heart became boisterous.
Your laughter is a song whose words are drowned in the
tunes, an odour of flowers unseen.
It is like moonlight rushing through your lips' window
when the midnight moon is high up in your heart's
sky.
I ask for no reason, I forget the cause, I only know that
your laughter is the tumult of insurgent life.

## MY OFFENCE

TRANSLATED BY SIR RABINDRANATH TAGORE FROM A
BENGALI POEM BY DEVENDRANATH SEN.

WHEN you smilingly held up to me, my sweet, your
child of six months, and I said, "Keep him in
your arms,"
Why did a sudden cloud pass over your face, a cloud of
pent-up rain and hidden lightning?
Was my offence so great?
When the rose-bud, nestling in the branch, smiles back
to the laughing morn, is there any cause for anger if I
refuse to steal it from its leaves' cradle?
Or when the Kokil fills the heart of the spring's happy
hours with love-dreams, am I to blame if I cannot
conspire to imprison it in a cage?

## THE UNNAMED CHILD

TRANSLATED FROM THE BENGALI OF DEBENDRA SEN
BY SIR RABINDRANATH TAGORE

SHE is a child of six months, lacking the dignity of a
name.

She is like a dewdrop hanging on the tip of a Kamini bud ;
like the peep of the first moon through the tresses of the
night ; like a pearl in the earring of the tiniest little fairy.

Her elder sister clasps her to her breast, crying, " You are
sweet as my new pet doll,"—

and her baby brother likens her to a pink sugar drop.

Thus while the whole household casts about in vain for
a simile to fit her, she nods her head opening her eyes
wide.

## POEMS

### BY SIR RABINDRANATH TAGORE

THE axe begged humbly, " O thou mighty oak,
Lend me only a piece of thy branch—
Just enough to fit me with a handle."

The handle was ready, and there was no more wasting of
time.

The beggar at once commenced business—and hit hard
at the root,

And there was the end of the oak.


The favourite damsel said, " Sire, that other wretched
queen of thine,

Is unfathomably deep in her cunning greed.

Thou didst graciously assign her a corner of thy cowshed,

It is only to give her chances to have milk from thy cow
for nothing."

The king pondered deeply and said, " I suspect thou hast
hit the real truth.

But I know not how to put a stop to this thieving."

The favourite said, " 'Tis simple.  Let me have the royal cow

And I will take care that none milk her but myself."

Said the beggar's wallet, " Come, my brother purse,
Between us two the difference is so very small,
Let us exchange! " The purse snapped short and sharp,
" First let that very small difference cease! "

The highest goes hand in hand with the lowest.
It is only the commonplace who walks at a distance.
The thirsty ass went to the brink of the lake
And came back exclaiming, " O how dark is the water! "
The lake smiled and said, " Every ass thinks the water
    black,
But he who knows better is sure that it is white."

Time says, " It is I who create this world."
The clock says, " Then I am thy creator."

The flower cries loudly, " Fruit, my fruit,
Where art thou loitering—Oh how far! "
" Why is such a clamour? " The fruit says in answer,
" I ever live in your heart taking form."

The man says, " I am strong, I do whatever I wish."
" Oh what a shame! " says the woman with a blush.
" Thou art restrained at every step," says the man.
The poet says, " That is why the woman is so beautiful."

" All my perfume goes out, I cannot keep it shut."
Thus murmurs the flower and beckons back its breath.
The breeze whispers gently, " You must ever remember
    this—
It is not your perfume at all which is not given out to
    others."

The water in the pitcher is bright and transparent;
But the ocean is dark and deep.
The little truths have words that are clear;
The great truth is greatly obscure and silent.

A little flower blooms in the chink of a garden wall.
She has no name nor fame.
The garden worthies disdain to give her a glance.
The sun comes up and greets her, "How is my little
  beauty?"

Love comes smiling with empty hands.
Flattery asks him, "What wealth didst thou win?"
Love says, "I cannot show it, it is in my heart."
Flattery says, "I am practical. What I get I gather in
  both hands."

"Who will take up my work?" asks the setting sun.
None has an answer in the whole silent world.
The earthen lamp says humbly from a corner,
"I will, my lord, as best as I can."

The arrow thinks to himself, "I fly, I am free,
Only the bow is motionless and fixed."
The bow divines his mind and says, "When wilt thou
  know the truth,
That thy freedom is ever dependent on me?"

The moon gives light to the whole creation,
But keeps the dark spot only to herself.

"Restless ocean, what endless speech is thine?"
"It is the question eternal," answered the sea.
"What is there in thy stillness, thou ancient line of hills?"
"It is the silence everlasting," came the answer.

In the morn the moon is to lose her sovereignty,
Yet there is smile on her face when she says,
"I wait at the edge of the western sea
To greet the rising sun, bow low, and then depart."

The word says, "When I notice thee, O work,
I am ashamed of my own little emptiness."
The work says, "I feel how utterly poor I am;
I never can attain the fulness which thou hast."

If you at night shed tears for the lost daylight
You get not back the sun but miss all the stars instead.

I ask my destiny—What power is this
That cruelly drives me onward without rest?
My destiny says, "Look round!" I turn back and see
It is I myself that is ever pushing me from behind.

The ashes whisper, "The fire is our brother."
The smoke curls up and says, "We are twins."
"I have no kinship," the firefly says, "with the flame—
But I know I am more than a brother to him."

The night comes stealthily into the forest and loads its
    branches
With buds and blossoms, then retires with silent steps.
The flowers waken and cry—"To the morning we owe
    our all."
And the morn asserts with a noise, "Yes, it is doubt-
    lessly true."

The night kissed the departing day and whispered,
"I am death, thy mother, fear me not.
I take thee unto me only to give thee a new birth
And make thee eternally fresh."

Death, if thou wert the void that our fear let us imagine,
In a moment the universe would disappear through the
    chasm.
But thou art the fulfilment eternal,
And the world ever rocks on thy arms like a child.

Death threatens, "I will take thy dear ones." The thief
    says, "Thy money is mine."
Fate says, "I'll take as my tribute whatever is thine own."
The detractor says, "I'll rob you of your good name."
The poet says, "But who is there to take my joy from
    me?"

*Iran*

## IRANIAN LITERATURE

THE greatest glory and distinction of Iranian poetry and prose consists in the excellence with which the poet detaching himself from the world writes of the world—in much of it, more especially when a Singer's effusions are touched by the Sufi doctrines, " he is in the world but not of the world." Facility of expression in his mother tongue, and delicate shades of meaning which Persian words can import to a composition, has given the Iranian a power equalled only by the Arabs; so that when he sings of love, or wine, or the beloved he means a divine scene, the amorous does not enter into it. In the war ballads or poems in praise of hero-Kings the flight of imagination has taken him up to regions where few if any other set of Oriental writers have so far reached. Translations in this collection are from; Issac Adams, Professor C. E. Wilson, S. Robinson, Edward FitzGerald, G. Bell and Sir William Jones.

## LOVE OF MAJNUN

### BY NIZAMI

MAJNUN was the son of a chieftain and Laili the daughter of a humble Arab who, nevertheless, possessed all the pride of his desert race. Laili was so beautiful and charming that when Majnun first gazed upon her flashing dark eyes, and

> The soft expression of her face,
> Destruction stun his burning brain
> Nor rest he found by day or night—
> She was forever in his sight.

As Laili's people were accustomed to wandering in the desert, they one day folded their tents and went to the mountains with their families and cattle, leaving no trace of their march, and cutting off every possible way for the two lovers to communicate with each other. Majnun became almost insane in the vain search after his love through the groves and glens of the wilderness and the solitary rocks of the mountains. At length his father, alarmed by his condition, took an organized band and went in search of their tribe. Finding them in the mountain stronghold he made preparations of marriage for his son to the maiden, but in such a conceited and haughty way that he received a very cold and unfavourable message in response. The chieftain, indignant and full of anger, took his homeward trip, when poor

> Majnun saw his hopes decay,
> He beat his hands and garments tore,
> He cast his fetters on the floor
> In broken fragments and in wrath
> Sought the dark wilderness path;
> And there he went and sobbed aloud,
> Unnoticed by the gazing crowd.

Once, while wandering near the camps of the Arabs, he was seen by some relations of Laili, who represented him as an insane youth of the desert. The maiden, recognizing her lover in their description, rejoiced over the tidings, though she feared to go out to meet him, dreading her father's wrath but anxiously

> From morn to eve she gazed around
> In hopes her Majnun might be found.

Once, while sitting at a fountain under a shady cypress tree near the encampment with bright hopes of chancing to see her beloved, she mournfully sang her faithfulness:

> Oh faithful friend and lover true,
> Still distant from thy Laili's view;
> Still absent, still beyond her power
> To bring thee in her fragrant bower.
> Oh ! noble youth, still thou art mine,
> And Laili, Laili, still is thine.

While she was thus chanting her love song under the cool shade of the tree a stranger, a princely youth, by name Ibu-sallaam, passed by. His eyes rested upon the crimson lips and beaming softness of her dark eyes. Electrified by her grace and beauty, he hurried to her father with a plea for his daughter's hand. Because of his kingly apparel and dazzling ornaments he was favoured by the father of Laili who gave his consent to the proposed union. The poor Majnun may wander, threatened and tried to induce his friend to fight the cruel Arab, but all is in vain. The contract is signed and the father has pledged his word of honour. The new lover brings his costly gifts, a long line of camels, all laden with embroidered robes, beautiful rugs and carpets, silks of all kinds and the most valuable gems to be laid at the bride's feet. The rattle of the drums and the shrieks of the pipes, the music for the marching steeds, announces the coming of the bridegroom, dressed in the richest cassimere, and smiling at each step like the rising sun. The wedding takes place in due time, although against the maiden's will, those pitiful pleadings were unheard and uncared for by any mortal. Still she cherishes Majnun's memory; the tenderest feeling, though the wife of Ibu-Sallaam now.

> Deep in her heart a thousand woes
> Disturbed her day and night's repose;
> A serpent at its very core,
> Writhing and gnawing evermore,
> And no relief—a prison room
> Being now the lonely sufferer's doom.

The rolling years and the whirling months did not bring any soothing to the heartache of Laili. She sat quietly in her prison tower, watching the circling of the sun by day and the flashing of the stars by night, with but a fainting hope in her sad heart for her Majnun. Once, while sitting in her chamber, meditating on her fate, she heard an unusual noise below; shrieks and wailing cries, a great confusion in the family. A messenger entered with a death note announcing the death of Ibu-Sallaam. Although the message was a star of hope and a benediction to her heart, yet to fulfil the Arab law she assumed the garments of woe and wept with the rest.

> But all the burning tears she shed
> Were for Majnun, not the dead.

When the prescribed years of mourning were fulfilled she was freed from her rock bound tower. She called her trusty servant boy and sent a hasty message to Majnun. She appointed a time and place for the two lovers to meet in communion sweet. She made her way through groves of palms and bowers of roses, not stopping until she saw the haggard form of her lover. Stepping gently to his side she laid her hand upon his arm and said:

"Ah, Majnun, it is thy Laili that has come." As he recognized the familiar voice and the gentle touch, overcome with emotion, he fainted at her feet.

> His head which in the dust was laid,
> Upon her lap she drew, and dried
> His tears with tender hand, and pressed
> Him close and closer to her breast;
> "Be here thy home, beloved, adored;
> Revive, be blest—Oh! Laili's Lord!"
>
> At last he breathed, around he gazed,
> As from her arms his head he raised;
> "Art thou," he faintly said, "a friend
> Who takes me to her gentle breast?
> Dost thou in truth so fondly bend
> Thine eyes upon a wretched distressed!
>
> "Are these thy unveiled cheeks I see?
> Can bliss be yet in store for me?
> Is this thy hand, so fair and soft?
> Is this, in sooth, my Laili's brow?
>
> "In sleep these transports I may share,
> But when I wake—'tis all despair!
> Let me gaze on thee—e'en though it be
> An empty shade alone I see.
> How shall I bear what once I bore,
> When thou shalt vanish as before?"

To this Laili responded quickly and readily:

> Here in this desert join our hands,
> Our souls were joined long, long before;
> And if our fate such doom demands,
> Together wander evermore.
> Oh, Majnun! never let us part.
> What is the world to thee and me?
> My universe is where thou art:
> And is not Laili all to thee?

Majnun, knowing that, according to the Arab law, he could not make her his wife, with tearful eyes and faltering voice, answered :

> How well, how fatally I love,
> My madness and my misery prove ;
> All earthly hopes I could resign—
> My life itself to call thee mine.
> But shall I make thy spotless name
> That sacred spell—a word of shame ?
> Shall selfish Majnun's heart be blest,
> And Laili prove the Arab jest ?
>
> The city's gates though we may close,
> We cannot still our conscience's throes.
> No, we have met, a moment's bliss
> Has dawned upon my gloom in vain ;
> Life yields no more a joy like this,
> And all to come can be but pain.

He clasped her close to his aching heart, and kissed her sorrowfully his last good-bye.

Accompanied by her servant she went back to her home and lived a most solitary life. The time of life's sunset drew rapidly nigh. She called her mother to her bedside and entreated that when she was dead Majnun might be allowed to weep over her grave.

After she was gone, the faithful servant took the tidings to the poor love-stricken Majnun. He made his way weepingly to the grave and mourned over her for weeks. At last he was found with his head resting upon the tomb and the peaceful touch of death upon his brow.

Laili's tomb was opened and they laid the still heart beside her own.

> One promise bound their faithful hearts—one bed
> Of cold, cold earth united them when dead.
> Severed in life, how cruel was their doom
> Ne'er to be joined but in the silent tomb.

Another of Nizami's productions is his story of Shirin and Farhad, two other lovers, whose devotion and sad life is no less thrilling and sentimental than that of Laili and Majnun. Some of the Persian scholars even admire it more. Shirin was the betrothed of the King Khosroe Parwiz and Farhad was a famous sculptor in his employment. These two fell in love with each other, and the king becoming aware of it, promised to give her to him if he could execute the impossible task of bringing to the city the abundant waters of the mountains. Farhad set himself to the herculean labour, and to the horror of the king, nearly accomplished it, when Khosroe Parwiz dreading the advancing necessity of losing Shirin, or being dishonoured, sent to inform him of her death. Being at the time on top of a precipice, urging on the work of the aqueduct, the news filled him with such ungovernable despair that he threw himself down and was killed.

∾∾∾∾∾∾∾∾∾∾∾∾∾∾∾∾∾∾∾∾∾∾

# PROLOGUE TO A BATTLE

## BY NIZAMI

*T*HE graceful procession of the azure sphere;
   The regular circling of sun, moon, and stars;
Think not that they were determined in idle sport,
Or that this fair pavilion was spread out for nothing!
Not a thread in its curtain was woven-in without a meaning,
Though the end of the thread be not visible to us.
Who knows, what will befall us on the morrow?
Of that which is seen what will become unseen?
With whom Destiny will make a compact?
Of whom his star will make for itself sport
Whom they will carry from his house dead?
On whose head will be placed the crown of Fortune?
Who knows, on the dust which is now stirred up,
What blood of heroes will to-morrow be poured forth?

BAHRAM SITS ON TUESDAY IN THE RED DOME, AND THE
DAUGHTER OF THE KING OF THE FOURTH CLIMES TELLS
HIM A STORY.

### BY NIZAMI

*W*HEN came December's month, upon a day short as
a night is in the month of June,—

The best of all the seven days of the week, Tuesday
its happy and auspicious name,

The day of Mars, and martial too its hue;—on such
a day Bahram, namesake of both,

Adornment, red with red together, leagued, and to the
Red Dome hastened at the dawn.

The fair Slavonian rosy-red of cheek, in hue like fire,
like water all benign,

Ran up to meet the king, and homage paid, and with
her sleeve swept from his cheek the dust.

For service worshipful she then prepared,—'tis sweet
to see a moon adore the sun.

When night had raised its gilded globe on high, and
dimmed the lustre of the solar cup,

She, honeyed apple, sweet and rosy-hued, was asked
by him to tell a cheerful tale.

The charming one resisted not his will; she cast pearls
from cornelian at his feet:

You, to whose Gate the sky as threshold serves; orb
of the sun and of the moon your tent;

Higher than every pearl that one can bore, better than
every word that one can speak.

No one so bold as to approach you near;—blind be
the man who is too blind to see!

She, having ended this, her prayerful speech, gave
purest rubies to the ruby mine.

### STORY

She said, In Russia's broad domains there was a town
ın beauty like a beauteous bride.

A king in it, a fosterer of good, who had a daughter bred in luxury.

A heart-beguiler, witching by her glance, of roseate cheeks, and cypress-slender form.

Face lovelier than the moon in beauty bright, in sweetness lips more sweet than sugar is.

All strength of heart she took from those who sued; sugar and taper near her were put out.

Sugar, before her small a sugary mouth, in heart was more contracted than her waist.

The musk afflicted at her curling locks; on thorns the rose and basil at her face.

High-statured like the cypress in the grove; like lamp and taper radiant of face.

The freshness of her face more fresh than Spring; than picture lovelier her lovely tints.

The drowsy jonquil languorous for her; the grace of eglantine her humble slave.

All men the dust beneath her servants' feet; the rose prepared to serve her slaves as slave.

Besides her beauty and her smiling grace, she had the ornament of learning too.

Knowledge of every order she had gained; and had perused a leaf on every art;

Had read the world's famed books on magic lore, on sorcery and other secret things.

Over her face she'd drawn a veil of locks; and was averse to all command to wed.

For she who in her time's unmatched, unique, how can it fit that she be mated, paired?

When that the rumour spread throughout the world that from the heavens a huri had appeared,

And that the moon and sun had borne a child, Venus had given it milk through Mercury.

An eager longing for her rose in each; each one with deprecation urged his suit.

One backed his claim with gold and one with strength; she on the instant hid her gold from view.

The father from the suit of men so famed, to which he saw that idol did not yield,

Was helpless, knowing not what means to adopt,—how, with apponents hundred, " nard " to play.

The lovely girl to strict seculsion vowed, seeing the urgency of those who sued,

Sought out a lofty mountain in those lands, far from the fear of damage as the sky.

She had a castle built, so strong and fit that from the mount's pith a new mount seemed born.

She made excuses, asked her father's leave to make her preparations for the road.

Her loving father, though he was distressed at parting from her, gave her leave to go.

So that when far his honey from the hive, the bees might not swarm in by roof and door ;

Also, that with the treasure in a fort, the watchman might not be disturbed by thieves.

Then that incastelled beauty, for her ease, saw to the proper ordering of the fort.

When she had built a castle of such strength, she went and treasure-like remained in it.

Her treasure thus secured, to her was given the name of " Lady of the Castle-keep."

Her castle thwarted treasure-pillagers, for, iron-built, 'twas as the " Brazen Fort."

She a Slavonian princess in that fort-of princesses naught like it had been dreamt.

She'd closed the road to those who took the road ; she'd foiled the wish of those whose wish was law.

The accomplished princess was on every theme most fertile in device and quick in thought.

She knew the constitution of the stars, their temperaments together she'd compared.

She'd fully mastered all the temperaments ; she'd taken in her hand the fragrant wine.

So that the treatment of all dry and moist, how water is made hot and dire made cold,

How men behave towards their fellow-men, how to community community.

All that may help and further culture too, all that may add adornment to mankind,—

Of all this she had gathered knowledge true, she, who in form was woman, man in mind.

As she became content within those walls, she cast all thought of mankind from her heart.

Upon the road to that high-towering fort she set with cunning skill some talismans.

Each talisman a form of iron and stone, each bearing in its hand a glittering sword.

So that whoever reached that dangerous pass, by the swords' strokes at once was cut in two.

Except the watchman of the fort, each one who went that way was foiled and overthrown.

The watchman too, though an initiate, took not the road except with reckoned steps.

For if he happened to take one wrong step, his head would from his body severed fall.

A talisman would strike him with a sword ; the moon, his life, would hide behind a cloud.

The fortress-gate, which towered to the sky, was hidden like the portal of the sky.

Though a serveyor searched it for a month, he'd find it no more than the heaven's gate.

That fairy-faced one, dweller in the fort, of China's studios was a painter skilled.

When she engaged in painting with the brush, she tied knots on the water like a shell.

With the black paint, as 'tis with huris' locks, she painted darkest shadow upon light.

When she was high-established in that house, and the house shone by that high-'stablished Moon,

She took the brush, and on a piece of silk painted a full-length portrait of herself.

And then above the silken portrait wrote in finest characters the ensuing words :

Whoever in the world may wish for me, with such a castle as is my abode,

Let him, not speaking from afar, come in, moth-like no simple gazer at the light.

A brave man may gain access to such fort; no coward can have any business here.

Whoever wishes for the beauteous one, must have not only one but thousand lives;

Must boldly set his mind upon the road, and four conditions strictly must observe.

The first condition of this wedlock then is that he have fair fame and beauty too.

The second, that by knowledge he has gained, he loosen on this road the talismans.

The third condition is that having loosed from their connections all the talismans,

He show where is the portal of this fort, that he become my mate by door, not roof.

If he the fourth condition would fulfil, then let him take the pathway to the town,

That I may come unto my father's court, and question him upon some learned themes.

If he should answer me in fitting mode, then I will wed him as good faith requires.

That honoured man shall be my husband then, for that which I have promised must be done.

And whosoe'er in these conditions fails, false to the terms, his blood be on his head!

Who holds this admonition in esteem,—he has the alchemy of happiness.

But he who cannot penetrate my words,—though he be great, he shortly shall be small.

When she had done preparing thus her page, she gave it to a fitting messenger.

She said, Arise, and take this page with you; go and take all the cover from this plate.

Go to the city gate, in some high place upon the tollhouse fasten this my note;

That anyone, of army or of town, whose wish may fall upon so fair a one,

May take the road on the conditions named, and either be the castellan or die.

The servant then departing with the note, followed an intricate and winding road.

He fixed the beauty's portrait on the gate, so that her lovers there might look on it;

That whoso should desire her might arise, and rashly with his own hand shed his blood.

When by each reigning prince and sovereign crowned was gathered of this story some account,

Led by desire inspired by that wild news, people appeared from all the parts around.

Each one urged by the fervour of his youth abandoned to the winds his precious life.

Whoever for the sake of her set out but incurred destruction through the falchion's strokes.

Not one who strove by judgment and by schemes could loose those talismans, the castle's guard.

And he who had some slight success in this,—even his spells reached not the remedy.

Though sundry of the talismans he loosed, he had not any power with the rest.

From want of proper judgment and of sense, disgraced, as but a warning did he serve.

Thus many handsome youths were brought to death without at all attaining to their wish.

No one had found deliverance from that road; no road was there but that of loss of head.

Each head cut off of those exalted ones,—they hung it up upon the city gate;

Till heads so many were cut off, that in the city, eaves on eaves were formed.

When round the world you look in every place, you find the towns adorned by festive scenes;

The trouble of the huris, fairy-faced, with heads, not festive scenes, adorned the town.

Upon her head how many heads there were which had not reached the shadow of her door!

Among the great in rank, the monarchs' sons, there was a handsome youth of noble mind.

Astute and powerful, beautiful and brave; the wolf and lion victims of his sword.

One day he left the city for the chase, to gain such joy as early spring invites.

On the town-gate he saw a honeyed page; around it hundred thousand poison flasks.

A portrait painted on a silken ground, one which should please the eyes, beguile the heart.

A face which from its loveliness and grace, took in a moment from him self-restraint.

He uttered fervent blessings on a reed from whose point came such characters as those.

Around the portrait, which adorned the world, round, head to foot, a hundred heads were hung.

He said, How from this shark-infested pearl can I escape? No place as refuge serves.

If from this love-affair I hold my hand, such self-restraint will bring on me distress.

And if my heart renounce not this desire, I lose my head, my wish still unfulfilled.

Although a lovely form is on the silk, snakes in the ring are, apines among the dates.

Forsooth, so many heads have been cut off; would that some business too had been achieved!

Take it that I too lose my head,—what gain? A harmless being killed and blood-defiled.

If from this cord I do not hold my hand, my head must be and will be bound by it.

Though I be bold enough to encounter death, how can I ever bid adieu to life?

Again he said, This silk is fairies' work, painted in order suitors to attract.

Before the spells of fairy such as this one must not go without some magic power.

Until by magic I annul her spells, I should not take up lightly this affair.

I must procure a means from small and great that from the wolf's jaw may escape my sheep.

He would grasp a business hastily,—the order of his business gets confused.

But in your action dwell not on the small, in order that great loss be not incurred.

Perform this mode of music with the world : take slowly, give out forcibly and quick.

My heart is more unbalanced than my mind; my liver much more blighted than my heart.

How then with such a heart can I be gay? What can I bring to thought from such a mind?

He spoke these words and for a time was sad, and from his bosom heaved a bitter sigh.

He shed tears as he gazed; he saw cloth, sword, and on the basin saw, as 'twere, his head.

This love, as 'twas, he hid within his heart, the thought and care he had he told to none.

Thus he was night and day with anguished heart; nor night was night to him, nor day was day.

With utter longing he at every dawn would wend his way unto the city-gate;

Would see that wondrous portrait on the gate : tomb of Farhad, and palace of Shirin.

Though for the lock a hundred thousand keys he sought, he still could not find any clue.

He saw a thread with thousand thousand ends, but the right end, the clue, remained unknown.

Then he discarded pride from the affairs, and turned himself to search and scrutiny.

He sought in every land expedients by means of which the tight knot might be loosed.

Although he sped about on every side, he could not loose it from its tangled state.

Until at last he heard news of a sage, a demon-binder of angelic kind.

One who could bridle every untamed horse; who to all learning had attained in full.

Subservient to him every fellow-sage; opened by him all doors just claim might close.

When of that learned man the noble youth heard news from men experienced and wise.

To that Simurgh of sun-like majesty he sped like bird which flies from mount to mount.

He found him like a garden in full bloom. Where? In a cave most desolate and drear.

He touched his saddle-straps as lily might; he girt himself for service like the rose.

Through his good fortune and most happy state much knowledge did he gather from that Khizr.

When from the spring he's drunk full many a draught, he spoke a word upon his fixed resolve,

And of the fay-like girl, the lofty fort, the people's fate caused by her sorcery.

The talismans she'd set upon her road; her casting down before her thousand heads—

All he related there before the sage; in naught did he the matter hide from him.

The sage informed him then of what was fit, in secret calculations for the affair.

The prince thus found the remedy he sought, then full of anxious care retraced his steps.

In a few days regaining steadiness, he set himself to think about the affair.

He gathered every needful instrument for the business in that narrow pass.

He sought a spiritual relationship which should relieve in this his hard emprise.

According as his estimate came out he formed his plan for every talisman.

And first, to further his pursuit he sought favour from those of spiritual power.

He dressed in red, for blood's involved, said he; this plaint is from the sky's oppressive act.

Since he was soon to enter seas of blood, he made his garments, as his eyes, blood-stained.

All care for his own safety he resigned.—Then cries of disapproval rose from all.

He said, I take not for myself this pain ; nay, rather, I avenge unnumbered heads.

Either I'll loose this yoke from people's neck, or sacrifice my life in the attempt.

When for this work he'd dipped his clothes in blood, he took his sword, and pitched his tent without.

All who became acquainted with the affair,—that one of lion heart had come to avenge,

Sent fervent aspirations forth with him, that he should soon succeed in that emprise.

Their aspirations and his pure, calm mind, were as steel armour to encase his frame.

Then afterwards, with plea to be excused, he asked the king's permission to depart.

Then set out on the road towards the fort, keeping in mind the plans for his affair.

When he arrived quite near a talisman, he made a stroke and then a gap appeared.

And by the magic of that charm sublime the talisman's connection he dissolved.

Each talisman he saw upon the road,—he cast it headlong down into the pit.

When he had thus removed them from the mount, he put their swords upon the mountain-peak.

Then he went quickly to the castle wall, and beat a drum there with a leathern strap.

He studied eagerly the sound it made, having in this prepared a keen device.

For since to crevices the sound was clue, the door by means of crevices was found.

When she became aware of these events, the moon-faced beauty sent someone to say :

You who make breaches and who open roads, you whom good fortune guides to his desire,

Since you have loosened first the talismans, and then
correctly found the treasure-door,

Turn to the city now like running stream, and two days
wait with patience if you can,

Till to the city to my sire I come, and there subject you
to a searching test.

About four searching things I will question you; give
answer to these questions if you can.

My love will then be yours, no plea will be admissible
against relationship.

When the man saw that he had found success, he turned
back and went forward on the road.

From the high fort when to the town he came, he took
the silken portrait off the gate.

He folded it and gave it to a slave;—blessings and praise
gained life, and trouble died.

Then all the heads upon the city-gate indignantly he
took down from their cords.

The people of the town applauded him, and with the
slain men's bodies buried them.

Followed by thousand blessings he went home, while
minstrels raised their voices high in song.

The townsmen in his honour scattered coins; from
all the roofs and doors they scattered them.

All of them swore on oath that should the king consent
not to the union of the twain,

They would at once bring down the king, and make
that prince their ruler and their sovereign.

For one was cruel and cut off their heads; the other,
brave and kindly, saved their heads.

And on her side the lovely princess too joyed in the
suit of her prospective mate.

And soon as night, from pods of blackest mush, rubbed
perfume on the litter of the moon,

She, sitting in her little gay in heart,—the wind the
driver of her cavalcade,—

From mountain pass unto the palace came; which
gained the mountain's majesty from her.

Her father seeing her grew bright and gay; nor did she hide from him the state of things.

All that had happened to her, good and bad,—she told him all her story end to end.

About those cavaliers through her cast down; who dug a pit, fell into it themselves.

Until the story came to where the prince had of a sudden lost his heart to her.

How to the mount he came, and firmness showed; how he broke, one by one, the talismans.

How he became successful with the fort, and failed not in the stipulations made.

Having fulfilled of four conditions three, let us now see how 'twill be with the fourth.

The king enquired of her, What is the fourth? That of the fair should one, not twenty be.

The honey-lipped one said, With fortune's lead, I mean to set four problems hard to solve.

And if by him my problems should be solved, the crown will then be placed upon his head.

But if he should break down upon this road, then he will pitch his tent where he well knows.

'Twere fitting that to-morrow at the dawn, the king should take his place upon the throne;

Should then invite the prince to be his guest; whilst I behind the curtain should be hid.

Then I some mystic questions would prepare, for him to answer with maturest thought.

The king said, we will do so, it is well; whate'er is done by you by me is done.

To these their words they added not a word, but sought their rooms and then retired to rest.

Next morn at dawn when that the azure sphere over the rocks the ruby's lustre shed;

When in these seven " nard "—boards of six squares, a wheat-ear sown came up a single grain,

Like the Great Kings, the king arranged a Court, and girded tight his waist in servitude.

He gathered an assembly of the famed, of those esteemed for piety and truth.

Then when the royal guard was formed in rank, he made his Court a hospitable hall.

The prince he then invited as his guest, and scattered precious pearls upon his head.

Then golden trays were set down in the hall; the hall in straits through store of food profuse.

Since all one wished was on the tray, it was, rather than tray, supplier of desires.

The foods which were to right and left of them,—each person ate of that which he desired.

The food partaken of in measure due, and nature thus refreshed with nutriment,

The king ordained that in a private hall they should assay the gold refined by fire.

When he went in he gave up his own seat, and made his guest be seated at his place.

He sat before his daughter then to see what further play she'd with her suitor make.

She who might teach Tarazian puppets play, behind the curtain gave a puppet-show.

She took off from her ears two cryptic pearls, and gave them to a treasurer and said,

Convey these to our guest without delay, and when they've been conveyed, his answer bring.

The messenger at once went to the guest, and that which she had brought she showed to him.

When the man carefully had weighed the pearls, the secret of them found place in his mind.

Three other pearls he added to those two, pearls which were worthy to consort with them.

Then he consigned them to the messenger, and sent her back to that exalted dame.

When she whose heart was stone saw those fine pearls, she took a stone up then and weighed the pearls.

On seeing that their weight was quite correct, with the same stone she pounded them to dust;

A little sugar added to the pearls, so that the pearls and
sugar were commixed.

The envoy took them and rejoined the guests; the
guest again divined the subtlety.

He asked the servant for a glass of milk; he poured
both into it and said, here, take.

The servant to her lady then returned, and near her
placed the present she had brought.

The lady took the milk and drank it up, and made a
paste then of the residue.

She weighed it with the weights in use before; the
weight was not diminished by a hair.

Then from her hand at once she took a ring, and gave
it for the trusty girl to take.

The wise man took it from the servant's hand, then on
his finger placed it with respect.

He gave a world-illuming pearl most rare, for night a
lamp, in brightness like the day.

The girl of huri race then speeded back, and gave to
rarest ruby rarest pearl.

The lady put the pearl upon her hand, and from her
necklace took apart the pearls.

Until she found a pearl a mate for his, for night a lamp,
of the same kind as his.

She threaded them together on one string, this one
and that as one, exactly alike.

The servant went, gave pearls unto the sea,—rather
she gave the pleiads to the sun.

When the wise man had seen them, in those two united
he could find no difference.

Twixt those bright pearls no difference there was in
light and sheen—none save duality.

He asked the servants for a blue-glass bead, for to those
two no pearl could be a third.

He placed the little bead among the pearls; he gave,
that she who brought might take them back.

The lady, seeing bead and pearls conjoined, propitious,
sealed her lips and sweetly smiled.

She, comprehending, took the pearls and bead, fixed
bead on wrist, and in her ears the pearls ;

Then to her sire said, Rise, arrange the affair, for I
have played with fortune now enough.

Behold, now, how my fortune favours me, when I can
choose a lover such as this.

Now have I found a match in one whose match no
other person is in his own land.

I who have wisdom and approve the wise, in wisdom
am inferior to him.

Her father, when he heard these pleasant words, said
to the fay, O you of angel kind,

The converse which I've witnessed at this time,—its
face behind a veil has been concealed.

All that in secret converse has occurred, you must
successively narrate to me.

She, nurtured in a thousand hopes, then raised the
cryptic curtain of the mystery.

She said, When first I set my wits to work, the two
pearls I unloosened from my ears.

Under the symbol of those lustrous pearls I said, Life's
but two days, these wisely use.

He, who three others added to the two, said, Though
'twere five 'twould also quickly pass.

Then I, who added sugar to the five, and ground in one
the sugar and the pearls,

Meant that this life, polluted by desire, is like the pearls
and sugar ground in one.

By incantation and by alchemy, who can each from
the other set apart ?

He, who poured milk upon the mixture then, so that
one melted and the other stayed,

Meant that the sugar mixed up with the pearls would
from them with a drop of milk divide.

I, who drank up the sugar from his cup, was but a
suckling when compared with him.

My sending him a wing was meant to show that in his
wedding me I acquiesced.

The pearl bestowed by him occultly showed that, like the pearl, his match could not be found.

I from my necklace added then a pearl to point out that I was myself his match.

Examining, he saw not in the world a third one that resembled those two pearls.

Thereafter he obtained a blue glass-bead; and added it against the evil eye.

I, who disposed the bead upon myself, thus showed myself devoted to his will.

His blue glass-bead, as seal upon my heart, is on my treasury the treasure-seal.

For solving thus the five close mysteries I honour and acknowledge him as king.

When the king thus beheld the wild colt tamed, the whip no longer in a state undressed,

In method excellent he set himself all rites prescribed by wedlock to perform;

Saw to the sweetmeats of her marriage-feast; and portioned Venus, to Canopus wed.

He made a banquet like the field of heaven; perfumed the hall with aloes-wood and musk.

He had all done to adorn the marriage-feast; with rose he seated cypress and went forth.

He joined together two of joyous heart, and then departed, leaving them alone.

When the prince saw his captivating bride, saw that a heavenly huri was his mate,

Sometimes he kissed her cheek, at times her lips; at times pomegranates tasted, sometimes dates.

Postremo adamas margaritas superavit; falco avis phasianae pectori superincubuit.

He saw his blue glass-bead upon her wrist, and love for him in her two languorous eyes.

Ejus margaritas cum sigillo non reliquit; margaritarum sigillum thesauro detraxit.

He lived with her, enjoying his desires. He dressed in red, a symbol of her cheeks.

For he had taken on that previous day redness of clothes as omen of success.

Since by that red he had escaped from black, he ever with red gems adorned himself.

Since then in red his fortune had been cast, the name was giv'n to him " King in Red."

Red's an ornament which delights the eyes; the value of red gems is due to this.

Gold, which the name, red sulphur, has received, has its best title in the title, " red."

The vital spirit is diffused with blood, and this is with the grace of life bright red.

Those persons in whom beauty may be found,—the source of this, their beauty, is of red.

When this delightful story reached its end, and roses red had filled the air with scent,

By reason of the roses strewed about Bahram's face brightened red like fragrant wine.

Extending then his hand to the red rose, he took her to his arms, in comfort slept.

# THE PATH OF MEDITATION
## BY NIZAMI

IT was a night like a gem-adorned morning,
   Implored in many a morning prayer,
The world resplendent with a brilliant moonlight,
The earth emptied of all its blackness,
The terrestrial bazaar relieved from its clamour,
The ear reposing from the jingling of bells,
The night-watchers with heads confused with drowsiness,
The nigh-at-hand dawn still steeped in moisture.
I had withdrawn my hand from worldly business,
And shackled my feet in the fetters of meditation :
My mind expanded, but my eyes sealed,
And my heart burning in the paths of expectation,
Like one who hath selected a likely station,
And waiteth for the prey to fall into the snare.
My head had found a place on the tip of my knee,
The ground beneath my head, the sky beneath my feet ;
No steadiness was there in the pulses of my limbs,
My head seemed to be changed into a footstool ;
My thoughts rambled inconstantly on their way,
And wandered from side to side, and in circle within circle :
My body was squeezed as it were into a corner,
And sought for nourishment in the fields of the spirit,
Now gathering examples from yet unread tablets,
Now searching for lessons in the pages of the ancients.
Then fell a fire as of a lamp into my garden (my heart),
And my garden was scathed as with a fiery scar ;
I melted like wax in the presence of the sun,
And my eyes were closed as with wax in sleep,
In such wise that enchanters might learn by me
How they might shut up all eyes in slumber.
Through such perplexing traverses of thought,
The clear brain was dissipated in my head,
And from its agitation proceeded a dream ;
And in that dream I beheld a fair garden,
And in that varied garden I plucked fresh dates,

And gave of them to every one whom I saw,
From that sweet dream came the gathering of dates,
Which filled my brain with fire and my mouth with water.
Then called the Muezzin to the first prayer,
PRAISE BE TO GOD! THE EVER-LIVING AND THE NEVER-
DYING!
And then there burst from me a sudden groan,
And instead of vacuity I fell into thoughtfulness;
I lighted up again the night-illuming taper,
And thoughts like my taper were burning within me.
At last the morn of felicity dawned upon me,
And I awoke to new life with the morning breeze;
My heart entered into eloquent converse with my tongue,
Like Marüt with Zahra in the mystical story.
" Why is it needful to sit so long without occupation?
I will take in hand afresh the unfinished embroidery;
I will introduce into my song a yet unknown melody;
I will salute anew the spirit of the olden times;
I will again remove the taper from the moth;
I will raise from the seed so goodly a tree,
That every one who shaketh down fruit from its branches
May pronounce a blessing on him who planted it:
But on condition that a handful of worthless fellows
Should not plunder the goods of their neighbours."
I am he who is the head of the sharp-witted,
The prince of those who are setters of jewels (poets).
They all pluck the ears, though I have sowed the grain;
They all are but house-furbishers, I am the house-holder:
In all four quarters I lay out my wealth,
But never am I secure against these street-robbers.
Where is the shopkeeper in all these quarters,
Whose shop is not breached on many a side?
Yet, like the ocean, why should I fear the stealing of a drop,
When my cloud renders back more than I bestow?
Though thou shouldst kindle three hundred lamps like
the moon,
The brand would still show that the light was stolen from
the sun.

〜〜〜〜〜〜〜〜〜〜〜〜〜〜〜〜〜〜〜〜〜〜〜〜

BAHRAM SITS ON FRIDAY IN THE WHITE DOME, AND THE
  DAUGHTER OF THE KING OF THE SEVENTH CLIME TELLS
  HIM A STORY.

### BY NIZAMI

ON Friday when this willow arched and high whitened
  its mansion through the rising sun,
The king adorned with ornaments of white, went forth
in pride and joy to the White Dome.
Venus upon the Sign of the Fifth Clime played the
five turns in honour of the king.
Until the Greeks attacked the Ethiop van, the King
indulged in pleasure without stint.
When night with sky-prepared collyrium gave brightness to the eyes of moon and stars,
He, from that loving and soul-caressing bride, associate
of the night, born of the dawn,
Requested that with dulcet fluted tones she would
evoke the echoes of her Dome.
When she, that fair one, blessings had invoked both
on the king and on his lofty throne,—
Such blessings as increase prosperity, and may become
so great a throne and crown,—
She said, Since you demand a pleasing tale, this one
occurs to me of those I know.

### STORY OF THE MASTER

Thus said my mother, a true, worthy dame,—old
women may be wolves, a lamb was she,—
Once an acquaintance one of my own age, took me
as guest,—her tray be ever filled!
A well-replenished tray for us she set;—the foods!
what shall I say, when limitless?
Lamb, birds, Iraqian cumin-flavoured meat, round
bread-cakes, and thin flour and butter cakes.
Some species of "halva" which have no name: some
with pistachios, some with almond dressed.

Fruits, fine and delicate, to charm the taste; apples from Isfahan, and grapes from Rai.

Speak not of pomegranate, the drinker's fruit; pomegranate-bosoms filled the house entire.

When in a measure we had eaten food, we set out to regale ourselves with wine.

With constant laughter sociably we mixed; I and some story-tellers of my kind.

Each one told some event about herself, of something singular or paralleled.

Till came the turn to one of silvery breast, honey in milk, and milk on sugar poured;

A heart-beguiler such that when she spoke the birds and fish were by her accents lulled.

She from cornelian loosed a honey-fount, she made her lovers cry out and lament.

She said, There was a youth of honeyed speech, who scattered sugar through his grace of thought.

A Jesus when his knowledge he displayed; a Joseph when assemblies he illumed.

Able in knowledge and accomplishments, his lively apprehension best of all.

He had a pleasant garden like Iran, of equal beauty were the gardens round.

The earth with scent of roses was perfumed; its fruit were like the fruits of paradise.

The cypress like an emerald palace rose; a dove was on the throne of every branch.

Therein, not Kauser's stream, but that in which was life, a fountain of life's water flowed.

All hearts were centred in its pomegranates; its roses had no meditating thorns.

If in the garden there were any thorn, it was to guard it from the evil eye.

Water beneath the fresh young cypresses; around the flowing waters verdant growth.

Unnumbered birds upraising voices sweet in choral symphony throughout the air.

In cypress-trees fixed raptured to the spot, moved everyone undued with heart to song.

As an encompassing protecting line were raised by its four walls four heads of glass;

And by these structures, towering to the moon, the evil eye to it no access gained.

It ranged its cypresses, sowed jessamine; it pounded musk, steeped all in ambergris.

On every rich man's heart there was a brand from wish to have such garden for his own.

The young man every week by way of rest for recreation to the garden went.

One day at time of mid-day prayer he went to view the garden and its leafy groves.

He found the garden shut, stones at the gate; the gard'ner soothed to slumber by the harp.

Sweet singers giving voice to dulcet song—may praise and blessing on such voices rest!

The garden tuneful with melodious tones, the charmers striving for their best effects.

Swaying in dancing movements every tree; bereft of heart the fruits, of life the leaves.

The master when he heard the songs of love, losing all self-possession tore his robes.

He had no self-control to turn away, nor any key with which to unlock the gate.

He knocked much at the gate, no answer came;—the cypress dancing, and the rose asleep.

The garden he encompassed all around; in all the garden he could find no way.

When he could gain no access by his gate, he tore some stone out from the garden-wall.

He went inside to have a look around; with earnest observation to inspect;

To hear the melody of song and make his wish to see the garden his excuse;

To see how stood the garden, whence the sounds, and what had happened to the gardener.

Of all those roses who illumed the place, who in the garden present were that day.

Two jasmine-bosomed ones of silvery limbs were keeping order at the garden-gate;

So that no alien's eyes should dare to gaze upon those radiant Moons of huri face.

Then when the master enters by the hole, the girls found him devoid of shame and rude.

They raised their plectrums up and wounded him; they took him for a thief and bound him tight.

The man this ignominy suffered:—why? through fear of being charged with an offence.

After ill-treating him with nails and fists, they roughly then exclaimed against him thus:

You through whose brand the garden is displeased, were there no guard what gain could gardens show?

A thief who into others' garden goes,—in beating him the gardener does well.

We, who have somewhat wounded you with sticks,— 'tis well that we have tied you hand and foot.

Then too, perverse and stupid-minded man, you leave the gate and enter through the wall!

The man replied, The garden is my own; but of my branding is this brand on me.

A gate is at hand, wide as a lion's mouth, I leave the gate, and enter by the hole.

Whoever comes into his land like this, his land will too fall surely to the ground.

When the girls saw his nature they inquired into the features of the garden claimed.

They found him in his evidence correct; anger subsided, litigation fled.

The master of the garden better known,—the heart of each was drawn to love of him.

For he was handsome, young, and eloquent;—a woman's lost who sees such qualities.

They judged it well to be at peace with him, because they found him of congenial kind.

They were rejoiced to have him as a friend, and set to work to free him from his bonds.

They loosened from his hands and feet the bonds, and planted kisses on his hands and feet.

Many apologies they made to him, and in attention to his business joined.

Then with excuse might turn a foe to friend,—repair the breach too in the garden-wall,—

They brought some brambles and closed up the breach, and thus ended the night-attack of thieves.

With blandishments they sat before the youth, and offering explanations of the case.

Said, In this garden green, a flowery Spring,—may the proprietor enjoy its fruits!—

A feast there is by heart-ensnarers given, beauties of moonlight face, in nature kind.

All the most lovely women in the town, whose beauty seen gives light unto the eyes,

Have in the garden all together joined, tapers and pictures void of smoke and flaw.

As an excuse for having used you ill, and having thus cast dust upon our lot,—

Rise and step out a little while with us, that you may gain your wish from which you please.

Go to some nook well out of sight, and from the strewing of the roses gain some joy.

Any fair one on whom you fix your heart, to whom you give your love, whom you approve,

We will at once bring to your secret nook, that on your threshold she may place her head.

Those accents falling on the master's ears, his dormant passions woke and cried aloud.

Though in his nature he had continence, passion was to his nature not unknown.

A man, his human nature was beguiled : a man, he could not woman's wiles resist.

With those of jasmine bosom, silver form, he went, indulging in the highest hope.

Before those beauties of the heavenly fort there was a lofty upper room of bricks.

The master entered it and closed the door, and the two guides retired then from his side.

In the front centre of the room there was a hole, and through it shone a beam of light;

And owing to this hole the master's eye beheld a narrow source and spacious stream.

In the plantation of the garden was a lawn full of the forms of cypress-grove.

Each beauty there, enlivening the heart, upraised her voice in sweet commingled sound.

In gardens pomegranates and apples too fail not, still less when gard'ners use them well.

But when a dragon in their treasure lurks, their oranges are shrivelled, hard and dry.

Beauties of silver limbs, pomegranate breast, were strewing roses upon every side.

Light to the eyes were all the honey-lipped, sweeter than all the ripe fruits of the place.

Pomegranate breasts and chins like apples there he saw, and other apples held as naught.

A stream flowed over it like sparkling tears; in it were fish untouched by injury.

And by that stream of surface fresh and bright the jasmine, lily, and narcissus grew.

Those beauties, velvet-cheeked, came towards the stream; they saw a spacious basin towering high.

The heat of the sun's rays had heated them; the sun-like water had been found by them.

They came with mien seductive to the stream, untying as they came their wrapper bands.

Their robes they took off and unveiled themselves, and showed like pearls in water by their grace.

They cast the water on their silvery necks, sometimes in blackness silver they concealed.

Together in the water moon and fish; confused with one another moon and fish.

When the moon into water "dirams" pours, where there is any fish it darts below.

But those Moons in their heart-entrancing grace made the fish rise for him, the master there.

With hands joined in a ring they danced awhile, mocking the jasmine in their loveliness.

Awhile in ranks opposed they scattered pearls; made pomegranate and orange valued high.

One came and made another fear a snake: A snake! she cried, whilst throwing out a curl.

Una dum alteri crurem natesque ostenderet dixit, Montem vide, et fissum terrae motu solum.

Columns in Bistun columnless they raised; killing Farhad with the sharp axe of love.

The milky stream which Shirin's palace had, in that delightful, pleasant basin rose.

The master saw; no self-control remained; but what avail? he had no friend or help.

He was as thirsty man to reason lost who water sees he has no power to reach;

Or epileptic who the new moon sees, and now jumps up and now sits down again.

He looked towards every cypress statured belle; a Resurrection, ne'er a stature saw.

His veins, full-blooded, through their ferment drew from his whole being cries and clamour loud.

Standing there like a thief concealed from sight;— that which you know in such state as you know,—

His bird through aperture, his snake through hole, wished among them audaciously to dart.

The fair-faced washed the roses' faces clear, and looked like jasmine in silk rosy vests.

They put on silken robes of azure hue, and in their brightness seemed to upbraid the moon.

With them, the loveliest player of the harp, was one of Grecian face and Ethiop locks.

A sun with full chin like a crescent moon, her lips by none e'er tasted honeyed dates.

Her glances sharper than an arrow's point, than sugar-candy sweeter still her smiles.

Like laden cypress pomegranates were dipped in water, water dipped in pomegranates.

With one lure she would capture thousand hearts; whoever saw her died before her face.

Whenever she began to touch the strings, love woke alert, and intellect was dimmed.

The master with that charmer of the world more charmed afar than watchmen are with light.

Although each one was like a radiant moon, in that assembly she was like a queen.

The ascetic in his heart strayed from the path: the laxness see! fine moral usages!

After a time those two musk-deer-eyed belles, who when in anger had the lightning's fire,—

Who roused the musk-deer in that new Khoten, and showed the musk-deer to the cheeta swift.

Advanced to speak with him in honeyed tones, their muslin veiling crowns of majesty.

They saw the master in the curtained place; as keepers of the curtain questioned him.

Said they, To which of all these lovely ones of huri race does most incline your heart?

The beauty there who pleased the master most, he pointed out to those two lovely ones.

Ere he had spoken out they both sprang up: as deer, nay rather raging lions, sped.

That beauty, fairy-born, with many a wile, with words sung to the harp they led away.

In manner such, that no one might suspect, that might not peril, but advance the affair.

When they had brought the marvel to the room,—the marvel see! they closed the door of heaven.

Although he knew not he was mate for her, she mate for him, and easy him emprise,

Twas so, for those fair harpers who had sped, had harmonised his business like a harp.

Those stores of grace and beauty had before told her in detail all the master's case.

That charming one, endowed with fairy face, had fixed her heart on him as yet unseen.

His beauty when she saw him, drew from her iron from silver,—silver which was gold.

The master, lost to self-control through love, addressed the cypress straight in chiding tones.

He asked, What is your name? Fortune, she said. Said he, Where is your place? She said, The throne.

What is your curtain? Music, answered she. And what your business. Coquetry, she said.

He said. What is your source? She answered, Light. He said, The evil eye be far from you!

A kiss you'll give, said he? Sixty, she said. He said, Come, is it time? She said. It is.

Said he, Shall you be gained? She answered, Soon. He said, Was this in view? She said, It was.

The master's heart with strong emotion stirred, he lost all bashfulness and diffidence.

He seized the lovely charmer's harp-like locks, embraced her tightly, strained as his heart-strings.

He kissed and tasted lips as sugar sweet, gave kisses one to ten, till ten times ten.

The kisses were as fire to stir his heart; the fervent heat gave keenness to his aim.

He wished to taste the sweetness of the Spring, and from the fount of life to take the seal.

When at the onager the lion sprang, and drew it forcibly beneath its claws,—

The place was weak, and, suffering violence, breaches were opened in its loosening bricks.

The chamber was an old one and came down,—let not the business of the good end ill!

Both this and that one by a hair escaped; this to one side, that to another sprang.

That they should not be seen upon that road, they went some distance from that fruitful tract.

The man retired from it, and in his pain went to a quiet place and suffered grief.

The girl went then and with her comrades sat, with wrinkled brow like those who suffer pain.

She set before her mind her past distress; took up her harp and put it on her lap.

When she brought out the sweet plaint of the harp, with plaints she drove her lovers all distraught.

She said, Be salutation from my harp by the strings dulcet plaint to lovers given.

She touched the string and thus began to sing: The Jadas tree had come, the flowers bloomed;

The cypress had drawn out its lofty form, the rose's smile displayed a box of sweets.

The nightingale arrived, sat on its branch; the day of making love had brightly dawned.

The Gard'ner to the garden fragrance gave; joyous he came and on its beauties gazed.

He saw a cup of wine and took it up, but then there fell a stone which broke the cup.

You who have pillaged me of all I had,—only by you can my affairs come right.

Although I am ashamed of what I've done, my heart to separation is averse.

Her mode of music gave her confidants full information of her secret thought.

They went away oppressed with anxious care; they went and saw the master who had gone.

The master, like a slave who butter steals, had naught but shame to follow on the feast.

He crept behind a narrow river's bank, 'neath cypress, willow, box, and poplar-tree.

Confounded at his injudicious plans,—the yellow wall-flow'r from his lilies sprang.

They sought to know that which he had in mind; and he told all to those two confidants.

Those secret agents felt it due from them to bring the loved one to the lover there.

Thence they returned, and opened out the way; so the rose-water to the rose they sent.

That friendly one, sweet songstress, came to him, renewing for her lover love once more.

The master took her hand and then advanced unto a certain place that he thought fit.

Branches upon branch the branches of the trees, forming aloft innumerable thrones.

He sped beneath the branch of a high tree; with joy of heart he made a pleasant seat.

With love he drew the heart-ensnarer close; close to his bosom as the heart it held:

A cypress free with graceful, swaying gait, one like the jasmine on Samanian rug.

He took her to his bosom and rejoiced; the cypress made a compact with the rose.

The moon-faced beauty on the master's breast, he well inclined, all self-restraint deposed.

His piece on house-securing all intent, his partner prompt to carry off the stakes.

He was all eagerness to take the fort, and quench with water all the fire of love.—

It chanced a field-mouse near has seen some gourds suspended from the lofty branch above.

It flew up to the string like any bird, and cut the strings which held them with its teeth.

Such a calamity fell on the ground! each gourd in figure like a kettle-drum.

The noise of such a drum went many miles;—a drum,— what drum? the drum to sound retreat.

The noise, disturbing, with continued clash, tore from the panther's claws the deer away.

The master thought the inspector with a stick, the censor with a stone had come to attack.

Leaving his shoes behind, he ran away; he went about his business once again.

That idol also went with thousand fears back to her intimates in music skilled.

A short time after she unveiled her heart, joining the music of the harp to song.

She thus sang, Lovers on a time have said, A lover went to visit her he loved.

He wished to the extent of his desire by union with her happiness to gain.

To take her to his arms as love dictates: sweet in the arms of cypress the red rose!

Then through her swelling bosom and her chin, an apple eat, pomegranate from her breast.

Ad locum ubi thesaurus asservatur manus protendere voluit ut thesauri portam aperiret;

Saccharum cum saccharo indurato miscere voluit, et salice rubra tuplipae sanguinem effundere—

When suddenly a tumult brought distress, so that so fine an entertainment failed.

It is not well you offer me false tones; I will not cease to play true tones for you.

O you whose every throw has been unfair, as one who throws with fairness make a throw.

A moth is left here anxious for the light; a thirsty one far from the fount of life.

When this ode had been sung her confidants, as sympathizers understood its aim.

They went with deprecation to the youth, and found him stretched full length on the ground.

They found him lying, resting on the ground, greatly abashed and much distressed at heart.

With kindly treatment then and friendliness the cause of such dejection they inquired.

Questioned about his state, he told the tale: even in hell 'twould raise a bitter sigh.

Then those devisers by device, their own, gave him deliverance from his gloomy thoughts.

From his contracted heart they loosed the bonds, heartened one out of heart by promises.

Be in this business more expert, said they; you love, 'tis true, but be more loving still.

At the due time make such a place your nest that no calamity may fly to it.

We surely from afar will hold the place, and we will guard the road like sentinels.

Then for the business they returned to her again of cypress form and rose-like cheeks.

So that once more she went with charming gait; she found the master soon and soothed his heart.

She came, relieved him of his load of grief; the master, seeing this, lost mastership.

He seized her ringlets like a drunken man; and in the garden sought a quiet nook.

There was a distant corner of the place, a heap of jasmine there a dome of light.

The jasmine raised its standard to a wall; above there was a wood, below, a cave.

The master found no better place than that, so in it he prepared a pleasant couch.

He plucked the jasmine and arranged it well, then brought his love in comfort to the place.

Pudore omisso ejus strophii ligamentun, pariterque vestimenti alterius de quo mentionem facere non licet ligamentum solvit.

He drew a heap of roses to his breast, blanched almonds sugar-coated sweet to taste.

Specillo pixi qua collyrium conditur nondum immisso,—the curved dome played them still another trick.

Some foxes in recesses of the cave had come together in pursuit of game.

A wolf had followed close and barred their road, to separate each from the other one.

The foxes knowing that he fed on all,—a terrible and great calamity,—

With terror took to flight, the wolf behind, their only road across the master's bed.

They started up to do as best they could,—in front the foxes, and the wolf behind.

The master's court had fallen all away, he saw a hostile camp, and bounded off.

Truly he knew not what had happened there; covered with dust he ran from side to side.

His heart in sore anxiety and pain to know how best to quit the garden soon.

Then met him there those two of cypress form, who pomegranates, narcissi, had bestowed,—

Then grasping his beloved by her skirt,—she pearl-like 'twixt two water-dragons placed.

They shouted at her, What deceit is this? What demon this among your qualities?

How long will you disturb and vex the youth, killing him with rancour him who loves you so?

No person on a stranger, sure, would play, with show of sympathy, a trick like this!

This night how often have you left him thus! How much deceit and fraud have you employed!

She offered pleas and swore that they were true; they would not listen to the truth from her.

Till in distress the master came to them; he saw the dawn between a pair of shears;

Covered with shame at their severe reproofs, receiving blows from this one, slaps from that.

He said, Beware now! Take your hands from her! Do not distress my friend who is distressed.

Since from a radiant moon no sin has come, so must you sing a better air to her.

If in such want of faith be any sin, hands should be laid on those ashamed of it.

Her nature is quite pure of any sin; any offence committed is from me.

The clever and sharp-witted of the world are all devoted servants of the pure.

The grace of God has given my affairs immunity from harm and from mischance.

And all those harms which broke my spirit so, which came and heaped mischance upon mischance,—

Since my good fate had given me continence,—they gave me freedom from so ill an act.

He whom the demon brings not to his aims is good in grain, naught that is good does ill.

But he who puts his heart on action base,—saving your presence, base of birth is he.

A beauty with so fairy-like a face,—no person can refrain from loving her :

No man especially, who has some youth, the feelings of a man, some love in him.

But still when chastity protects the road, one cannot think of going to meet sin.

No one can eat fruit from the fruitful tree on which a single evil eye may look.

The eyes of hundred kinds of beasts of prey were on us, hence our business turned out ill.

What's gone has gone, of that I will not speak ; thus will I spoil not that which still I have.

I now repent of all both hid and clear, and from the Ruler of the world accept.

That if He grant me still a time to live,—since she of sugar lips receives her slave,—

As lawful wife I'll take her as my bride, treat her with more devotion than before.

The agents seeing how it was with him, were awed at his God-fearing piety.

They put their heads before him on the ground ; they said, Be blessings on a faith so pure.

Faith in which seeds of goodness have been sown, and which from evil disposition's kept.

How many are the griefs which seemed as griefs ! they were thought griefs, but comforts were in fact.

How many too, the pains which come on man, and still a remedy is in the pain.

The lovely ones put coquetry aside, confounded at the puppet-playing sphere.

When from the mountain rose the fount of light, it banished from the world the evil eye.

Dawn, like the spider of the astrolabe, unto the world's
pole spun its gossamer.

Bearing a lamp a breeeze arose and bore the gard'ner
from the garden to the town.

The master raised his standard in control, released
from that subjection and those bonds.

From last night's fire of love-essays his heart was
cauldron-like to ebullition brought.

When to the town he came, he sought at once to carry
out in faithfulness his aim.

The Moon of last night he induced to come, assigned
the portion as the law commands.

Margaritam imperforatam coralio perforavit : experrectus
est gallus, piscis requievit.—

If in the world you look from bird to fish,—this same
affection will be found in all.

Good fortune has to find a limpid stream! he drank
of water lawful then to him.

Pure as the radiant sun he found a spring, bright, clear
as jasmine, and, as silver, white.


In whiteness is the bright light of day ; by whiteness
too the moon illumes the world.

In colour is an artificial taint, except in whiteness,
which is pure, unstained.

Man when bestained is in a hopeless state ; whiteness,
the sign is of his purity.

Then when in adoration men engage, it is the mode
that they should dress in white.


She, jasmine-bosomed, ending thus her words, the
monarch gave her place upon his breast.

Thus many a night in comfort and in joy he went and
tarried in the Domes in turn.

The sky, constructor of the lofty domes, opened the
doors of the Seven Domes to him.

## ISKANDAR'S CONVERSATION WITH THE BRAHMINS

### BY FIRDUSI

ISKANDAR asked the Brahmins about their sleep and
their food; How they enjoyed their days of tran-
quility; and how they supported the dust of the battle :
" What is your portion of the delights of the world,
For Fortune never separateth the poison and the anti-
dote ? "
One of the sages replied : " O Conqueror of the world!
No one speaketh here of fame or of battle.
We have no wants as to clothing, reposing, or eating.
Since man cometh naked from his mother,
He ought not to be very delicate in the matter of
raiment.
Hence he will return naked to the earth.
And here he will find a place of fear, and of sickness, and
of anxiety.
The ground is our bed, and our covering the sky,
And our eyes are set upon the road,
Waiting for that which Time may bring with it.
The ambitious man laboureth excessively for something
Which, after all, is little worth the labour ;
For when he leaveth this temporary place of refuge,
He must leave behind him also his crown and his treasures.
His sole companions will be his good deeds,
And he and all that he hath will return to the dust."
One of the Brahmins said to him : " O Monarch,
Close thou for us the door of Death."

He replied : " With Death, vain are all petitions!
What rescue can there be from the sharp claws of that
dragon ?
For wert thou of iron, from them thou couldst not escape.
Youthful as he may be, he who remaineth long here
Will from old age find no deliverance."

The Brahmin answered : " Then, King,
Puissant, and learned, and worthy of empire,
Since thou knowest that for death there is no remedy,
And that there is no worse affliction than old age,
Why give thyself so much pains to win the world ?
Why madly persevere to smell its poisoned flower ?
The misery thou hast caused will remain after thee ;
The fruits of thy trouble and thy treasure will go to thine
    enemies."

# FROM NUSHIRVAN'S LETTER TO HIS
## SON HORMUZ

*I* HAVE thought it meet to write this serious letter to
my child,
Full of knowledge and true in the faith:
May God give him happiness and a prosperous fortune!
May the crown and throne of empire be his in perpetuity!
In a fortunate month, and on a day of Khurdad (light-
giving),
Under a happy star and brilliant omens,
We have placed on thine head a crown of gold,
As we in like manner received it from our father,
And we remember the blessing which the happy Kobad
Conferred on our crown and throne.
Be thou vigilant; be master of the world; be intelligent;
Be thou of a generous disposition, and do harm to no one.
Increase thy knowledge, and attach thyself to God;
And may He be the guide to thy soul.
I inquired of a man whose words were excellent,
And who was mature in years and in intellect:
" Who amongst us is the nearest to God?
Whose path towards Him is the clearest? "
He replied: " Choose knowledge,
If thou desirest a blessing from the Universal Provider:
For the ignorant man cannot raise himself above the
earth;
And it is by knowledge that thou must render thy soul
praiseworthy."
It is by knowledge that the King becometh the ornament
of his throne:
Gain knowledge, therefore, and by thy throne victorious!
Beware thou become not a promise-breaker;
For the shroud of the promise-breaker will be the dust.
Be not a punisher of those who are innocent;
Lend not thine ear to the words of informers.
In all thy business let thine orders be strictly just;
For it is by justice that thy soul will be rendered cheerful.

Let thy tongue have no concern with a lie,
If thou desirest that thou shouldst reflect a splendour on
thy throne.
If any one of thy subjects accumulate a fortune,
Preserve him from anxiety about his treasure ;
For to take aught from his treasure is to be the enemy of
thine own :
Rejoice in that treasure which thou has gained by thine
own care.
If the subject shall have amassed wealth,
The monarch out to be his sustainer ;
Every one ought to feel secure in thine asylum,
However exalted he may be, or however humble.
Whoever doeth thee a kindness, do him the same ;
Whoever is the enemy of thy friend, with him do battle.
And if thou comest to honour in the world,
Bethink thee of pains of body, and sorrow, and calamity,
Wheresoever thou are, it is but a halting-place ;
Thou must not feel secure, when thou sittest down in it.
Seek, then, to be deserving ; and seat thyself among the
wise,
If thou desirest the favours of Fortune.
When thou placest on thine head the diadem of sovereignty,
Seek ever the better way beyond that which is good.
Be charitable to the wretched ; keep thyself far from all
that is bad ;
And fear for the calamity which thou permittest.
Sound the secret places of thine own heart,
And never show a magnanimity or justice which is only
on the surface.
Measure thy favours according to merit ;
And listen to the counsels of those who have seen the
world.
Be inclined to religion, but keep thine eye on the Faiths,
For from the Faiths proceed jealousies and anger amongst
men.
Manage thy treasury in proportion to thy treasure,
And give thy heart no anxiety about its increase.

Regard the actions of former kings,
And take heed that thou be never otherwise than just.
Where are now the diadems of those Kings of kings?
Where are those princes, those great ones so favoured by
    Fortune?
Of their acts they have left nothing behind them but the
    memory:
That is all; for this transient resting-place remaineth to
    no one.
Give not command recklessly to spill blood,
Nor lightly engage thine army in war.
Walk in the ways of the Lord of Sun and Moon,
And hold thyself afar from the works of demons.
Keep this Letter before thee night and day,
And sound reason perpetually in thy heart.
If thou doest in the world what deserveth remembrance,
Thy name will not perish for lack of greatness.
The Lord of Goodness be ever thy refuge;
May earth and time be ever favourable to thee;
May sorrow have no domination over thy soul;
And may the hand of cheerfulness for thee never be
    shortened!
May fortune be ever thy slave;
And may the heads of those who wish evil to thee be
    abased!
May the star of thy destiny ascend to the ninth heaven;
And may the Moon and Jupiter be the protectors of thy
    throne!
May the world be irradiated from the splendour of thy
    crown;
And may kings be servants in thy court!
When he had written this Letter, he consigned it to his
    treasury,
And continued to live in this transitory world in fear and
    trembling.

# THE GULISTAN
# ON LOVE AND YOUTH

### BY SADI

THEY asked Hussain Maimundi, how it was that Sultan Mahmüd, who had so many handsome slaves, each one of whom was of rare beauty, should have no heart-felt affection for any of them, except for Iyäz, one who had no excess of comeliness. He replied: "Hast thou not heard that whatever touches the heart will look fair to the eye?"

If any one regardeth another with the eye of dislike,
Though he were formed in the image of Joseph,
He would yet be looked upon as one of the unlovely;
And if thou regardest a demon with the eye of desire,
He would appear in thine eye an angel and a cherub.
Whomsoever the Sultan regardeth with partiality,
All that he doeth badly is sure to be well done;
And whomsoever the monarch discardeth from his presence,
Will never be caressed by any one of the household.
There was a handsome and virtuous youth
Who was betrothed to a beautiful girl;
I have read that, as they were sailing on the great sea,
They fell together into a whirlpool.
When a sailor came to seize his hand, and save him from perishing in that extremity,
He called out from the midst of the threatening waves:
"Leave hold of me and take the hand of my beloved."
Every one admired him for that speech, and when he was expiring he was heard to say:
"Learn not the tale of love from that light-minded man who forgetteth his beloved in the hour of danger."

## THE GULISTAN

## MAXIMS FOR THE CONDUCT OF LIFE

ℛICHES are for the comfort of life, not life for the amassing of riches. I asked a wise man, Who is the fortunate, and who is the unfortunate man? He replied: "He is the fortunate who sowed and reaped, and he is the unfortunate who died and enjoyed not. Offer no prayer in behalf of that worthless wretch who did nothing but spend his life in the accumulation of wealth which he used not!

Wouldst thou be the better for worldly possessions be beneficent to others, as God as been beneficent to thee. The Arabs say: " Give, and account it not an obligation, for the advantage of it will come back to thyself."
Wherever the tree of liberality has rooted itself, its stem and its branches will ascend to the sky.
If thou hast hopes of eating of its fruit, deem it not an obligation that thou didst not lay the axe to its root.
Be thankful to God that he has prospered thee to thy good,
And has not shut thee out from a share in His favours.
Think not that thou conferrest an obligation in serving the Sultan;
Recognise the obligation he has conferred upon thee by placing thee in his service.

Two persons took trouble in vain, and laboured without advantage; he who gained wealth which he enjoyed not, and he who gathered knowledge which he did not apply. Whatever amount of science you may possess, if you reduce it not to practice you are still ignorant. The beast which you load with a few books is not on that account a learned man or a philosopher. What knows that empty skull, whether it be carrying precious volumes or firewood?

Three things are not stable without three things: wealth without traffic; learning without discussion; and a kingdom without government.

Thou shouldst speak such words between two enemies that, should they become friends, thou wilt not need be ashamed. A quarrel between two persons is like a fire, and he who malevolently reports their words is like one who supplies fuel to the flame. Speak softly to your friends, that the blood-thirsty enemy may not overhear. Be on your guard when you speak before a wall, that there be not an ear behind the wall.

Whilst an affair can be arranged with money, it is not right to endanger life; nor till every device has failed does it become law to lay hands upon the sword.

The wicked man is a captive in the hand of an enemy, for whithersoever he goeth, he cannot free himself from the grasp of his own punishment.
If the wicked man should seek refuge in heaven from his anguish,
He would still be in anguish from his own evil disposition.

Hearest thou news which will afflict a heart, be thou silent, and let another bear it. O nightingale! bring thou the good news of the spring; leave to the owl the tidings of evil.
He who offers advice to a self-conceited man needs himself advice from another.

An affair succeeds through patience, and over-haste ends in disappointments. I have seen with my own eyes in the desert the slow man pass by the quick one, the wind-footed courser fall exhausted through its speeds, and the camel-driver, though tardily, push on to the end.

To the ignorant man nothing is better than silence, and were he aware of this he would no longer be ignorant.

When you are not possessed of perfection or excellence,
It is better that you keep your tongue within your mouth.

The tongue bringeth disgrace upon men. The nut without a kernel is light in weight.

The beast will not learn of thee how to speak; learn thou of the beast how to be silent.

Whoever reflecteth not before he answereth,
Will probably utter inappropriate words.
Either adorn thy speech with the intelligence of a man,
Or sit in silence like a dumb animal.

Whoever entereth into argument, in order to display his learning, with a man more learned than himself will thereby be taught that he is unlearned. Though thou mayest be well informed, if one wiser than thyself take up the discourse, be not thou ready to start objections.

Publish not the secret faults of others, for you inflict disgrace upon them, and procure thereby no honour to yourself.

He who readeth and doth not practise resembleth the man who driveth the oxen but scattereth not the seed.

Were every night a night of power, THE NIGHT OF POWER would lose its worth. Were every pebble a ruby, the ruby and the pebble would be of equal value.

It is very easy to deprive the living of life;
To give back life to him from whom thou hast taken it is impossible.
The archer should be patient ere he draw the bow,
For when the arrow hath left the bow it returneth no more.

What wonder is the nightingale loses its spirit, if a crow is the companion of his cage?

The friend who it hath taken a lifetime to acquire, it is not right to estrange in a moment. How many years doth it require to turn the stone into a ruby? Take heed lest with another stone thou grind it down in an instant.

I heard a fellow of mean disposition slandering a person of distinguished rank. I said: "O sir, if thou art unfortunate, why is it a crime to be one of the fortunate? O do not invoke misery on the envious man, for the condition of that man is misery in itself. What need for pursuing one with enmity, who has such an enemy perpetually at his heels?"

I asked a wise man to give me a word of counsel. He said to me: "Take heed how you commit yourself with an ignorant man, for if you are possessed of knowledge you will become an ass, and if you are without knowledge, your folly will become still greater."

The bird will not alight upon the seed,
If it see another bird caught in the snare.
Take thou warning from the misfortunes of others,
That thou give no occasion to others to take warning from thee.

The poor man whose end is good is better than the king whose end is evil.
The sorrow which thou bearest before enjoyment
Is better than the enjoyment which precedeth sorrow.
A holy man in his prayers was wont to say: "O God, have mercy on the bad, for on the good Thou hast already had mercy, in that Thou hast created them good."

Feridün ordered his Chinese embroiderers to embroider around his pavilion: "Thou who are of an understanding heart, be good to the wicked, for the good are great and happy of themselves."

Two persons died, carrying with them vain regrets: he who had wealth which he never enjoyed, and he who had knowledge of which he made no use.

No one ever saw a man who had merit, but was miserly, that people did not expatiate on his faults; but if a generous man hath two hundred defects, his generosity will cover them all.

Generosity and kindness make the man; think not that it is his material image. To gain all the wealth of the world is not virtue; try if thou canst conquer a single heart.

The truly wise man practiseth humility; the bough full of fruit inclineth its head towards the ground. It is in those of high estate that humility appeareth to most advantage; in the beggar it is only the mark of his profession.

## SHABLI AND THE ANT

### BY SADI

*L*ISTEN to one of the qualities of good men, if thou art thyself a good man, and benevolently inclined!

Shabli, returning from the shop of a corn-dealer, carried back to his village on his shoulder a sack of wheat.

He looked, and beheld in that heap of grain an ant which kept running bewildered from corner to corner,

Filled with pity thereat, and unable to sleep at night, he carried it back to its own dwelling, saying:

"It were no benevolence to wound and distract this poor ant by severing it from its own place!"

Soothe to rest the hearts of the distracted, wouldst thou be at rest thyself from the blows of Fortune.

How sweet are the words of the noble Ferdusi, upon whose grave be the mercy of the Benignant One!

"Crush not yonder emmet as it draggeth along its grain; for it too liveth, and its life is sweet to it."

A shadow must there be, and a stone upon that heart, that could wish to sorrow the heart even of an emmet!

Strike not with the hand of violence the head of the feeble; for one day, like the ant, thou mayest fall under the foot thyself!

Pity the poor moth in the flame of the taper; see how it is scorched in the face of the assembly!

Let me remind thee, that if there be many who are weaker than thou art, there may come at last one who is stronger than thou.

# KEEP YOUR OWN SECRET

## BY SADI

SULTAN TAKISH once committed a secret to his slaves, which they were enjoined to tell again to no one.

For a year it had not passed from his breast to his lips; it was published to all the world in a single day.

He commanded the executioner to sever with the sword their heads from their bodies without mercy.

One from their midst exclaimed: "Beware! slay not the slaves, for the fault is thine own.

"Why didst thou not dam up at once what at first was but a fountain?—What availeth it to do so when it is become a torrent?"

Take heed that thou reveal not to anyone the secret of thy heart, for he will divulge it to all the world.

Thy jewels thou mayest consign to the keeping of thy treasurer; but thy secret reserve for thine own keeping.

Whilst thou utterest not a word, thou hast thy hand upon it; when thou hast uttered it, it hath laid its hand upon thee.

Thou knowest that when the demon hath escaped from his cage by no adjuration will he enter it again.

The word is an enchanted demon in the pit of the heart, let it not escape to the tongue and the palate.

It is possible to open a way to the strong demon; to retake him by stratagem is not possible.

A child may untether "Lightning" but a hundred Rustams will not bring him to the halter again.

Take heed that thou say not that which, if it come to the crowd, may bring trouble to a single individual.

It was well said by his wife to an ignorant peasant: "Either talk sensibly or hold thy tongue."

# HOW TO BRING UP A SON

### BY SADI

WHEN thy son hath passed his tenth year, say to him: "Sit apart from strangers."

It is not well to kindle a fire near cotton, for whilst thou closest thine eyes thy house may be burning.

If thou desirest that thy name should remain in its place, teach thy son understanding and knowledge.

If he possess not wisdom and knowledge thou wilt die, and no one will remain after thee.

Oft-times hath the son had to bear hardships in the end, when he hath been too tenderly natured by his father.

Keep him within bounds of prudence and moderation; if thou holdest him dear, indulge him not in delicacies.

In his childhood thou must give him chastisement and instruction; must teach the good and the evil by threats and by promises.

To the young learner praise, and commendation, and "Well-done!" are better than chiding and frightening in the master.

Teach to thy pupil some kind of handicraft, hast thou in thy hand all the wealth of Karün;

For what knowest thou, whether some shift of Fortune will not turn him out of his home to a distant land?

Place no reliance on present prosperity, for thy wealth may no longer remain in thy hand.

Let his hand be but skilful at some trade, and why should he stretch out the hand of necessity to any one?

Thy purse of silver and gold may come to an end; the purse of the artisan will never be empty.

Dost thou not know how Sadi attained his wishes?

He roamed not over plains, nor divided seas:

In his youth he bore cuffs from his elders, and in his age God gave him recreation.

Whoever submitteth his neck to authority, doth it not frequently happen that he cometh to authority himself?

The child who hath never felt the austerity of the teacher will have to learn from the severity of life.

Be good to the child, and treat him with kindness, that his eye may not be directed to look for it from others.

Whoever doth not himself sympathise with his child will make others sympathise, and gain him a bad name.

Take heed that thou commit him not to a vicious teacher, for he will make him as vicious and led-astray as himself.

Thou canst not find him a blacker book than that good-for-nothing fellow, to blacken him ere his face is blackened by his beard.

Fly from that man so lost to honour, that his unworthiness causeth worthy men to weep.

If his son hath sat in the society of Kalenders' say to his father : " Hope no good of him.

" Cry not Alas! over his death or ruin ; for it is well that the degenerate one should die before his father."

## SADI AND THE RING

### BY SADI

*I* RECALL to my memory, how, during the life of my father—may the rain of mercy every moment descend upon him!—

He bought for me in my childhood a tablet and a writing-book, and for my finger a golden seal-ring.

As it happened, a pedlar came to the door, and in exchange for a date carried off the ring from my hand;

For a little child cannot estimate the value of a seal-ring, and will easily part with it for anything sweet.

And thou, too, dost not estimate the value of a life, who throwest it away in luxurious indulgencies.

In the resurrection, when the righteous arrive at the lofty place, and are raised from the damp pit to the region of the Pleiades,

Will thy head not be bowed down in abasement, when all *thy* works shall be assembled before thee?

O brother, be ashamed now to do the deeds of the bad, that thou mayest not need to be ashamed in the face of the good.

On that day when inquest shall be made into deeds and words, and the body even of those who have striven after holiness shall tremble,

With what excuse for thy sins wilt thou hear *thy* summons, when the very Prophets will be overwhelmed with terror?

# JOSEPH AND ZULAIKHA

## INVOCATION

### BY JAMI

ℰXPAND for me, O God, the blossom of hope.
Show me a rose from the Eternal Garden!
Cause my garden to smile from the lips of that rose-bud,
And invigorate my brain with the sense of its perfume!
In this abode of affliction, where is no rest,
Make me ready to acknowledge the multitude of Thy
mercies!
Fill my mind full of thoughts to Thy praise,
Make thanksgiving the business of my tongue!
Give me for a spear the power of my reason,
In the battle-field of words give me the victory!
Thou has made my heart a treasure-house—jewel upon
jewel:
Let my tongue duly weigh the jewels of my heart!
Thou has placed in my navel the musk-pod of musk,
Let my musk spread its fragrance from Kaf to Kaf!
Give to my reed a sugar-sweet tongue to write my poem:
Shed over my book an amber-diffusing perfume!
For the object of my words has not yet been attained,
And nothing but a name has yet been left of its story.
In this the wine-house of pleasant histories
I find not an echo of this sweet melody.
The guests drank their wine, and forthwith departed—
Departed, and left only the empty wine-jars.
Of those who are seasoned or unseasoned in such banquets,
I see not one whose hand holds a goblet of this wine:
Come then, Jami, throw off thy timidity;
Be it clear, or the dregs only, bring to us what thou hast!

## LOVE

### BY JAMI

*A* HEART which is void of the pains of love is no heart;
   A body without heart-woes is nothing but clay and
   water.
Turn thy face away from the world to the pangs of love,
For the world of love is a world of sweetness.
Let there not be in the world an unloving heart!
Let not the pangs of love be less in the bosom of any one!
Heaven itself is confused with longings after love;
Earth is filled with tumult at the clamours of its passion.
Become the captive of love, in order to become free;
Lay its sorrows to thy heart, that thou mayest know its
   gladness.
The wine of love will inebriate and warm thee,
Will free thee from coldness and devotion to self.
In the memories of love the lover renews his freshness,
In his devotion to it he creates for himself a lofty fame.
If Mejnun had never drunk the wine from this cup,
Who would have spread his name throughout both
   worlds?
Thousands of the wise and learned have passed away,
Passed away—forgotten, because strangers to love;
No name or trace remains of their existence,
No history of them is left on the records of Time.
Many are the birds of beautiful forms,
Which the people closes its lips and refuses to speak of;
When those who have hearts tell stories of love,
The stories they tell are of the Moth and the Nightingale.
In the world thou mayst be skilled in a hundred arts,
Love is the only one which will free thee from thyself.
Turn not thy face from love, even if it be shallow,
It is thy apprenticeship for learning the true one;
If thou dost not first learn thine A.B.C. on thy slate,
How wilt thou be ever able to read a lesson from the
   Koran?

I heard of a scholar who besought a teacher
To assist him in treading the path of his doctrine;
The teacher replied: " Thou hast never yet stirred a foot
   in the way of love;
Go—become a lover, and then appear before me;
For till thou hast tasted the symbolical wine-cup,
Thou wilt never drain the real one to the lees."
No! thou must not stay lingering over the image,
But quickly transport thyself over this bridge:
   If thou desirest ever to reach the inn,
Thou must not remain standing at the bridge-head.
Praise be to God! that so long as I have dwelt in this
   monastery,
I have been a nimble traveller in the road of love!
When the mid-wife first divided the navel-string,
She divided it with the knife of love;
When my mother first put my lips to her breast,
She gave me to suck the blood-tinged milk of love;
Although my hair is now white and milk,
The savour of lost still dwells in my mind.
In youth or in age there is nothing like love;
The enchantment of love breathes upon me for ever.
" Jami," it says, " thou hast grown old in love;
Rouse up thy spirit, and in love die!
Compose a tale on the pleasures of love,
That thou mayst leave to the world some memorial of thy
   existence:
Draw thou a picture with thy delicate pencil,
Which, when thou quittest thy place, may remain in thy
   stead."

## ZULAIKHA'S FIRST DREAM

### BY JAMI

*A* NIGHT it was, sweet as the morning of life,
Joy-augmenting like the days of youth!
Fish and fowl rested from motion,
Business drew its foot within the skirt of its garment.
Within this pleasure-house, full of varieties,
Nought remained open save the eye of the star.
Night—the thief—robbed the sentinel of his under-
standing,
The bell-ringer stilled the tongue of the bell;
The hound wound its tail round its neck like a collar,
And in that collar stifled its baying;
The bird of night drew out its sword-like feathers,
And cut off its tuneful reed (i.e. its throat) from its morning
song;
The watchman on the dome of the royal palace
Saw in imagination the drowsy poppy-head,
And no longer retained the power of wakefulness—
The image of that poppy-head called him into slumber.
The drummer no longer beat his tymbal,
His hand could no longer hold to the drum-stick.
The Muezzin from the minaret no longer cried,
"Allah! Allah! the Ever-Living!
Roll up your mattresses, ye nightly-dead, and neglect not
prayer!"
Zulaikha, of the sugar-lips, was enjoying the sweet slumber.
Which had fallen on her soft narcissus-like eyes:
Her head pressed the pillow with its hyacinthine locks,
And her body the couch with its roseate burthen.
The hyacinthine locks were parted on the pillow,
And painted the roseate cheek with silken streaks;
The image-seeing eye was closed in slumber,
But another eye was open—that of the soul:
With that she saw suddenly enter a young man—
Young man, do I say?—rather a spirit!
A blessed figure from the realms of light,

Beauteous as a Huri, borne off from the Garden of the
    Seventh Heaven,
And had robbed trait by trait of each beauty, excellence,
        and perfection,
Copying, one by one, every alluring attraction.
His stature was that of the fresh box-tree ;
The free-cypress in its freedom was a slave compared with
    his ;
His hair from above hung down like a chain,
And fettered, hand and foot, even the judgment of the
    wise ;
From his brow shot so resplendent a flash of light,
That sun and moon bent to the ground before him ;
His eyebrows, which might have been a high-altar for
    the saintly,
Were an amber-scented canopy over the sleeper's eyes ;
His face was as the moon's from its station in Paradise ;
From his eyelashes darted arrows to pierce the heart ;
The pearly teeth within the ruby lips
Were lightning flashing from a roseate evening sky ;
The smiles of his ruby-lips were sweet as sugar—
When he laughed, his laugh was the lustre of the Pleiades
The words of his mouth were sugar itself.
When this vision rose before the eyes of Zulaikha,
At one glance happened that which needs must happen :
She beheld excellence beyond human limits,
Seen not in Peri, never heard of in Huri.
From the beauty of the image and charm of its perfection—
She became his captive, not with her one but with a hundred
    hearts ;
Fancy made his form the ideal of her mind,
And planted in her soul the young shoot of love.

### SILENT SORROW

On the morrow, when the raven of light had taken its
    upward flight,
And the cock was crowing its morning carol,
And the nightingales had ceased their soul-moving chant,

And had withdrawn from the rose-bush the veil of the
rose-bud,
And the violet was washing its fragrant locks,
And the jessamine was wiping the night-dew from its
face,
Zulaikha still lay sunk in sweet slumber,
Her heart-look still fixed on her last night's altar;
Sleep it was not—rather a delightful bewilderment—
A kind of insanity from her nocturnal passion!

Her waiting-maids impress the kisses on her feet,
Her damsels approach to give the hand-kiss;
Then she lifteth the veil from her dewy tulip-cheeks,
And shaketh off the sleep from her love-languishing eyes;
She looketh round on every side, but seeth not a sign
Of the roseate image of her last night's dream.
For a time she withdrew like a rose-bud into herself;
In the grief of not beholding that slender cypress-form,
She would have rent the clothes off her body to pieces,
Had not shame withheld her hand in the presence of
others,
And restrained her foot within the skirt of patience:
So she kept the secret tight within her bosom,
As in a ruby-mine the hard stone encases the ruby;
And though she was gulping down in her heart the rose-
red blood,
She showed not outwardly an action of emotion.
Her lips recounted her stories to her maidens,
But her heart, whilst she recounteth them is full of lamenta-
tions;
Her mouth to her companions talketh sweetly as sugar,
But her heart, like the sugar-cane, is full of hard knots;
Her tongue to her friends still telleth its tale,
But a hundred sparks flash from the wounds of her passion;
Her looks fall on the figures of rivals,
But her heart remaineth fixed on the only beloved one.
No longer were the reins of her heart in her own hands,
For wherever she was, she was with the heart-stealer.

No longer now hath she a wish beyond her friend,
Nor except with her friend had she any rest.
If she sayeth a word, to her friend she sayeth it;
And if she formeth a wish, from her friend she seeketh it.
A thousand times riseth to her lips the desire of her heart,
That night would come to that day of weariness—
The night which cometh so agreeably to lovers—
The night which keepeth the secrets of lovers:
Therefore all the day the night is their desire;
For this guardeth the veil, and that uplifteth it.

When night came she turned her face to the wall of
    sorrow,
She stooped her back like a crooked lyre;
She strung her harp with the chords of tears,
And tuned it in accord with her own heart's sadness;
She rent her bosom with its tuneful wailings,
And runneth through ever note of sighs and lamentings;
She setteth her friend in fancy before her face,
And poureth out from her lips and eyes words and pearly
    tears:
From what mine doest thou come, thou pure gem,
That hast given me this power of scattering jewels?
Thou hast stolen my heart, but told me not thy name,
Nor left me a sign of the spot where thou dwellest!
I know not of whom I can ask thy name!
I know not whither to go to inquire thy habitation!
If thou are a king, what is thy name?
If thou art a moon, what is thy station?
Forbid it, that another should become captive like me,
For I have no longer in my hand either my heart or my
    lover!
I saw a vision which has broken my sleep,
And drawn out pure blood from heart and eyes;
Now I no longer know what sleep is,
My heart is consumed by a perpetual glow!
How is it that, as when thou castest water on fire,
Thou too dost not become warm and agitated!

I was a rose from the rose-bed of youth,
Moist and fresh as from the Fountain of Life;
No rough wind had ever blown on my head,
Never had a thorn punctured my foot;
With a single soft glance thou gavest me over to the
  wind,
Thou hast planted a thousand thorns in my couch!
A body a hundred times softer than a rose-leaf,
How should sleep visit it on a bed of thorns?"
So all the night long she passed in moanings,
Uttering her complaints to the vision of her friend;
But when the night was gone, to avoid suspicion,
She washed the tears from her blood-suffused eyes;
On her lips, still moist from the cruel struggle of the night,
She impresseth deeply the seal of silence;
She maketh her bed gay with the fresh rose-leaves,
And enliveneth her pillow with the silvery cypress.
In such wise passed she her days and nights,
Nor changed her habit by a single hair.

## SHAIKH AHMAD, THE SON OF KHIZRUYA, BUYS "HALVA" FOR HIS CREDITORS ON THE INSPIRATION OF GOD MOST HIGH.

### BY JALALUDDIN RUMI

*T*HERE was a Shaikh who was always in debt through the generosity for which he was famous.

He incurred countless debts with the great and rich, and spent the money on the poor of the world.

He had also built a monastery by debt incurred—he had bestowed energy, money, and the monastery for the love of God.

God used to pay his debts from every quarter. For "the Friend" God turned sand into flour.

The Prophet has said, "Two angels continually utter the following prayer in the streets:

'O God, give a worthy successor to the lavish, And O God, give destruction to the miserly.'"

This applies especially to that lavish man who expends his life: who sacrifices his throat to God.

Like Ishmael, presents his throat; the knife then can do his throat no harm.

Therefore in this respect the martyrs are alive and happy; do not look simply at the body as an infidel would.

For God has given them eternal life as a return for their self-sacrifice: a life free from grief, pain and misery.

The indebted Shaikh continued this practice for years: he took from some, and gave to others, like a business agent.

He went on sewing seeds until the day of death, so that he might be on the day of death a glorious lord.

When the Shaik's life reached its end: when he saw in himself the signs of death,

His creditors sat all together around him—whilst the Shaikh was softly melting away like a candle.

The creditors had become hopeless and morose; and the pain of their hearts was added to the pain of his lungs.

The Shaikh said to himself, " See these suspicious people ! Has not God four hundred gold dinars ? "

At that time a boy cried " halva " outside the house : he boasted of the " halva " in the hope of " Dangs."

The Shaikh nodded to his servants to go and buy the whole of the "halva " ;

Thinking to himself that when his creditors should eat the " halva," they would not, for a short time, look so bitterly at him.

The servant immediately went out to the door in order to buy all the " halva " from the boy.

He said to him, " For how much will you sell the 'halva' in a lump ? " The boy answered, " Half a ' dinar ' and a few odd coins."

He rejoined, " No ! Do not ask too much from Sufis ; I will give you half a ' dinar '—say no more."

The boy put the tray before the Shaikh.—See now something of the mysterious secrets of the Shaikh.

He made a sign to the creditors, signifying, " Behold this food is an offering ; eat and enjoy it ; I give it you."

When the tray was empty the boy took it. He said, " Give me the money, O wise man."

The Shaikh answered, " Whence can I get money ? I am a debtor, and I am on the way too to inexistence."

The boy through grief cast the tray upon the ground ; he raised lamentations and wept and sobbed.

The boy wept with cries of distress at the imposition ; he said, " Would that both my legs had been broken so that I had not come to this place !

Would that I had wandered about a bath fire-place ; and that I had not passed the door of this monastery !

Parasite Sufis, fond of dainty morsels ! Dogs in heart who wash their faces like cats ! "

From the boy's outcry people of all sorts collected there, and a crowd gathered round the boy.

The boy came up to the Shaikh and said, " O harsh Shaikh, know for certain that my master will beat me to death.

If I go to him empty-handed, he will kill me. Do you sanction this?"

And the creditors too, with strong disbelief in the Shaikh, turned their faces towards him, and asked what was the meaning of this trick.

"You have," said they, "consumed our property; you bear to the future state our grievances against you; for what other reason then was this other wrong super-added?"

Till afternoon prayers the boy wept; the Shaikh closed his eyes, and did not look at him.

The Shaikh heedless of harsh words and opposition, had drawn his face under the coverlet like the mood.

Happy in eternity without beginning, happy in death, rejoicing-careless of blame and of the words of high and low.

He in whose face the Beloved sweetly smiles,—what injury can he suffer from the sourness of face of others?

He whose eyes the Beloved kisses,—how can he suffer from the Sky and its anger?

On a moonlight night when the moon is above "Simak," what does it care for dogs and their barking?

The dog accomplishes its function; and the moon fulfils its office of diffusing light by its face.

Everyone accomplishes his own little business; the water does not lose its purity through a bit of stick or straw.

The bit of stick or straw floats inconspicuously on the surface of the water; the pure water flows on calm and undisturbed.

Mustafa cleaves the moon at midnight; and the Bu Lahab through malice talks nonsense.

Can the dog's bark ever reach the moon's ear—especially a moon which is the elect of God?

The king drinking till dawn on the banks of a stream, and in ecstasy with music, is unaware of the croakings of frogs.

The division of the boy's claim among them would have been only a few " dangs "; but the influence of the Shaikh's mind prevented that generosity.

So that nobody might give anything to the boy.—The powers of " Pirs " is greater even than this.

The time of afternoon prayers came on, when a servant arrived with a tray in his hand from a man generous as Hatim.

A man of wealth and means, who sent the Pir a present, being aware of his case.

Four hundred " dinars," and on the side of the tray another half " dinar " in a piece of paper.

The servant approached and showed honour to the Shaikh, and put the tray before the incomparable Shaikh.

When the Shaikh unveiled the face of the tray, the people beheld that miracle of his.

Sighs and groans at once arose from all, whilst they said, " O chief of Shaikhs and Kings of the Path, what miracle is this?

What mystery is this, what predominant power again is this, O lord of the lords of mystery?

We did not know; pardon us; most rambling and senseless indeed are the words which have escaped us.

We who blindly hit about with staffs shall necessarily break lamps.

We, like deaf people, without having heard a single address, from our own mere conjecture give answer in idle and inapplicable words.

We have not taken counsel from Moses, who was shamed by unbelief in Khizr:

Unbelief notwithstanding he had such eyes as reached the heights: such eyes that the light of them penetrated the heavens.

Through folly, O Moses of the time, have the eyes of a mill-mouse opposed your eyes."

The Shaikh answered, " All that talk and babble I forgive: I make it no wrong against you.

The secret of this matter was that I petitioned God; He necessarily showed me the right path.

He said, 'Although that " dinar " is little, still the return of it is dependent upon the clamour and lamentation of the boy.

Until the confectioner boy weep, the sea of my mercy is not agitated.' "

The boy, O brother, is the pupil of your eye: know well that the object of your desire is dependent upon your lamentation.

If you wish that that robe of honour should come to you, then make the pupil of your eye weep over your body.

# RUBÁ'IYÁT

## BY OMAR KHAYYÁM

OMAR KHAYYÁM, the astronomer-poet of Persia, was born at Naishapur in the latter half of the eleventh century and died in the first quarter of the century succeeding. He is supposed to have been a tent-maker originally, but was pensioned by an old schoolfellow who had become Vizier, so that he had leisure in which to study, and he became famous as a scientist, and was one of those employed to reform the calendar.

Edward FitzGerald (1809–83) made himself and Omar famous by his free English translation. It was published anonymously in 1859 at 5s., but, proving apparently a failure, the unsold copies soon found their way into the penny box. Few poems in the English language have, however, proved so popular.

In his illuminating *Note on Omar*, the late Professor York Powell wrote : " When FitzGerald put Omar into English he did more than he knew. He revealed to us in fixed and memorable form a white, broad tract of thought many moderns and a few ancients had described, but only in vague and cloudy delineation." And again : " Omar is not often a preacher, seldom a prophet, occasionally a frank counsellor, always a friend. He had learnt to be content to accept men and things as they are. He would have men charitable and sincere. He had no ethical advice beyond this. He recognized that the ultimate explanation is beyond our comprehension, though he did not trouble himself to doubt its existence. He had done with systems and universal theories. He laughed at creeds and mocked at superstitions, but he welcomed facts with a gentle and humorous smile. He had no malice, no grudge against life. He was companionable in his hours, never inhuman. Of the hermit or the ascetic there was no trace in him. He was not the man to shudder at the beauty of women or the splendours of the earth and heavens, because mutability has set her seal upon them all."

### I

Awake! for Morning in the Bowl of Night
Has flung the Stone that puts the Stars to Flight;
   And Lo! the Hunter of the East has caught
The Sultan's Turret in a Noose of Light.

### II

Dreaming when Dawn's Left Hand was in the Sky
I heard a Voice within the Tavern cry,
   "Awake, my Little ones, and fill the Cup
Before Life's Liquor in its Cup be dry."

### III

And, as the Cock crew, those who stood before
The Tavern shouted—"Open then the Door!
   You know how little while we have to stay,
And, once departed, may return no more."

### IV

Now the New Year reviving old Desires,
The thoughtful Soul to Solitude retires,
   Where the WHITE HAND OF MOSES on the Bough
Puts out, and Jesus from the Ground suspires.

### V

Iram indeed is gone with all its Rose,
And Jamshyd's Sev'n-ring'd Cup where no one knows;
   But still the Vine her ancient Ruby yields,
And still a Garden by the Water blows.

### VI

And David's Lips are lock't; but in divine
High-piping Pehlevi, with "Wine! Wine! Wine!
   Red Wine!"—the Nightingale cries to the Rose
That yellow Cheek of her to incarnadine.

### VII

Come, fill the Cup, and in the Fire of Spring
The Winter Garment of Repentance fling:
   The Bird of Time has but a little way
To fly—and Lo! the Bird is on the Wing.

### VIII

And look—a thousand Blossoms with the Day
Woke—and a thousand scatter'd into Clay:
 And this first Summer Month that brings the Rose
Shall take Jamshyd and Kaikobad away.

### IX

But come with old Khayyám, and leave the Lot
Of Kaibobad and Kaihosru forgot:
 Let Rustum lay about him as he will,
Or Hatim Tai cry Supper—heed them not.

### X

With me along some Strip of Herbage strown
That just divides the desert from the sown,
 Where name of Slave and Sultan scarce is known,
And pity Sultan Mahmud on his Throne.

### XI

Here with a Loaf of Bread beneath the Bough,
A flask of Wine, a Book of Verse—and Thou
 Beside me singing in the Wilderness—
And Wilderness is Paradise enow.

### XII

" How sweet is mortal Sovranty "—think some:
Others—" How blest the Paradise to come! "
 Ah, take the Cash in hand and waive the Rest;
Oh, the brave Music of a distant Drum!

### XIII

Look to the Rose that blows about us—" Lo,
Laughing," she says, " into the World I blow:
 At once the silken Tassel of my Purse
Tear, and its Treasure on the Garden throw."

### XIV

The Worldly Hope men set their Hearts upon
Turns Ashes—or it prospers; and anon,
 Like Snow upon the Desert's dusty Face
Lighting a little Hour or two—is gone.

### XV

And those who husbanded the Golden Grain,
And those who flung it to the Winds like Rain,
   Alike to no such aureate Earth are turn'd
As, buried once, Men want dug up again.

### XVI

Think, in this batter'd Caravanserai
Whose Doorways are alternate Night and Day,
   How Sultan after Sultan with his Pomp
Abode his Hour or two, and went his way.

### XVII

They say the Lion and the Lizard keep
The Courts where Jamshyd gloried and drank deep:
   And Bahram, that great Hunter—the Wild Ass
Stamps o'er his Head, and he lies fast asleep.

### XVIII

I sometimes think that never blows so red
The Rose as where some buried Caesar bled;
   That every Hyacinth the Gardens wears
Dropt in its Lap from some once lovely Head.

### XIX

And this delightful Herb whose tender Green
Fledges the River's Lip on which we lean—
   Ah, lean upon it lightly! for who knows
From what once lovely Lip it springs unseen!

### XX

Ah, my Beloved, fill the cup that clears
TO-DAY of past Regrets and future Fears—
   TO-MORROW?—Why, To-morrow I may be
Myself with Yesterday's Sev'n Thousand Years.

### XXI

Lo! some we loved, the loveliest and the best
That Time and Fate of all their Vintage prest,
   Have drunk their Cup a Round or two before,
And one by one crept silently to Rest.

### XXII

And we, that now make merry in the Room
They left, and Summer dresses in new Bloom,
   Ourselves must we beneath the Couch of Earth
Descend, ourselves to make a Couch—for whom?

### XXIII

Ah, make the most of what we yet may spend,
Before we too into the Dust descend;
   Dust into Dust, and under Dust, to lie,
Sans Wine, sans Song, sans Singer, and—sans End!

### XXIV

Alike for those who for TO-DAY prepare,
And those that after a TO-MORROW stare,
   A Muessin from the Tower of Darkness cries
"Fools! your Reward is neither Here nor There!"

### XXV

Why, all the Saints and Sages who discuss'd
Of the Two Worlds so learnedly, are thrust
   Like foolish Prophets forth; their Words to Scorn
Are scatter'd, and their Mouths are stopt with Dust.

### XXVI

Oh, come with old Khayyám, and leave the Wise
To talk; one thing is certain, that Life flies;
   One thing is certain, and the Rest is Lies;
The Flower that once has blown for ever dies.

### XXVII

Myself when young did eagerly frequent
Doctor and Saint, and heard great Argument
   About it and about: but evermore
Came out by the same Door as in I went.

### XXVIII

With them the Seed of Wisdom did I sow,
And with my own hand labour'd it to grow;
   And this was all the Harvest that I reap'd—
"I came like Water, and like Wind I go."

### XXIX

Into this Universe, and *why* not knowing,
Nor *whence*, like Water willy-nilly flowing:
   And out of it, as Wind along the Waste,
I know not *whither*, willy-nilly blowing.

### XXX

What, without asking, hither hurried *whence?*
And, without asking, *whither* hurried hence!
   Another and another Cup to drown
The Memory of this Impertinence!

### XXXI

Up from Earth's Centre through the Seventh Gate
I rose, and on the Throne of Saturn sate,
   And many Knots unravel'd by the Road;
But not the Knot of Human Death and Fate.

### XXXII

There was a Door to which I found no Key:
There was a Veil past which I could not see:
   Some little Talkawhile of ME and THEE
There seemed—and then no more of THEE and ME.

### XXXIII

Then to the rolling Heav'n itself I cried,
Asking, " What Lamp had Destiny to guide
   Her little Children stumbling in the Dark?"
And—" A blind Understanding!" Heav'n replied.

### XXXIV

Then to this earthen Bowl did I adjourn
My Lip the secret Well of Life to learn:
   And Lip to Lip it murmur'd—" While you live
Drink!—for once dead you never shall return."

### XXXV

I think the Vessel, that with fugitive
Articulation answer'd, once did live,
   And merry make; and the cold Lip I kiss'd
How many Kisses might it take—and give!

### XXXVI

For in the Market-place, one Dusk of Day,
I watch'd the Potter thumping his wet Clay:
   And with its all obliterated Tongue
It murmur'd, " Gently, Brother, gently, pray!"

### XXXVII

Ah, fill the Cup :—what boots it to repeat
How Time is slipping underneath our Feet:
   Unborn TO-MORROW and dead YESTERDAY,
Why fret about them if TO-DAY be sweet!

### XXXVIII

One Moment in Annihilation's Waste,
One Moment, of the Well of Life to taste—
   The Stars are setting and the Caravan
Starts for the Dawn of Nothing—Oh, make haste!

### XXXIX

How long, how long, in infinite Pursuit
Of This and That endeavour and dispute?
   Better be merry with the fruitful Grape
Than sadden after none, or bitter, Fruit.

### XL

You know, my Friends, how long since in my House
For a new Marriage I did make Carouse:
   Divorced old barren Reason from my Bed,
And took the Daughter of the Vine to Spouse.

### XLI

For " IS " and " IS-NOT " though with Rule and Line,
And " UP-AND-DOWN " without, I could define,
   I yet in all I only cared to know,
Was never deep in anything but—Wine.

### XLII

And lately, by the Tavern Door agape,
Came stealing through the Dusk an Angel Shape
   Bearing a Vessel on his Shoulder; and
He bid me taste of it; and 'twas—the Grape!

### XLIII

The Grape that can with Logic absolute
The Two-and-Seventy jarring Sects confute :
　　The subtle Alchemist that in a Trice
Life's leaden Metal into Gold transmute.

### XLIV

The mighty Mahmud, the victorious Lord,
That all the misbelieving and black Horde
　　Of Fears and Sorrows that infest the Soul
Scatters and slays with his enchanted Sword.

### XLV

But leave the Wise to wrangle, and with me
The Quarrel of the Universe let be :
　　And, in some corner of the Hubbub coucht,
Make Game of that which makes as much of Thee.

### XLVI

For in and out, above, about, below,
'Tis nothing but a Magic Shadow-show,
　　Play'd in a Box whose Candle is the Sun,
Round which we Phantom Figures come and go.

### XLVII

And if the Wine you drink, the Lip you press,
End in the Nothing all Things end in—Yes—
　　Then fancy while Thou art, Thou art but what
Thou shall be—Nothing—Thou shalt not be less.

### XLVIII

While the Rose blows along the River Brink,
With old Khayyám the Ruby Vintage drink :
　　And when the Angel with his darker Draught
Draws up to Thee—take that, and do not shrink.

### XLIX

'Tis all a Chequer-board of Nights and Days
Where Destiny with Men for Pieces plays :
　　Hither and thither moves, and mates, and slays,
And one by one back in the Closet lays.

**L**

The Ball no Question makes of Ayes and Noes,
But Right or Left as strikes the Player goes;
   And He that toss'd Thee down into the Field,
He knows about it all—He knows—He knows!

**LI**

The Moving Finger writes; and, having writ,
Moves on: nor all thy Piety nor Wit
   Shall lure it back to cancel half a Line,
Nor all thy Tears wash out a word of it.

**LII**

And that inverted Bowl we call The Sky,
Whereunder crawling coop't we live and die,
   Lift not thy hands to It for help—for It
Rolls impotently on as Thou or I.

**LIII**

With Earth's first Clay They did the Last Man's knead,
And then of the Last Harvest sow'd the Seed:
   Yea, the first Morning of Creation wrote
What the Last Dawn of Reckoning shall read.

**LIV**

I tell Thee this—When, starting from the Goal,
Over the shoulders of the flaming Foal
   Of Heav'n Parwin and Mushtara they flung,
In my predestin'd Plot of Dust and Soul.

**LV**

The Vine had struck a Fibre; which about
If clings my Being—let the Sufi flout;
   Of my Base Metal may be filed a Key,
That shall unlock the Door he howls without.

**LVI**

And this I know: whether the one True Light,
Kindle to Love, or Wrath-consume me quite,
   One Glimpse of It within the Tavern caught
Better than in the Temple lost outright.

### LVII

Oh Thou, who didst with Pitfall and with Gin
Beset the Road I was to wander in,
    Thou wilt not with Predestination round
Enmesh me, and impute my Fall to Sin?

### LVIII

Oh, Thou, who Man of baser Earth didst make,
And who with Eden didst devise the Snake;
    For all the Sin wherewith the Face of Man
Is blacken'd, Man's Forgiveness give—and take!

．　　．　　．　　．　　．

## Kuza-Nama

### LIX

Listen again. One Evening at the Close
Of Ramazan, ere the better Moon arose,
    In that old Potter's Shop I stood alone
With the clay Population round in Rows.

### LX

And, strange to tell, among the Earthen Lot
Some could articulate, while others not:
    And suddenly one more impatient cried—
"Who is the Potter, pray, and who the Pot?"

### LXI

Then said another—"Surely not in vain
My Substance from the common Earth was ta'en,
    That He who subtly wrought me into Shape
Should stamp me back to common Earth again."

### LXII

Another said—"Why, ne'er a peevish Boy,
Would break the Bowl from which he drank in Joy;
    Shall He that made the Vessel in pure Love
And Fancy, in an after Rage destroy!"

### LXIII

None answer'd this; but after Silence spake
A Vessel of a more ungainly Make:
 "They sneer at me for leaning all awry;
What! did the Hand then of the Potter shake?"

### LXIV

Said one—"Folks of a surly Tapster tell,
And daub his Visage with the Smoke of Hell;
 They talk of some strict Testing of us—Pish!
He's a Good Fellow, and 'twill all be well."

### LXV

Then said another with a long-drawn Sigh,
"My Clay with long oblivion is gone dry:
 But, fill me with the old familiar Juice,
Methinks I might recover by and by."

### LXVI

So while the Vessels one by one were speaking,
One spied the little Crescent all were seeking:
 And then they jogg'd each other, "Brother, Brother!
Hark to the Porter's Shoulder-knot a-creaking!"

.  .  .  .  .

### LXVII

Ah, with the Grape my fading Life provide,
And wash my Body whence the Life has died,
 And in a Winding-sheet of Vine-leaf wrapt,
So bury me by some sweet Garden-side.

### LXVIII

That ev'n my buried Ashes such a Snare
Of Perfume shall fling up into the Air,
 As not a True Believer passing by
But shall be overtaken unaware.

### LXIX

Indeed the Idols I have loved so long
Have done my Credit in Men's Eye much wrong:
 Have drown'd my Honour in a shallow Cup,
And sold my Reputation for a Song.

### LXX

Indeed, indeed, Repentance oft before
I swore—but was I sober when I swore?
   And then and then came Spring, and Rose-in-hand
My thread-bare Penitence apieces tore.

### LXXI

And much as Wine has play'd the Infidel,
And robb'd me of my Robe of Honour—well,
   I often wonder what the Vintners buy
One half so precious as the Goods they sell.

### LXXII

Alas, that Spring should vanish with the Rose!
That Youth's sweet-scented Manuscript should close!
   The Nightingale that in the Branches sang,
Ah, whence, and whither flown again, who knows!

### LXXIII

Ah Love! could thou and I with Fate conspire
To grasp this sorry Scheme of Things entire,
   Would not we shatter it to bits—and then
Re-mould it nearer to the Heart's Desire!

### LXXIV

Ah, Moon of my Delight who know'st no wane,
The Moon of Heav'n is rising once again:
   How oft hereafter rising shall she look
Through this same Garden after me—in vain!

### LXXV

And when Thyself with shining Foot shall pass
Among the Guests Star-scatter'd on the Grass,
   And in thy joyous Errand reach the Spot
Where I made one—turn down an empty Glass!

## SONGS OF HAFIZ

### BY HAFIZ

*L*AST night I dreamed that angels stood without
  The tavern door, and knocked in vain, and wept;
They took the clay of Adam, and, methought,
Moulded a cup therewith while all men slept.
Oh dwellers in the halls of Chastity!
You brought Love's passionate red wine to me,
Down to the dust I am, your bright feet stept.

For Heaven's self was all too weak to bear
The burden of His love God laid on it,
He turned to seek a messenger elsewhere,
And in the Book of Fate my name was writ.
Between my Lord and me such concord lies
As makes the Huris glad in Paradise,
With songs of praise through the green glades they flit.

A hundred dreams of Fancy's garnered store
Assail me—Father Adam went astray
Tempted by one poor grain of corn! Wherefore
Absolve and pardon him that turns away
Though the soft breath of Truth reaches his ears,
For two-and-seventy jangling creeds he hears,
And loud-voiced Fable calls him ceaselessly.
That, that is not the flame of Love's true fire
Which makes the torchlight shadows dance in rings,
But where the radiance draws the moth's desire
And sends him forth with scorched and drooping wings.
The heart of one who dwells retired shall break,
Rememb'ring a black mole and a red cheek,
And his life ebb, sapped at its secret springs.

Yet since the earliest time that man has sought
To comb the locks of Speech, his goodly bride,
Not one, like Hafiz, from the Face of Thought
Has torn the veil of Ignorance aside.

# Iran

Forget not when dear friend to friend returned,
Forget not days gone by, forget them not!
My mouth has tasted bitterness, and learned
To drink the envenomed cup of mortal lot;
Forget not when a sweeter draught was mine,
Loud rose the songs of them that drank that wine—
                    Forget them not!

Forget not loyal lovers long since dead,
Though faith and loyalty should be forgot,
Though the earth cover the enamoured head,
And in the dust wisdom and passion rot.
My friends have thrust me from their memory;
Vainly a thousand thousand times I cry:
                    Forget me not!

Weary I turn to my bonds again.
Once there were hands strong to deliver me,
Forget not when they broke a poor slave's chain!
Though from mine eyes tears flow unceasingly,
I think on them whose rose gardens are set
Beside the Zindeh Rud, and I forget
                    Life's misery.

Sorrow has made her lair in my breast,
And undisturbed she lies—forget them not
That drove her forth like to a hunted beast!
Hafiz, thou and thy tears shall be forgot,
Lock fast the gates of thy sad heart! But those
That held the key to thine unspoken woes—
                    Forget them not!

Arise! and fill a golden goblet up
Until the wine of pleasure overflow,
Before into thy skull's pale empty cup
A grimmer Cup-bearer the dust shall throw.
Yea, to the Vale of Silence we must come;
Yet shall the flagon laugh and Heaven's dome
Thrill with an answering echo ere we go!

Thou knowest that the riches of this field
Make no abiding, let the goblet's fire
Consume the fleeting harvest Earth may yield!
Oh Cypress-tree! green home of Love's sweet choir,
When I unto the dust I am have passed,
Forget thy former wantonness, and cast
Thy shadow o'er the dust of my desire.

Flow, bitter tears, and wash me clean! for they
Whose feet are set upon the road that lies
'Twixt Earth and Heaven: "Thou shalt be pure," they
    say,
"Before unto the pure thou lift thine eyes."
Seeing but himself, the Zealot sees but sin;
Grief to the mirror of his soul let in,
Oh Lord, and cloud it with the breath of sighs!

No tainted eye shall gaze upon her face,
No glass but that of an unsullied heart
Shall dare reflect my Lady's perfect grace.
Though like to snakes that from the herbage start,
Thy curling locks have wounded me full sore,
Thy red lips hold the power of the bezoar—
Ah, touch and heal me where I lie apart!

And when from her the wind blows perfume sweet,
Tear, Hafiz, like the rose, thy robe in two,
And cast thy rags beneath her flying feet,
To deck the place thy mistress passes through.

The margin of a stream, the willow's shade,
A mind inclined to song, a mistress sweet,
A Cup-bearer whose cheek outshines the rose,
A friend upon whose heart thy heart is laid:
O Happy-starred! let not thine hours fleet
Unvalued; may each minute as it goes
Lay tribute of enjoyment at thy feet,
That thou may'st live and know thy life is sweet.

# *Iran*

Let everyone, one upon whose heart desire
For a fair face lies like a burden sore,
That all his hopes may reach their goal unchecked,
Throw branches of wild rue upon his fire.
My soul is like a bride, with a rich store
Of maiden thoughts and jewelled fancies decked,
And in Time's gallery I yet may meet
Some picture meant for me, some image sweet.


Give thanks for nights spent in good company,
And take the gifts a tranquil mind may bring;
No heart is dark when the kind moon doth shine,
And grass-grown river-banks are fair to see.
The Saki's radiant eyes, God favouring,
Are like a wine-cup brimming o'er with wine,
And him my drunken sense goes out to greet,
For e'en the pain he leaves behind is sweet.


Hafiz, thy life has sped untouched by care,
With me towards the tavern turn thy feet !
The fairest robbers thou'lt encounter there,
And they will teach thee what to learn is sweet.


Where are the tidings of union? that I may arise—
Forth from the dust I will rise up to welcome thee!
My soul, like a homing bird, yearning for Paradise,
Shall arise and soar, from the snares of the world set
    free.
When the voice of thy love shall call me to be thy slave,
I shall rise to a greater far than the mastery
Of life and the living, time and the mortal span:
Pour down, oh Lord! from the clouds of thy guiding
    grace,
The rain of a mercy that quickeneth on my grave,
Before, like dust that the wind bears from place to
    place,
I arise and flee beyond the knowledge of man.

When to my grave thou turnest thy blessed feet,
Wine and the lute thou shalt bring in thine hand to me,
Thy voice shall ring through the folds of my winding
    sheet,
And I will arise and dance to thy minstrelsy.
Though I be old, clasp me one night to thy breast,
And I, when the dawn shall come to awaken me,
With the flush of youth on my cheek from thy bosom
    will rise.
Rise up! let mine eyes delight in thy stately grace!
Thou art the goal to which all men's endeavour has
    pressed,
And thou the idol of Hafiz's worship; thy face
From the world and life shall bid him come forth and
    arise!

## GHAZELS

### BY HAFIZ

COME, for Hope's strong castle is built on weak foundations; bring wine, for the fabric of life is unstable as is the wind.

I am the slave of His wishes, who under the azure vault is free from the shadow of dependence.

Shall I say, when yesternight I was utterly intoxicated in the wine-house, what glad message was brought to me by an angel from the unknown world?

"O lofty-sighted royal falcon, whose seat is on the tree of Paradise, not in this nook of misery should be thy rest.

"For thee are sounding the melodious voices from the Ninth Heaven! How thou art fallen into this place of snares I cannot conceive!"

I will give thee a piece of counsel: keep it in mind and reduce it to practice; for it is a precept which I have preserved in my memory for my aged guide:

"Seek not for the fulfilment of its promise from this perfidious world, for this old hag has been the bride of a thousand wooers."

Let not the cares of the world consume thee, and let not my advice depart from thee, for I received it in affection from one who had been a pilgrim in many lands:

"Be content with what hath been given, and smooth thy ruffled brow; for the door of choice will not be opened either to thee or me."

In the smile of the rose is no sign of promise, or of performance: lament, thou loving nightingale, for there is room for lamentation.

Why, feeble poetisers, be envious of Hafiz, because God hath given him the power to pour out sweet words and to win all hearts?

In the hour of dawn the bird of the garden thus spoke to a freshly-blown rose: "Be less disdainful, for in this garden hath bloomed many a one like thee."

The rose smiled and said: "We have never grieved at hearing the truth, but no lover would speak so harshly to his beloved!"

To all eternity the odour of love will never reach the brain of that man who hath never swept with his brow the dust from the sill of the wine-house.

Dost thou desire to drink the ruby-tinted wine from that gold-begemmed goblet, how many a pearl must thou first pierce with the point of thine eyelashes!

Yesterday, when in the Rose Garden of Irem, the morning-breeze with its gentle breath began to disturb the hair of the spikenard;

I exclaimed: "O throne of Jemshid, where is thy magic world-reflecting mirror?"—and it replied: "Alas! that that watchful Fortune should be slumbering!"

The words of love are not those that come to the tongue; O Cup-bearer, cut short this asking and answering.

The tears of Hafiz have cast patience and wisdom into the sea: how could it be otherwise? The burning pangs of love how could he conceal?

## A PERSIAN SONG OF HAFIZ

SWEET maid if thou wouldst charm my sight,
   And bid these arms thy neck infold;
That rosy cheek, that lily hand,
Would give thy poet more delight
Than all Bocara's vaunted gold,
Than all the gems of Samarcand.


Boy, let yon liquid ruby flow,
And bid thy pensive heart be glad,
Whate'er the frowning zealots say:
Tell them, their Eden cannot show
A stream so clear as Rocnabad,
A bow'r so sweet as Mosellay.

O! when these fair perfidious maids,
Whose eyes our secret haunts infest,
Their dear destructive charms display;
Each glance my tender breast invades,
And robs my wounded soul of rest,
As Tartars seize their destin'd prey.

In vain with love our bosoms glow:
Can all our tears, can all our sighs
New lustre to those charms impart!
Can cheeks, where living roses blow,
Where nature spreads her richest dies,
Require the borrow'd gloss of art?

Speak not of fate :—ah! change the theme,
And talk of odours, talk of wine,
Talk of the flow'rs that round us bloom;
'Tis all a cloud, 'tis all a dream;
To love and joy thy thoughts confine,
Nor hope to pierce the sacred gloom.

Beauty has such resistless pow'r,
That ev'n the chaste Egyptian dame
Sigh'd for the blooming Hebrew boy;
For her how fatal was the hour,
When to the banks of Nilus came
A youth so lovely and so coy!

But ah! sweet maid, my counsel hear:
(Youth should attend when those advise
Whom long experience renders sage)
While musick charms the ravish'd ear,
While sparkling cups delight our eyes,
Be gay; and scorn the frowns of age.

What cruel answer have I heard!
And yet, by heav'n, I love thee still:
Can aught be cruel from thy lip?

Yet say, how fell that bitter word
From lips which streams of sweetness fill,
Which nought but drops of honey sip?

Go boldly forth, my simple lay,
Whose accents flow with artless ease
Like orient pearls at random strung;
Thy notes are sweet, the damsels say,
But O! far sweeter, if they please
The nymph for whom these notes are sung.

Japan

## Japanese Literature

IT is related in an Indian literary composition, that a poet stopped after reading each stanza of his poems, hoping to gain the attention of his patron who continued to play with the coloured fish in the garden pond. At last, the patron, noticing the chagrin of the poet, said : " Continue your recitation, any verse worthy of it will surely detach me from this game! " Most Indo-Iranian poetry contrives to invade the mind of the hearer by its obvious force. Not so the Japanese. It demands a wrapped attention from one who might be privileged to hear it from the very start : thus it is that inattentive reading of the Japanese poetry leaves one cold and indifferent. Its meaning must be sought, contemplation should be given to it or it has nothing to impart one " bent on passing an idle hour." Poems included herein are from the translation of F. Victor Dickins and Clay MacCaulay.

## ANGELS OF EARTH

O YE Winds of Heaven!
　　In the paths among the clouds
Blow, and close the ways,
　　That we may these virgin forms
Yet a little while detain.

## SECRET LOVE

Lo the gathered waves
　　On the shores of Sumi's bay!
E'en in gathered night,
　　When in dreams I go to thee,
I must shun the eyes of men.

## THE MOUNTAIN WIND

SINCE 'tis by its breath
　　Autumn's leaves of grass and trees
Broken are and waste,
　　Men may to the mountain-wind
Fitly give the name, "The Wild."

## PURSUIT AND POSSESSION

FOR thy precious sake,
　　Once my eager life itself
Was not dear to me.
　　But 'tis now my heart's desire
It may long, long years endure.

## A VIEW AT SEA

O'ER the wide sea-plain,
　　As I row and look around,
It appears to me
　　That the white waves, far away,
Are the ever-shining sky.

## IN DOUBT

*I* FEAR me thou wilt break the pact
   Thou mad'st with me—thy love will pass
Away from me, whom thoughts distract,
   As tangled as the unkempt mass
     My ravel tresses show,
That o'er my waking pillow flow.

## THE TRANSFIGURED PAST

*I* F I long should live,
   Then perchance, the present days
May be dear to me ;—
   Just as past time fraught with grief
   Now comes fondly back in thought.

## A PRISONER OF LOVE

*F* OR but one night's sake,
   Short as is a node of reed
Grown in Naniwa bay,
   Must I, henceforth, long for him
   With my whole heart, till life's close ?

## ON FALLEN FLOWERS

*N* OT the snow of flowers,
   That the hurrying wild-wind drags
Round the garden court,
   Is it that here, withering, falls :—
That in truth is it, myself.

Turkey

## Turkish Literature

OTTOMAN poetry and prose shows much the same passion
for portraying the human soul as do the Iranian or Indian
literatures. Possessing a rich language, the Turkish poet admits
of no impediments in moulding thought for a particular effect,
thus is capable of presenting his subject in several points of
view, like the facets of a diamond. It also shows philosophical
devoutness as in the included Composition of Bahlool Dana
where the skill of the narrator strives to prove how most
pleasures, like flower, when gathered, die : for the rest it can
be said that the Ottoman poet, perhaps more so than others,
have been more successful in imparting a personality to their
melodies and song, and the following quotations from the
translations of S. Lane-Poole.

## A GHAZEL OF SELIM I

*D*OWN in oceans from mine eyen rail the tears for grame
 and teen,
Acheth still my head for all the dolour that my feres have
 seen,
That the army of my visions o'er the flood, my tears,
 may pass,
Form mine eyebrows twain a bridge, one-piered, with
 arches two beseen.
Clad in gold-bespangled raiment, all of deepest heavenly
 blue,
Comes the ancient Sphere each night-tide, fain to play
 my wanton quean.
Lonely had I strayed a beggar through the realms of
 strangerhood,
Had not pain and woe and anguish aye my close com-
 panions been.
O thou Sphere, until the Khan Selim had nine full beakers
 drained,
Ne'er did he, on all earth's surface, find a faithful friend,
 I ween.

## ODE ON SPRING

### BY MESIHI

ᕼARK, the bulbul's blithesome carol: 'Now are come
 the days of spring!'
Merry bands and shows are spread in every mead, a maze
 o' spring.
There the almond-tree bescatters silvern showers, sprays
 o' spring.
 Drink, be gay; for soon will vanish, biding not, the
 days o' spring!

Rose and tulip bloom as beauties bright o' blee and
 sweet o' show,
Who for jewels hang the dew-drops in their ears to gleam
 and glow.
Deem not thou, thyself beguiling, things will aye continue so.
 Drink, be gay; for soon will vanish, biding not, the
 days o' spring!

 .  .  .  .  .

While each dawn the clouds are shedding jewels o'er the
 rosy land,
And the breath of morning's zephyr, fraught with Tartar
 musk, is bland,
While the world's delight is present, do not thou unheeding stand;
 Drink, be gay; for soon will vanish, biding not, the
 days o' spring !

 .  .  .  .  .

With the fragrance of the garden, so imbued the musky
 air,
Every dew-drop, ere it reacheth earth, is turned to attar
 rare ;
O'er the garth, the heavens spread the incense-cloud's
 pavilion fair.
 Drink, be gay; for soon will vanish, biding not, the
 days o' spring!

 .  .  .  .  .

# TWO GHAZELS

## BY FUZULI

### I

*O* MY loved one, though the world because of thee my
foe should be,
'Twere no sorrow, for thyself alone were friend enow
for me.

Scorning every comrade's rede, I cast me wildly midst of
love;
Ne'er shall foe do me the anguish I have made myself
to dree.

Dule and pain shall never fail me, long as life and frame
aby;
Life may vanish, frame turn ashes: what is life or frame
to me !

Ah, I knew not union's value, parting's pang I ne'er had
borne;
Now the gloom of absence lets me many a dim thing
clearly see.

Yonder Moon hath bared her glance's glaive; be not
unheeding, heart;
For decreed this day are bitter wail to me, and death to
thee.

O Fuzuli, though that life should pass, from Love's way
pass not I;
By the path where lovers wander make my grave, I pray
do ye.

### II

Whenso'er I call to mind the feast of union 'twixt us
twain,
Like the flute, I wail so long as my waste frame doth
breath retain.

'Tis the parting day; rejoice .thee, O thou bird, my soul,
for now
I at length shall surely free thee from this cage of pine
and pain.

Lest that any, fondly hoping, cast his love on yonder
  Moon,
Seeking justice 'gainst her rigour, unto all I meet I plain.
Grieve not I whate'er injustice rivals may to me display;
Needs must I my heart accustom Love's injustice to
  sustain.
Well I know I ne'er shall win to union with thee, still
  do I
Cheer at times my cheerless spirit with the hope as fond
  as vain.
I have washed the name of Mejnun off the page of earth
  with tears;
O Fuzuli, I shall likewise fame on earth through dolour
  gain.

# FROM A KASIDA IN PRAISE OF SULTAN MURAD IV

### BY NEF'I

THE early springtide breezes blow, the roses bloom at
    dawn of day;
Oh! let our hearts rejoice; cup-bearer, fetch the bowl
    of Jem, I pray.
The gladsome time of May is here, the sweetly scented
    air is clear,
The earth doth Eden-like appear, each nook doth Irem's
    bower display.
'Tis e'en the rose's stound o' glee, the season of hilarity,
The feast of lovers fair and free, this joyous epoch bright
    and gay.
So let the goblet circle fair, be all the taverns emptied bare,
To dance let ne'er a toper spare, what while the minstrels
    chant the lay.
A season this when day and night the tavern eyes the
    garth with spite;
Though drunk, he loved a winsome wight, excused were
    Mekka's guardian gray.
Oh! what shall now the hapless do, the lovelorn, the
    bewildered crew?
Let beauties fetch the bowl anew, to spare the which
    were shame to-day.
Be bowl and lovesome charmer near, and so the hour
    will shine with cheer;
And he indeed will wise appear who maketh most of mirth
    and play.
That toper's joy in truth were whole who, drunken and
    elate of soul,
With one hand grasped the tulip bowl, with one the
    curling locks did fray.
Cup-bearer, lay those airs aside, give wine, the season
    will not bide,
Fill up the jar and hanap wide, nor let the beakers empty
    stay.

Each tender branchlet fresh and fine hath hent in hand its
cup of wine.

Come forth, O cypress-shape, and shine; O rosebud-
lips, make glad the way.

Of this say not 'tis joy or pain; grieve not, but pass
the bowl again;

Submit to Fate's eternal reign; and hand the wine without delay.

For wine of lovers is the test, of hearts the bane, of souls
the rest,

The Magian elder's treasure blest, th'adorn o' th' idol's
festal tray.

'Tis wine that guides the wise in mind, that leadeth lovers
joy to find;

It blows and casts to every wind, nor lets grief's dust the
heart dismay.

A molten fire, the wine doth flow; in crystal cup, a tulip
glow:

Elsewise a fragrant rosebud blow, new-oped and sprent
with dewy spray.

So give us wine, cup-bearer, now, the bowl of Jem and
Kay-Khusrau;

Fill up a brimming measure thou, let all distress from
hearts away.

Yea, we are lovers fair and free, for all that thralls of
wine we be,

Lovelorn and stricken sore are we, be kind to us nor say
us nay.

For Allah's sake a goblet spare, for yonder moon's that
shineth fair,

That I with reed and page prepare the Monarch's praises
to assay.

That Sun of empire and command, that Champion-
horseman of the land,

As blothe as Jem, as Hatim bland, whom all the folk
extol alway,

That Dread of Rum and Zanzibar, who rides Time's
dappled steed in war,

Who hunts the foeman's hordes afar, Behram, Feridun-
fair in fray,
That Monarch of the Osman race, whose noble heart
and soul embrace
Arabian Omar's saintly grace and Persian Perviz' glorious
sway.
Sultan Murad, of fortune bright, who crowns doth give
and kingdoms smite;
Both emperor and hero hight, the Age's Lord with Jem's
display.

.    .    .    .    .    .

## TWO GHAZELS

### BY NEDIM

#### I

*L*OVE distraught, my heart and soul are gone for nought
    to younglings fair,
All my patience and endurance spent on torn and shredded
    spare.
Once I bared her lovely bosom, whereupon did calm and
    peace
Forth my breast take flight, but how I wist not, nay, nor
    why nor where.
Paynim mole, and paynim tresses, paynim eyes, I cry ye
    grace;
All her cruel beauty's kingdom forms a Heathenesse, I
    swear.
Kisses on her neck and kisses on her bosom promised she;
Woe is me, for now the Paynim rues the troth she pledged
    while-ere.
Such the winsome grace wherewith she showed her locks
    from neath her fez,
Whatsoever wight beheld her gazed bewildered then and
    there.
" Sorrowing for whom," thou askest, " weeps Nedim so
    passing sore ? "
Ruthless, 'tis for thee that all men weep and wail in drear
    despair.

#### II

O my wayward fair, who thus hath reared thee sans all
    fear to be ?
Who hath tendered thee that thus thou humblest e'en the
    cypress-tree ?
Sweeter than all perfumes, brighter than all dyes, thy
    dainty frame ;
One would deem some fragrant rose had in her bosom
    nurtured thee.
Thou hast donned a rose-enwrought rich brocade, but
    sore I fear

Lest the shadow of the broidered rose's thorn make thee
  to dree.
Holding in one hand a rose, in one a cup, thou camest,
  sweet;
Ah, I knew not which of these, rose, cup, or thee, to take
  to me.
Lo, there springs a jetting fountain from the Stream of
  Life, methought,
When thou madest me that lovely lissom shape o' thine
  to see.

# THE ROSE OF ISTAMBOUL

## By Bahloal Dana

ONLY twenty-three, but already he had three wives. These had been thrust upon him by family and political exigencies. His first wife, Zara, was six years older than he, a cumbrous, over-sensible woman. Ayesha, the second, had been the young widow of a wealthy and childless pasha who had left her everything, and such a prize Seyd's mother could not resist for him. Danäe was a Greek, a prisoner in the last rebellion, given him by his General as a reward. He could not refuse her, and his native chivalry denied any other arrangement save marriage.

He had wished for none of these women, all three had been thrust upon him. They were content enough, but although he was kind, considerate and friendly with all three, he cared for none of them. He cared only for the beauty of the spiritual. He told himself that he should have been a Sufi, one of those poet-priests whose hermit lives are given over to the ecstasy of the contemplation of the divine.

But this evening, as he stepped to his barge through the most beautiful garden on the banks of the Golden Horn, Seyd realized that hermitage was really unnecessary to ecstatic thinking and living. Here was Paradise at his very gate.

Through the white columns of the Byzantine ruins standing where the garden met the sea, glowed the island-bearing sapphire of the Bosphorus, a plane of light beneath a turquoise sky dashed with thin gold. The lineaments on the marble capitals were clear as in the sculptor's thought, and the stony wreaths of ivy, myrtle and pine which clustered the shattered pillars seemed only not to move

and grow because no wind vexed the night's first rapture.
It was good to live not for vitality's sake, but for the sake
of that essence of the seraphic which drenches the airs
of that golden place.

The light barge, under the compelling hands of its four
negro rowers, thrust its nose towards the jutting lands
which almost meet at the bay's entrance. Seyd lit a chi-
bouque, and lay back in the cushions, taking in the magic
of the evening. A frail drift of opal cloud held the upper
sky, and the stars through this gazed as women's eyes
through veiling. Women's eyes! He smiled rather bitterly.
To him there had always seemed more of devil than angel
in womankind. They were not serene, they had no depths
of mind or soul, they were prone to obsessions and gross
superstitions which clung to them like weed to the body
of a ship. They were spirits of impulse, hating and loving
in a breath. Allah alone knew why He had created them.
Foolish men were captured by their little coquetries, but
wise men avoided the snare of them, as they avoided all
that was not good for the soul's life.

The barge shot through the harbour's mouth and
continued its course round the coastal fringe of silver sand
lying without the Horn. The heaped miracle of Istamboul
rose behind him, a mountain of minarets and rainbow
domes, lofting into the illimitable turquoise of the Eastern
night. At the spectacle of it, beautiful as a wreck of Paradise
his eyes overflowed with tears. When Nature and Man set
hands to the same canvas what, with the aid of Allah,
could they not achieve?

The barge drew shoreward, and toward a small jetty.
Seyd landed, and told the negroes to wait. He walked
inland by a narrow path, plunging into a little wood where
a small ruined mosque stood in deserted whiteness. Although it was roofless and long deserted, although the
incense of prayer seldom ascended here, Seyd piously
removed his peaked shoes before he entered. Some rain-
water, limpid as aquamarine, lay in the shattered basin,
and in this he made his ablutions.

Seating himself on one of the tilting flagstones, he began to pray, devoutly, utterly oblivious to all his surroundings. This indeed was life, this communion with the Merciful, the Compassionate, Sultan and Soveriegn of the Universe, of the seas and the stars, of men and of angels. The power of the Divine interpenetrated every fibre of him, overflowing into his spirit in mystical golden rapture, making his heart blossom in love and the comprehension of heaven. He could understand how the Patriarchs and Prophets who walked with God had endured material existence but for such moments as this, which brought a sense of the everlasting beauty and nobility of the bond betwixt God and man. This was indeed life, joy, victory!

A slight noise behind him disturbed his devotions. He turned his head. He rose quickly. Before him in the gathering shadows which fell like thick curtains upon the little mosque stood a woman heavily veiled. A sudden resentment seized him. To behold a woman there and at such an hour seemed monstrously inappropriate. Some crone, doubtless, who, with the privilege of age, came there to make secret devotions. Then he saw by her bare feet, white as alabaster, that she was a young woman. It was not meet that he should be there alone with her. He would go.

But as he made to do so, he found his way barred by a shapely arm.

" Stay, Seyd," she said in a deep rich voice that thrilled him to the deepest places of his blood. " Stay, for I am the answer to your prayer."

Amazed, he could scarcely speak. " How lady," he stammered. " I seem to known you, but. . . ." Then the truth of the matter rushed in upon him. This was some woman of love, some courtesan who had tracked him here, seeking to beguile him and bring him to shame, a ghoul, perhaps, sent by Eblis to destroy him, soul and body.

" Let me pass," he said sternly. Her answer was to raise her veil, and at the sight, Seyd gave back in amazed terror, for at once he knew that this was no mere mortal beauty, but a miraculous and elemental loveliness such as it is given given only to the inspired and the saintly to behold.

" Who art thou ? " he asked in great fear, his flesh shaking as though it would fall asunder and dissolve.

" Ask not my name, Seyd. Be content that I have been sent to thee in answer to thy unuttered prayers. Allah in His great mercy has understood that for thee and such as thee no mortal woman can suffice. But as it is necessary that the soul of woman should unite with that even of the most wise and pious of mankind, such as I have been raised up by Allah to attend them in order that the miracle of nature's unity may be made complete."

Seyd was silent for a long time. " Much of what you say is dark to me," he said at last. " It may be that in my dreams and even while in prayer I have sought the perfect woman, though I knew it not. But how am I to know whether you are of the divine or a demon from Eblis ? Sheitan sends strange and beautiful shapes to decoy the holy from their allegiance to Allah."

The woman laughed. " Nay seek, not to number me among the devils," she said, " for were I a demon I might not utter the name of Allah. Nor might I enter this holy mosque, deserted as it is. And that I am more than woman, you have but to look at me to be convinced. Come, Seyd, reject me not, for it is the will of Allah that you should love and cherish me, of Allah who would have nothing single, who has sent love into the world for all men's worship and acceptance."

As she spoke, she drew near, and, holding out her arms, folded him in an embrace so full of warm life and rapture, that, intoxicated, he returned it with almost equal ardour. His senses reeled at her kisses, his mood of cold insensibility fell from him like a garment outworn. For the first time he experienced the overwhelming miracle of love. The hours passed with dreamlike rapidity in the little mosque. Seyd, the passionless, the chilly hearted, felt himself transported as if to the seventh heaven of delight.

Profound as was the rapture of prayer, of communion with Allah, this was an experience more divine.

"You have not told me your name," he said, "but already I know it. For you are Mystery, whom all men love, but whose love few achieve while still in life."

"Mystery I am, as thou sayest, O Seyd," she replied. "Yet is that not all of me. I am something more, something you encounter every day, something you love well, and for which you would gladly give your life, yet which daily you tread under your feet."

"You are also Love, mayhap?"

"Yes. Love I am, Love the most profound, a love surpassing that of the mother for the son, the sailor for the sea."

A thin light broke through the canopy of the darkness.

"It is the hour before dawn," whispered the woman, "we must part, Seyd, my beloved. But come to me here soon. I shall keep tryst here each nightfall in the hope of meeting thee."

And so they parted with a lingering kiss. Seyd quickly made his way back to the barge, to find that his four negroes had long fallen asleep. Awaking them, he was rowed speedily home. All night he dreamed of the woman he had met in the ruined mosque.

When he rose the next day, it was to be assailed with doubt. Surely she must be a thing of evil, a ghoul such as the peasants spoke of, haunting ruined mosques and grave-yards, a lamia such as the old legends told of, seeking to lure men to destruction. Yet of evil in her he had seen not the least admixture. Her bearing, her speech were natural and unaffected. It was chiefly the comprehension of something elemental in her, some power indescribable, that nurtured his misgivings.

All that day he walked in his garden, deep in meditation. That his lady had entered a mosque showed at least that she was not a thing, an appearance, sent by the powers of Eblis for his destruction. Holy mullahs and imaums praying in the desert, had been beset by such, and through their influence, delivered over to the father of night. There was, of course, no imaginable test by which he could know absolutely that she was veritably a woman, unless he traced her to her dwelling-place. He recalled it as strange that when he had glanced back at the mosque when half-way to his barge that he had not seen her emerge from the only doorway the shrine had.

At nightfall after a troubled day, he ordered his caique once more, and was rowed to the little jetty. It was now almost quite dark, and as he entered the mosque, he saw a white shape bending to and fro in the actions of prayer. This dissolved his last fear that he had to deal with a creature unhallowed. Springing forward, he seized her in his arms, and was greeted with rapture.

" The day has been long," he said, " but its sorrows are over. I have thought of you through all the hours. I must know who you are—know your name."

" My name, beloved ? Call me the Rose of Istamboul if thou wilt, for indeed I have none other you may know."

" The Rose of Istamboul ! Truly that is a fair name enough, sweet, and so I shall call you, for the present at least. But when you become my bride, then I must know your true name."

" Your bride, Seyd ? Am I not already your bride ? Think you that the muttering of a few words by the imaum alone makes man and woman one ? "

" But I am resolved that you shall dwell in my house, moon of my eyes," cried Seyd in agitation. " Nay it must be so."

" Let us forget the thoughts of men for the present," she replied, clinging to him. " Let us remember only the elemental things—the things which make up real existence."

And so the night passed as that before it had done, and night after night Seyd met the Rose of Istamboul. He might not put aside his longing that they should share existence wholly, by day as well as by night. He craved to see her in his house, to eat with her, to share the common things of life with her, and often did he tell her so. But to his pleadings she was silent. When he spoke thus, not a word did she answer.

At length he resolved to discover her identity, to find out where she lived. He had never, so far, seen her come or go at their rendezvous. So one night after leaving her in the little mosque as usual, he waited in the shadow of the trees which surrounded it, intent on following her.

Nearly half an hour passed, and he had almost resolved to retrace his steps to see whether she still remained in the mosque, when she passed the spot where he had concealed himself. Creeping stealthily from his hiding-place, he followed her. She walked slowly for some considerable distance over the rough bent which stretched between the seashore and the city. Suddenly, the first ray of daylight throbbed across the sapphire dusk of night. Distracted from his intention for an instant by the beauty of the sight, an arrow of silver flying across an azure shadow, he cast his glance upward, and when he brought it back to the point where she had last appeared it was to find no trace of her. She had vanished as completely as though she had dissolved into the vapours of the morning which now began to rise from the plains behind the sea.

In a frenzy he ran onward, calling her name. " Rose, Rose of Istamboul, where are you ? " But nothing could he see except the level bent where sand lay at the roots of each tuft of coarse grass, nothing could he hear except the low wind of sunrise sighing across the waste.

Despondently, he returned to his barge, and was rowed homeward. He had become aware that Zara, his chief wife, was suspicious of his nightly movements. Although she made no complaint, she frequently looked at him with deep reproach. As for the others, for days at a time he scarcely saw them. All three had become repugnant to him. To free himself from them was impossible.

Then he recalled that this woman who had taken him body and soul had told him that she was more than woman, that she was, indeed, the answer to his prayer—a prayer

he had been unconscious of offering up. Of what folly
had he not been capable? That, good or evil, the Rose
of Istamboul was a creature of spiritual mould he was now
assured. Her disappearance on the seashore in the twinkling
of an eye proved as much. He must see her no more, he
must content himself with life as he found it; as a true
man should.

So no more he went to the mosque in the little wood.
Days passed, and, although grief gnawed at his heart as
a serpent, he kept his own house at nights. His wife Zara
was pleased with him, and even refrained from tormenting
the little Greek, Danäe, while the young but experienced
Ayesha, who had been married before to an elderly roue,
smiled secretly, and tittered when he went to the casement,
opening it on the view of the Golden Horn.

But he could not harden his heart against the Rose of
Istamboul, for the lure of her was such as it is not given
to man to resist, the lure of earth, of air, of nature, of the
deep indwelling life which lies in the soil's womb, in
the bodies of trees, in the breath of life which we call the
wind. All that the eye might see, all that the ear might
hear, recalled the miracle of her, who was compounded
of atoms and essences natural and delectable. The woods
were her hair, the planets her eyes, the sea her spirit. And
Seyd knew that she might not be escaped by any man,
because, as she had said, she was not only woman, but all
that woman in her essential native vigour and power and
divine sweetness brings to man in one body—the rapturous spirit of that earth of which he is himself a part, the
less vivid, the less daedal part, the nymphic fire that from
the oak conceives the dryad, that from the stream brings
forth the naiad, that pagan fury which not only receives
the life of which man is the vessel, but which has power,
like its mother the earth, to bring it to harvest and
fruition.

Stunned for a space by the revelation of what he had
lost, he leaped from his divan with the frenzy of a man
who had cast away a whole world. His slaves shrank

from him in terror when they beheld him. With speech-less gestures he commanded them to prepare the caique. They obeyed and in a few moments he was cleaving the waters of the Golden Horn once more, the foam rising upon the prow, turning into snow the reflected heaven of Bosphorus.

And so he came to the little mosque and found her there. Once more he was enfolded in her arms, he drank of her loveliness.

"Ah," she cried, gazing into his eyes with rapture, "all is well at last. You know Seyd, you understand. For I am what comes to all poets, I am the soil as woman, as bride, she who at last arises out of the earth they love better than themselves to cherish them and be with them always. I am the Rose of Istamboul!"

Miscellaneous

# MEETING OF THE EAST AND WEST

*By Nawab Zada of Sardhana*

QUITE apart from that wonderful poetry and philosophy which characterized the Semitic mind of the Arabic speaking peoples, the true Oriental thought is recognized to be that which has its origin in Persia. For a critical study of Persian literature I might refer those interested in it to the works exclusively devoted to that subject, because the wisdom of the East has more or less adequately been interpreted by some Western scholars in the translations of Omar Khayyám, Sadi, Hafiz and others. In the following review, however, I shall concern myself with a new phase of Persian poetry which seeks to establish the fact that in higher aspects of spiritual evolution the Sages of the East have been extremely close to the approved philosophical thought of the West. In drawing attention to this facet of the meeting ground of the East and the West, I am breaking new ground.

"The East is East and the West is West, and never the twain shall meet," sings Kipling with characteristic felicity and force. This assertion, it may be admitted, is, at least, a plausible one, especially in so far as it refers to individual tendencies and experiences. Average Easterners and average Westerners, who come into accidental contact, no doubt find themselves "poles apart," as the English saying goes. Their habits of life are not the same; they appear to have different habits of thought, and a different outlook on the world. Consequently their impressions of each other are, when untinged by fanatical race prejudice, always interesting, sometimes novel, and, perhaps, amusingly odd ; but they are rarely, be it borne in mind, based upon intimate knowledge or genuine sympathy in the wide sense of the term. Casual asquaintanceship may not be limited by Time ; it may extend over many years and never attain the stage of real or intimate friendship, for mankind is prone to maintain those terrible barriers that separate mind from mind and heart from heart. We are all disposed, more or less, to be tyrannized by pre-conceptions and first impressions, and to refuse to see more than may be seen at a glance, or, perhaps, to see more than we want to see. Besides, being very human, we are ever inclined to become slaves of such phrases as Kipling has coined simply because they are trenchant and make a marked appeal to our fellows, and it seems not to matter how superficial they may happen to be. This applies to Easterner as well as to Westerner. The clever saying is not necessarily final, or the product of clear thinking and exact knowledge.

R. L. Stevenson's impressions of the Chinamen on the American emigrant train may be cited as an example in this regard. It affords an excellent illustration of the human tendency to paint a word-picture which pleases artist and reader by its sheer novelty and cleverness and finish. "For my own part," wrote R. L. Stevenson in *Across the Plains*, in his charming style, "I could not look but with wonder and respect on the Chinese. Their fore-fathers watched the stars before mine had begun to keep pigs." (Antiquarians sharply question this statement, I am told.) "Gunpowder and printing, which the other day we imitated, and a school of manners which we never had the delicacy so much as to desire to imitate, were theirs in a long past antiquity. They walk the earth with us, but it seems they must be of different clay. They hear the clock strike the same hour, yet surely of a different epoch. . . . Heaven knows if we had one common thought or fancy all that way, or whether our eyes which yet were formed upon the same design, beheld the same world out of the railway windows." Here the impressionist is carried away by his workable theme. After all, these Chinese, who were not necessarily conscious of racial antiquity, were, like the other emigrants, just pursuing the heart-absorbing quest of wealth, as had done their ancestors who trod out those ancient trade routes of Eastern and Central Asia, greedier for gold than for knowledge. They had at least, therefore, one particular motive in common with the medley of races that crowded the dingy railway carriages, and, among them, there may have been, for all we know, an Oriental Stevenson to whom even his own countrymen seemed strange fellows. The literary Scotsman, it may be noted, regarded the Cornishmen in the same saloon as eccentric aliens.

No greater gulf lies between the Easterner and the Westerner than exists between different classes of society in a single country. There is little in common, for instance, in everyday interest, between slow-witted Hodge in his turnip-field and the alert, calculating speculator on the Stock Exchange, or between the profiteer with an eye for the main chance and the boy-poet musing in his dug-out over a sad last beautiful poem revealing a wonderful soul-history, ere his brief but noble life is brought to an end by a chance bullet. Such men are surely "poles apart." Each would reckon the other, if brought into sudden contact, a strange and, perhaps, a dull fellow.

The average Easterner is not a symbol of the East, nor is the average Westerner necessarily typical of the West. Average men represent commonplace conditions of life and thought ; they are puppets of environment. Not average men, but men endowed with a capacity for spiritual and intellectual development are those really capable of representing their race and country and of interpreting the inner life—"the life of life," as Shelley puts it—of which average men in all lands are but pale and sometimes distorted reflections. "All minds," says an Eastern poet, "reflect the Great Mind. Some, like a mirror, reflect the sun and rival it ; others have no light to return, but take of it what they can receive, like a stone or a clod of earth." The intellectual life of a country is not reflected by its stones or clods.

A first essential for the sympathetic understanding of East by West, or of West by East, is Knowledge. " Wherein lies happiness ? " asked the poet Keats and his answer was :

> " In that which becks
> Our ready minds to fellowship divine,
> A fellowship with essence."

The way to Knowledge is similarly oriented. It is to the Intellectual and not to the labourer, or the man of affairs, the so-called " hard-headed, practical man " who may be, outside his narrow sphere, quite a stupid man, that we look for a solution of the riddle propounded by Kipling. Are East and West really so far apart as Kipling would have us believe ? Do Easterners look on the world so differently from Westerners that it is not possible for them to find a common meeting ground ? It is really " begging the question " to set down such queries. In the only real life, the intellectual life, East and West are less far apart than some would apparently care to acknowledge. " The Easterner is a mystic, for one thing," urges some confident theorist. But there are many Western mystics in poetry and prose, for mysticism is, after all, temperamental in essence. What of Blake, Carlyle, Browning, Burke, William Law, Coleridge, Wordsworth, Shelley and a host of others that could be mentioned ? Plato was not an Indian, nor was Swedenborg, and the mystical Emerson was an American. The men who have done the thinking for the masses in East and West are not so far apart as are Anglo-Indian trader and native coolie, or as Thackeray's " Jeames " and his lordship whose clothing " Jeames " carefully folds and lays out as if nothing else mattered in life.

Those who would separate East from West forget that it is from the East that Europe has received the essential elements in its religious life. Nor was it merely from the " Near East "—from that wonderful land of Palestine, which "never produced anything of consequence except a great religious literature." For Palestine, as Western scholars have abundantly demonstrated, was itself debtor to Egypt, Babylonia and Persia, and even, as some would have it, to Buddhistic India, for traces of Buddhist ideas are, it would appear, embedded in Isaiah and the Psalms of David. Before Christianity achieved full sway in Europe, it struggled for supremacy with Persian Mithraism which, although overcome in time, has, the scholars assert, left undeniable traces on European religious thought. It was from the East that civilization entered Europe, flowing along trade routes from the cradles of civilization in Egypt and Babylonia. The spiritual and intellectual life of Europe has an Eastern basis ; what has flourished with vigour in the West is not necessarily wholly indigenous ; from the roots rises the sap which feeds the blossom and the ripe fruit. It is not too much to assume that the influence imported from the area of origin is still flickering amidst the local fuel. Even science which is regarded as essentially Western, is Eastern in origin. Astronomy has emerged from the débris of Babylonian astrology, and the débris was not wholly cast off even in Shakespeare's day and still clings in odd quarters. Western clocks tick out Babylonian echoes, for time is measured on the Babylonian system. The very world is measured by Babylonian degrees. Europeans use the Egyptian calendar as adjusted and re-adjusted in Rome. Geometry was invented by Pharao's pyramid builders. The Brahmanic Indians gave the world Algebra, and the Arabs carried it westward. What ancient traders established the gold standard of currency ? Was it the Egyptians or Babylonians ? Who introduced the agricultural mode of life ? What set of Easterners ? And who but the Easterners first formed settled communities and built great cities with temples and palaces and villas and even slums ? And who were the earliest seafarers and the earliest sculptors and philosophers and writers and publishers ? Who would be so bold as to assert that East and West are so far apart when all that the West cherishes is rooted in the East ? East and West met ages ago and still meet, and Time has made the East in our own day the heavy debtor of the West.

The gulf that separates the peoples with skins differently pigmented is, in a sense, wholly mythical. Men in all parts of the world are prone to imagine that gulfs really exist. In the British Isles a gulf is set between Saxon and Celt, which takes much searching to perceive, and between Englishmen and Irishmen, and between Scotsmen and Englishmen and in Scotland between Highlanders and Lowlanders, and even in the Highlands, as the summer tourist discovers, between west coast men and east coast men. Among the Easterners there are many similar gulfs ; there are Parsees, Hindus, Mussulmans, and so on, and numerous sub-divisions, and there are lands in which racial gulfs are bridged by the idea of nationality, as is the case in Europe. Between the Easterner and Westerner there is often found more in common than between two groups of Easterners. And in Europe East and West are sometimes more intimately associated than is one part of the West with another.

The Easterner who sojourns for a period in the West, with the purpose of devoting himself to the acquirement of a meed of Western knowledge, invariably looks for enlightenment, during his leisure hours, regarding the intellectual life of the British Isles, not by questioning " the hewers of wood and the drawers of water," but by perusing the works of great men—the real representatives of the West. English literature reveals to him the soul of the English-speaking peoples. When he begins to peruse English literature, he does so with a mind stored with a heritage of ideas, fashions and leanings that have come down through countless generations ; and, ere he happens on the light that shines here as elsewhere, he has to accustom himself to local modes of expression and to individual idiosyncrasies. He must master the language to appreciate not only the sense of the metrical line—for he will inevitably begin with the poet—but also its music and verbal beauty. His first impressions depend very much on which poet, or group of poets, chance or a friend's guidance may place in his way. He may choose to begin with the very latest, and find himself startled by the materialism of Masefield :

> " ' Splash water on him, chaps. I only meant
>     To hit him just a chip . . . '
> ' God send ; he looks damn bad,' the blacksmith
>     said."

He may turn from the " Widow in the Bye Street " and set himself to get through " Dauber " till an Eastern ray suddenly breaks through the squalor and brutality of a rough sea life in the lines :

> " Then in the sunset's flush they went aloft
> And unbent sails in that most lovely hour,
> When the light gentles and the wind is soft,
> And beauty in the heart breaks like a flower."

An Oriental may find himself in " Comus," from which I quote, in a veritable Eastern atmosphere, especially when reading Milton's lines on a song—that since first perusal have haunted the writer's mind with a sense of mystery and beauty ; they are not surpassed even by Hafiz for their imaginative and spiritual qualities. The lines I refer to are :

> " At last a soft and solemn breathing sound
> Rose like a stream of rich distilled perfumes,
> And stole upon the air, that even Silence
> Was took ere she was 'ware, and wished she might
> Deny her nature, and be never more,
> Still to be so displaced. I was all ear,
> And took in strains that might create a soul
> Under the ribs of Death."

Those Himalayan heights of poetry, " Paradise Lost " and " Paradise Regained " may be found too vast for pleasurable appreciation without prolonged study, but " Comus," " Lycidas," and the shorter poems readily reveal a mind which appeals to the East as profoundly as to the West.

If, by chance, the reader selects Swinburne, he may be puzzled by numerous splashing and glimmering obscurities, and rendered blind or breathless by long, dazzling lines such as :

> " Are thy feet on the ways of the limitless waters, thy
>       wings on the winds of the waste north sea ?
> Are the fires of the false north dawn over heavens
>       where summer is stormful and strong like thee ? "

With relief he turns to the jungle of beauty in Keats with its vivid word-pictures, sharply and swiftly outlines as in Eastern poetry :

> " Clear rills
> That for themselves a cooling covert make
> 'Gainst the hot season."

> .     .     .     .     .

> "The rocks were silent, the wide sea did weave
> An untumultuous fringe of silver foam,
> Along the flat, brown sands."

In Keats the " Eastern atmosphere " is often evident. He was a mystic whose religion was Beauty :

> " Beauty is truth, truth Beauty, that is all
>       Ye know on earth, and all ye need to know."

The introductory sketch to my volume of Keats' poems is touched with a feeling of regret because the poet lived among the flowers and ignored the English reservoirs of learning,—because he was merely a "sensuous poet." An

Eastern perceives that Keats was one of the most intellectual of English poets. To him Truth, which is God, was
revealed by divine beauty. He enters into this Beauty
and becomes a part of it. In his " Endymion," so strangely
neglected, he exclaims :

> " Behold
> The clear religion of heaven! Fold
> A rose-leaf round thy finger's taperness.
> And soothe thy lips ; hist, when the airy stress
> Of music's Kiss impregnates the free winds. . . .
> Feel we these things ?—that moment have we stept
> Into a sort of oneness and our state
> Is like a floating spirit's."

Keats was no mere sensuous writer. Like the Eastern
poets, he realized that Beauty is the essence of the Creator,
to whom he really calls in these exquisite lines in
" Endymion " :

> " Thou wast the deep glen ;
> Thou wast the mountain top, the sage's pen,
> The poet's harp, the voice of friends, the sun ;
> Thou wast the river, thou wast glory won ;
> Thou wast the clarion's blast, thou wast my steed,
> My goblet full of wine, my topmost deed :
> Thou wast the charm of women, lovely Moon! "

A deep sense of what may justly be called religious
fervour of great poetic intensity pulsated in the soul of
this mystical singer. His love of Beauty was adoration
of God.

But of all the English poets with whom the Easterner
makes early acquaintance, none impresses so readily, so
intimately and so permanently as the saintly Shelley, over
whom some writers still shake their heads, because of an
offence committed against a social convention, despite
all the sorrow it brought him. An Easterner can understand this point of view, but he cannot understand what

is meant by "Shelley's atheism." In the East the religious sage may be found speculating with even more freedom than did Shelley regarding the mysteries of life and death. Speculation was in the old days encouraged, in the East, and it is still regarded as an attribute of an independent mind. Who can understand the truth if he has never had a cloud of doubt overshadowing his mind? All of us have been loitering in the shadows. The honest man admits his doubts, the impulsive man is no less honest if he insists on them at some period in his life, and declares that the shadow is the only reality. Shelley did this, and it has not yet been forgotten by the orthodox who are "less forgiving than God and therefore somewhat ungodly," as an Eastern sage puts it.

"I never read Shelley because I detest atheistical writings," declared one of my English friends; another, a Scot, asserted, "There is nothing in Shelley but winds and water and birds and clouds." Yet Shelley was in the real sense a prophet and a teacher of humanity, one of the greatest minds England has produced, as well as one of its greatest singers, if not its very greatest, not excepting Shakespeare. For Shakespeare never wrote such lyrics as did Shelley and never revealed himself as a solitary pilgrim-thinker in the spiritual world, as did the author of "The Hymn to Intellectual Beauty." Shakespeare was concerned about human character. Shelley was more concerned about human destiny. It is necessary to draw this distinction because there are those who would deny to Shelley, as to Keats, those intellectual qualities which are necessary for the production of great poetry. Both were profound, spiritually-minded thinkers; they were also seers in the real sense; at any rate, in the sense understood in the East. A Persian critic would be inclined to place Shelley and Keats above Shakespeare and yet not fail to admire Shakespeare as much as does the English critic.

Shelley, far from being an atheist, believed that God pervaded all things. He saw the Divine Spirit in Nature, in the tree instinct with life, in the moving river, in the "still, snowy and serene" Mont Blanc, in the cloud, in the skylark, in man. Life was but an episode in the history of man, and Eternity was to him an enduring reality; he sings in the "Adonais":

> "The One remains, the many change and pass;
> Heaven's light forever shines, Earth's shadows fly;
> Life, like a dome of many-coloured glass,
> Stains the white radiance of Eternity,
> Until Death tramples it to fragments.—Die
> If thou wouldst be with that which thou dost seek!
> Follow where all is fled! . . .
> Why linger, why turn back, why shrink, my Heart?
> Thy hopes are gone before . . .
> No more let Life divide what Death can join
>     together."

Light and Beauty were to Shelley manifestations of divine truth, and Love was God's beauty gleaming in the heart of man. His was a lovely and inspiring creed— "pleasant if one consider it":

> "That Light whose smile kindles the Universe,
> That beauty in which all things work and move,
> That Benediction which the eclipsing Curse
> Of birth can quench not, that sustaining Love
> Which through the web of being blindly wove
> By man and beast and earth and air and sea,
> Burns bright or dim, as each are mirrors of
> The fire for which all thirst; now beams on me
> Consuming the last clouds of cold mortality."

Shelley believed in the immortality of the soul, which, as he held, existed before birth and will endure after death. In that wonderful poem, "Ginevra," he pictures the horrors of death:

> "When there is felt around
> A smell of clay, a pale and icy glare,
> And silence."

Death comes suddenly to his heroine:

> "The dark arrow fled
> In the moon."

He contemplates the earthly phenomena of death with horror, not devoid of grandeur.

> "Ere the sun through heaven once more has rolled,
> The rats in her heart
> Will have made their nest,
> And the worms be alive in her golden hair;
> While the spirit that guides the sun,
> Sits throned in his flaming chair,
> She shall sleep."

But that is not the whole story of human destiny as felt in the shadows:

> "In our night
> Of thought we know thus much of death—no more
> Than the unborn dream of our life before
> Their barks are wrecked on its inhospitable shore."

Shelley, like the spirit of his own "West Wind," searched the whole world for God and found Him in the mind of man, the greatest of all Divine gifts, for the gift of mind unites all with the One. The poet makes this clear in his strange poem "Julian and Maddalo," in which the Count says to his friend:

> "The words you spoke last night might well have cast
> A darkness on my spirit—if man be
> The passive thing you say, I should not see
> Much harm in the religious and old saws
> (Tho' I may never own such leaden laws)

Which break a teachless nature to the yoke :
Mine is another faith."

Then we are given a glimpse of the beautiful faith of
this saintly and mystical singer of England :

> " See
> This lovely child, blithe, innocent and free,
> She spends a happy time with little care
> While we to such sick thoughts subjected are
> As came on you last night—it is our will
> That thus enchains us to permitted ill—
> We might be otherwise—we might be all
> We dream of, happy, high, majestical.
> Where is the love, beauty and truth we seek
> But in our mind ? and if we were not weak
> Should we be less in deed than in desire ? "

Burns is usually referred to as a " love poet," but
Shelley was more truly that, for he sang of the Greater
Love, the Love which is God. This love, revealed in
beauty to the eye in Nature, was similarly revealed to him
in the beauty of character and the beauty of the ideals of
peace and justice. He dreamed of the return of the Perfect
Age when War would cease to be and men would perceive
that there are greater victories than can be won on the
battlefield, that there are higher ideals than blood-shedding
can bring to frail man.

> " The world's great age begins anew,
>     The golden years return.
> The earth doth like a snake renew
>     Her wintry weeds outworn :
> Heaven smiles, and faith and empires gleam
>     Like wrecks of a dissolving dream."
>
> .    .    .    .    .
>
> " Oh write no more the Tale of Troy,
> If earth Death's Scroll must be ! "

The difference between Shelley and the Brahmanic authors of the "Upanishads" is most marked in one particular respect. In the famous "Forest Books" of India, the sages are really agnostics. They despair of the human mind ever being able to solve the riddle of existence. They cannot tell aught of God except negatively. They know what God is not, but not what God is. Shelley is a seer with a positive knowledge of divine truth. To him Love and Beauty were synonymous with the Divine Being. He rejoices in the thought of all-pervading Love. The idea of Divine Love never occurred to the authors of the coldly speculative "Upanishads" who likewise were blind to Divine Beauty. The Brahmans realized that they could not sway the masses with their vague speculations, and they provided a host of gods and goddesses with as many attributes as there was need or demand for. But behind all their pantheons remains the haunting belief that nothing positively can be known regarding Narayana or Brahma, or whatever name they choose to apply to the unknown God. But Shelley had a definite message for humanity, and it was essentially a poetical message. He desired men and women to live noble lives which would reflect divine beauty and divine love, not by the performance of certain rites, not by the organization of creeds and cults, but by thinking and living in a manner worthy of their ideals. To be "one with Nature" meant to Shelley to be "one with God."

Like the Easterner, Shelley had a symbolizing mind. He thought in symbols. In Greek mythology he found, ready-made, a host of Deities whom he spiritualized and glorified. His "Prometheus" is not, however, the old Greek Prometheus at all. He is Shelley's symbol of the human intelligence struggling with the chains that bind him, and the poet's "Asia" is his ideal of Eternal Love. This Love, married to intelligence, produces a new and better world.

Shelley's tendency to deify Nature, which puzzled his critics, including his wife, is manifested in that beautiful

poem, " The Witch of Atlas," which, had it been composed
by an Indian Brahman, would have added another deity
to the Hindu Pantheon. In his lines " To Mary," written
because she objected to the " Witch," " upon the score
of its containing no human interest," he compares the
poem to Wordsworth's " Peter Bell," and says:

" If you unveil my Witch, no priest nor primate
  Can shrive you of that sin—if sin there be
  In Love, when it becomes idolatry."

Here we have the keynote of the poem, which is no
mere fantasy, and something more even than " one of
the most ' poetic poems ' in the English language," I
never weary of studying the " Witch ":

" So fair a creature, as she lay enfolden
  In the warm shadow of her loveliness."

" A lovely lady garmented in light
  From her own beauty—deep her eyes, as are
  Two openings of unfathomable night
  Seen through a Temple's cloven roof—her hair
  Dark—the dim brain whirls dizzy with delight,
  Picturing her form : her soft smiles shone afar,
  And her low voice was heard like love, and drew
  All living things towards this wonder new."

One reads with feelings of reverence, perceiving that
the lady is the symbol of that Love which to Shelley was
the Eternal Good. The beauty of the metrical music and
the abundant imagery intensify the spell of the poet's
dream :

" The deep recesses of her odorous dwelling
  Were stored with magic treasures—sounds of air,
  Which had the power all spirits of compelling,
  Folded in cells of crystal silence there ;
  Such as we hear in youth, and think the feeling
  Will never die."

This reference is to Shelley's youth, let us remember, when he had visions of Eternal Purpose which are not realized wholly in this life of ours. The Witch of the poet says to mortals:

> " Oh, ask not me
> To love you till your little race is run;
> I cannot die as ye must."

She revealed herself in all that is beautiful by night and day, in the clear heaven, among the stars, in the ravine with its roaring river and on the summits of lofty and lonely mountains. She hovered over mankind by night. The poet imagines her visions in the wonderful lines:

> " A pleasure sweet doubtless it was to see
> Mortals subdued in all the shapes of sleep.
> Here lay two sister twins in infancy;
> There, a lone youth who in his dreams did weep;
> Within, two lovers linked innocently
> In their loose locks which over both did creep
> Like ivy from one stem;—and there lay calm
> Old age with snow-bright hair and folded palm.

> " But other troubled forms of sleep she saw,
> Not to be mirrored in a holy song—
> Distortions foul of supernatural awe,
> And pale imaginings of visioned wrong;
> And all the code of custom's lawless law
> Written upon the brows of old and young:
> ' This,' said the wizard maiden, ' is the strife
> Which stirs the liquid surface of man's life.' "

She gives dreams to the sleepers, and each dream reveals the character of the dreamer. Those worthy of her love:

> " She did unite again with visions clear
> Of deep affection and of truth sincere."

Why this poem should be neglected, or regarded merely as a poet's fantasy, sorely puzzles an Easterner. It has more poetry and more beauty and more truth than can be found in a dozen of the " popular poems " so often reproduced in anthologies. " The Witch of Atlas " is worth more than many " Don Juans," and is more beautiful than a Dauber, more human than an " Everlasting Mercy," more spiritual than many " Idylls of the King." One must go back to half-forgotten Spenser, " the poet's poet," for such a glimpse of :

> " That soveraine light
> From whose pure beams all perfect beauty springs,
> That kindled love in every godly spright
> Even the love of God : which loathing brings
> Of this vile world and these gay-seeming things."

There is much in common between Shelley and Spenser, although the latter takes a longer time to tell his story. Compare, for instance, Shelley's " Hymn to Intellectual Beauty " and Spenser's " Hymne of Heavenly Beautie " in which the same message is given :

> " Him to behold, is on his workes to looke."

And yet Spenser is regarded by many as a poet who wrote musical verse mainly about such trifling and archaic things as fairies and ogres met by wandering knights of old romance. But the poets who followed him heard and understood him, and hailed him, as does Wordsworth, in his enchanting " Prelude " :

> " Sweet Spenser, moving through his clouded heaven
> With the moon's beauty and the moon's soft pace."

It cannot be said that Wordsworth is neglected. But he does not seem to appeal to his own countrymen in the same manner as he does to an Easterner, that is, as a seer like Shelley, Keats and Spenser. He knew himself to be a seer, and in his "Prelude" and "Excursion," which so many critics regard as "failures" because they forget that the poet's message is of more account than his manner of setting it forth, and that it could not be concentrated in a series of pretty songs. He required space for his great pronouncement to humanity—the memorable inspiring message he was sent into this world to deliver. A poet without a great message is a mere piper of empty tunes, a mere clasher of brazen cymbals, a mere idolator who bows the knee to Baal in the name of Art, or a noisy reveller in the train of Bacchus. The merely "popular poet" is usually the poet with least intelligence and smallest soul, the poet who strikes the right note of mediocrity for business purposes, or who makes pretty phrases out of trite ideas fashionable in his age, or who glorifies the weaknesses and excesses of mere sensual passion which conceal the Divine spark by its formless, exaggerated and obscuring cloudiness. There is no real beauty which is not a manifestation of the Divine—not the Divine who is a god of a cult—but the divine spirit which is revealed in beauty and love in the heart or in nature.

A manly godliness of spirit is apparent in all immortal verse. He who creates even a poem must bear resemblance to the Creator of all that is beautiful and good and true. Let us not have Art for Art's sake, but Art for God's sake—Art which interprets the Divine element in mankind.

That Wordsworth realized all this is abundantly shown in his autobiographical poem "The Prelude" which is, without doubt, the most wonderful autobiography ever written in any country. He gives his account of what Westerners call his "conversion" in the fourth book. It occurred during a "sober hour" on a dewy evening:

> "Gently did my soul
> Put off her veil, and, self-transmuted, stood
> Naked, as in the presence of her God.

> While on I walked, a comfort seemed to touch
> A heart that had not been disconsolate :
>                     I had inward hopes
> And swellings of the spirit, was rapt and soothed,
> Conversed with promises, had glimmering views
> How life pervades the undecaying mind
> How the immortal soul with God-like power
> Informs, creates, and thaws the deepest sleep
> That time can lay upon her."

Having acquired " clearer knowledge," Wordsworth saw a new world which was the old, for there was divine love in his heart. The artist in him had been awakened by a loving influence sent direct from God who loves all. Then he became godlike as he relates :

>                  " I loved,
> More deeply all that had been loved before,
> More deeply even than ever."

Addressing Coleridge, he declares that poets had a message for mankind :

> " Prophets of Nature, we to them will speak
> A lasting inspiration, sanctified
> By reason, blest by faith ; what we have loved
> Others will love and we will teach them how."

These thoughts might well be translated from Persian or Arabic. East and **West** are more closely akin than some writers and travellers appear to realize, and this is particularly true in reference to intellectual life.

The religious systems may differ, and divergent views may be entertained as to which religion is the true religion. But in the lands " somewhere East of Suez," as in England, the seer-poets who have lived near to God enable all to surmount barriers and reach those green places which form the garden of God. There all may feel as did the Irish poet :

" The stars sang in God's garden,
    The stars are the birds of God,
    The night-time is God's harvest,
    Its fruits are the words of God."

In the " garden of God " are those divinely-inspired singers from whom we have much to learn as Eastern and Western children of the same Creator. In His eyes East and West are one.

# THE SEVEN FOUNTAINS

## AN EASTERN ALLEGORY

### BY SIR WILLIAM JONES

Deck'd with fresh garlands, like a rural bride,
And with the crimson streamer's waving pride,
A wanton bark was floating o'er the main,
And seem'd with scorn to view the azure plain:
Smooth were the waves, and scarce a whisp'ring gale
Fan'd with his gentle plumes the silken sail.
High on the burnish'd deck a gilded throne
With orient pearls and beaming diamonds shone,
On which reclin'd a youth of graceful mien,
His sandals purple, and his mantle green;
His locks in ringlets o'er his shoulders roll'd,
And on his cheek appear'd a downy gold.
Around him stood a train of smiling boys
Sporting with idle cheer and mirthful toys;

Ten comely striplings, girt with spangled wings,
Blew piercing flutes, or touched the quiv'ring strings;
Ten more, in cadence to the sprightly strain,
Wak'd with their golden oars the slumb'ring main:
The waters yielded to their guiltless blows,
And the green billows sparkled as they rose.

Long time the barge had danc'd along the deep,
And on its glassy bosom seem'd to sleep;
And now a pleasant isle arose in view,
Bounded with hillocks of a verdant hue:
Fresh groves, and roseate bow'rs appear'd above
(Fit haunts, be sure, of pleasure and of love)
And higher still a thousand blazing spires
Seem'd with gilt tops to threat the heav'nly fires.
Now each fair stripling plied his lab'ring oar,
And straight the pinnace struck the sandy shore.

The youth arose, and, leaping on the strand,
Took his lone way along the silver sand;
While the light bark, and all the airy crew,
Sunk like a mist beneath the briny dew.

With eager steps the young advent'rer stray'd
Through many a grove, and many a winding glade:
At length he heard the chime of tuneful strings,
That sweetly floated on the Zephyr's wings;
And soon a band of damsels blithe and fair,
With flowing mantles and dishevel'd hair,
Came with quick pace along the solemn wood,
Where wrap'd in wonder and delight he stood:
In loose transparent robes they were array'd,
Which half their beauty his, and half display'd.

A lovely nymph approach'd him with a smile,
And said, " O, welcome to this blissful isle !
For thou art he, whom ancient bards foretold,
Doom'd in our clime to bring an age of gold:
Hail, sacred king, and from thy subject's hand,
Accept the robes and sceptre of the land."

" Sweet maid," said he, " fair learning's heav'nly beam
O'er my young mind ne'er shed her fav'ring gleam;
Nor has my arm e'er hurl'd the fatal lance,
While desp'rate legions o'er the plain advance:
How should a simple youth, unfit to bear
The steely mail, that splendid mantle wear! "
" Ah! " said the damsel, " from this happy shore
We banish wisdom, and her idle lore;
No clarions here the strains of battle sing,
With notes of mirth our joyful valleys ring.
Peace to the brave! O'er us the beauteous reign,
And ever-charming pleasures form our train."

This said, a diadem, inlay'd with pearls,
She plac'd respectful on his golden curls;

Another o'er his graceful shoulder threw
A silken mantle of the rose's hue,
Which, clasp'd with studs of gold, behind him
    flow'd
And through the folds his glowing bosom showed.
Then in a car, by snow-white coursers drawn,
They led him o'er the dew-besprinkled lawn,
Through groves of joy and arbours of delight,
With all that could allure his ravish'd sight;
Green hillocks, meads, and rosy grots he view'd
And verd'rous plains with winding streams bedew'd.
On ev'ry bank, and under ev'ry shade,
A thousand youths, a thousand damsels play'd;
Some wantonly were tripping in a ring
On the soft border of a gushing spring,
While some reclining in the shady vales,
Told to their smiling loves their am'rous tales:
But when the sportful train beheld from far
The nymphs returning with the stately car,
O'er the smooth plain with hasty steps they came,
And hail'd their youthful king with loud acclaim;
With flow'rs of ev'ry tint on the paths they strow'd,
And cast their chaplets on the hallow'd road.

    At last they reach'd the bosom of a wood,
Where on a hill a radiant palace stood,
A sumptuous dome, by hands immortal made,
Which on its walls and on its gates display'd
The gems that in the rocks of Tibet glow,
The pearls that in the shells of Ormus grow.
And now a num'rous train advance to meet
The youth descending from his regal seat;
Whom to a rich and spacious hall they led,
With silken carpets delicately spread:
There on a throne, with gems unnumber'd grac'd
Their lovely king six blooming damsels plac'd,
And meekly kneeling, to his modest hand
They gave the glitt'ring sceptre of command;

Then on six smaller thrones they sat reclined,
And watch'd the rising transports of his mind:
When thus the youth a blushing nymph address'd,
And, as he spoke, her hand with rapture press'd,

" Say, gentle damsel, may I ask unblam'd,
How this gay isle, and splendid seats are nam'd?
And you, fair queens of beauty and of grace,
Are you of earthly or celestial race?
To me the world's bright treasures were unknown,
Where late I wander'd pensive and alone,
And, slowly winding on my native shore,
Saw the vast ocean roll, but saw no more;
Till from the waves with many a charming song,
A barge arose, and gayly mov'd along;
The jolly rowers reach'd the yielding sands,
Allur'd my steps, and wav'd their shining hands:
I went, saluted by the vocal train,
And the swift pinnace cleav'd the waves again;
When on this island struck the gilded prow,
I landed full of joy; the rest you know,
Short is the story of my tender years:
Now speak, sweet nymph, and charm my list'ning ears."

" These are the groves, for ever deck'd with flow'rs,"
The maid replied, " and these the fragrant bow'rs,
Where love and pleasure hold their airy court,
The seat of bliss, of sprightliness, and sport;
And we, dear youth, are nymphs of heav'nly line,
Our souls immortal, as our forms divine:
For Maia, fill'd with Zephyr's warm embrace,
In caves and forests cover'd her disgrace;
At last she rested on this peaceful shore,
Where in yon grot a lovely boy she bore,
Whom fresh and wild and frolick from his birth
She nurs'd in myrtle bow'rs, and called him Mirth.
He on a summer's morning chanc'd to rove
Through the green lab'rinth of some shady grove,

Where by a dimpled riv'let's verdant side
A rising bank with woodbine edg'd he spied :
There, veil'd with flow'rets of a thousand hues,
A nymph lay bath'd in slumber's balmy dews ;
(This maid by some, for some our race defame,
Was Folly call'd, but Pleasure was her name :)
Her mantle, like the sky in April, blue,
Hung on a blossom'd branch that near her grew ;
For long disporting in the silver stream
She shun'd the blazing daystar's sultry beam,
And ere she could conceal her naked charms,
Sleep caught her trembling in his downy arms :
Born on the wings of love, he flew, and press'd
Her breathing bosom to his eager breast.
At this wild theft the rosy morning blush'd,
The riv'let smil'd, and all the woods were hush'd.
Of these fair parents on this blissful coast
(Parents like Mirth and Pleasure who can boast ?)
I, with five sisters, on one happy morn,
All fair alike, behold us now, were born.
When they to brighter regions took their way,
By love invited to the realms of day,
To us they gave this large, this gay domain,
And said, departing, Here let beauty reign.
The reign, fair prince, in thee all beauties shine,
And ah! we know thee of no mortal line."

She said ; the king with rapid ardour glow'd,
And the swift poison through his bosom flow'd :
But while she spoke he cast his eyes around
To view the dazzling roof, and spangled ground ;
Then, turning with amaze from side to side,
Sev'n golden doors that richly shone he spied,
Then said, " Fair nymph (but let me not be bold)
What mean those doors that blaze with burnish'd
     gold ? "
" To six gay bow'rs," the maid replied, " they lead
Where Spring eternal crowns the glowing mead,

Six fountains there, that glitter as they play,
Rise to the sun with many a colour'd ray."
"But the sev'nth door," said he, "what beauties
    grace ? "
" Oh, 'tis a cave, a dark and joyless place,
A scene of bloody deeds, and magick spells,
Where day ne'er shines, and pleasure never dwells :
No more of that. But come, my royal friend,
And see what joys thy favour'd steps attend."
She spoke, and pointed to the nearest door :
Swift he descends ; the damsel flies before ;
She turns the lock ; it opens at command ;
The maid and stripling enter hand in hand.

The wond'ring youth beheld an op'ning glade,
Where in the midst a crystal fountain play'd ;
The silver sands that on its bottom grew
Were strown with pearls and gems of varied hue,
The diamond sparkled like the star of day,
And the soft topaz shed a golden ray,
Clear amethysts combin'd their purple gleam
With the mild em'rald's sight-refreshing beam,
The sapphire smil'd like yon blue plain above,
And rubies spread the blushing tint of love.
" These are the waters of eternal light,
The damsel said, the streams of heav'nly sight,
See, in this cup (she spoke, and stoop'd to fill
A vase of jasper with the sacred rill)
See how the living waters bound and shine,
Which this well-polish'd gem can scarce confine! "
From her soft hand the lucid urn he took,
And quaff'd the nectar with a tender look :
Straight from his eyes a cloud of darkness flew,
And all the scene was open'd to his view ;
Not all the groves, where ancient bards have told
Of vegetable gems, and blooming gold,
Not all the bow'rs which oft in flow'ry lays
And solemn tales Arabian poets praise,

Though streams of honey flow'd through ev'ry mead,
Though balm and amber drop'd from ev'ry reed,
Held half the sweets that nature's ample hand
Had pour'd luxuriant o'er this wondrous land.
All flow'rets here their mingled rays diffuse
The rainbow's tints to these were vulgar hues;
All birds that in the stream their pinions dip,
Or from the brink the liquid crystal sip,
Or show their beauties to the sunny skies,
Here wav'd their plumes that shone with varying
    dyes;
But chiefly he, that o'er the verdant plain
Spreads the Gay eyes that grace his spangled train:
And he, that, proudly sailing, loves to show
His mantling wings and neck of downy snow;
Nor absent he, that learns the human sound,
With wavy gold and moving em'ralds crown'd,
Whose head and breast with polish'd sapphires glow,
And on whose wing the gems of Indus grow.
The monarch view'd their beauties o'er and o'er,
He was all eye, and look'd from ev'ry pore.
But now the damsel calls him from his trance;
And o'er the lawn delighted they advance:
They pass the hall adorn'd with royal state,
And enter now with joy the second gate.

   A soothing sound he heard (but tasted first
The gushing stream that from the valley burst)
And in the shade beheld a youthful quire
That touch'd with flying hands the trembling lyre:
Melodious notes drawn out with magick art,
Caught with sweet ecstasy his ravish'd heart;
As hundred nymphs their charming descants play'd,
And melting voices died along the glade;
The tuneful stream that murmur'd as it rose,
The birds that on the trees bewail'd their woes,
The boughs, made vocal by the whisp'ring gale,
Join'd their soft strain, and warbled through the vale.

The concert ends; and now the stripling hears
A tender voice that strikes his wond'ring ears;
A beauteous bird in our rude climes unknown,
That on a leafy arbour sits alone,
Strains his sweet throat, and waves his purple wings,
And thus in human accents softly sings:

" Rise, lovely pair, a sweeter bow'r invites
Your eager steps, a bow'r of new delights;
Ah! crop the flow'rs of pleasure while they blow,
Ere winter hides them in a veil of snow.
Youth, like a thin anemone, displays
His silken leaf, and in a morn decays.
See, gentle youth, a rosy-bosom'd bride,
See, nymph, a blooming stripling by thy side!
Then haste and bathe your souls in soft delights,
A sweeter bow'r your wand'ring steps invites."
He ceas'd; the slender branch from which he flew
Bent its fair head and sprinkled pearly dew.
The damsel smil'd; the blushing boy was pleas'd,
And by her willing hand his charmer seiz'd:
Soon the third door he pass'd with eager haste,
And the third stream was nectar to his taste.

His ravish'd sense a scene of pleasure meets,
A maze of joy, a paradise of sweets.
Through jasmine bow'rs, and vi'let-scented vales,
On silken pinions flew the wanton gales,
Arabian odours on the plants they left,
And whisper'd to the woods their spicy theft;
Beneath the shrubs that spread a trembling shade
The musky roes, and fragrant civets play'd.
As when at eve an eastern merchant roves
From Hadramut to Aden's spikenard groves,
Where some rich caravan not long before
Has pass'd, with cassia fraught, and balmy store,
Charm'd with the scent that hills and vales diffuse,
His grateful journey gayly he pursues;

Thus pleas'd the monarch fed his eager soul,
And from each breeze a cloud of fragrance stole.
But now the nymph, who sigh'd for sweeter joy,
To the fourth gate conducts the blooming boy:
She turns the key; her cheeks like roses bloom,
And on the lock her fingers drop perfume.

Before his eyes, on agate columns rear'd,
On high a purple canopy appeared;
And under it in stately form was plac'd
A table with a thousand vases grac'd,
Laden with all the dainties that are found
In air, in seas, or on the fruitful ground.
Here the fair youth reclin'd with decent pride,
His wanton nymph was seated by his side:
All that could please the taste the happy pair
Cull'd from the loaded board with curious care;
(But first the king had quaff'd the tempting stream,
That through the bow'r display'd a silver gleam:)
O'er their enchanted heads a mantling vine
His curling tendrils wove with am'rous twine;
From the green stalks the glowing clusters hung.
Like rubies on a thread of em'ralds strung,
With these were other fruits of ev'ry hue,
The pale, the red, the golden and the blue.
An hundred smiling pages stood around,
Their shining brows with wreaths of myrtle bound:
They, in transparent cups of agate, bore
Of sweetly sparkling wines a precious store;
The stripling sip'd and revel'd, till the sun
Down heav'n's blue vault his daily course had run,
Then rose, and, followed by the gentle maid,
Op'd the fifth door: a stream before them play'd.

The king impatient for the cooling draught
In a full cup the mystick nectar quaff'd;
Then with a smile (he knew no higher bliss)
From her sweet lip he stole a balmy kiss;

On the smooth bank of vi'lets they reclin'd;
And, whilst a chaplet for his brow she twin'd,
While his soft cheek her softer cheek he pres'd,
His pliant arms were folded round her breast.
She smil'd, soft lightning darted from her eyes,
And from his fragrant seat she bade him rise;
Then, while a brighter blush her face o'erspread,
To the sixth gate her willing guest she led.

The golden lock she softly turn'd around,
The moving hinges gave a pleasing sound:
The boy delighted ran with eager haste,
And to his lips the living fountain plac'd;
The magick water pierc'd his kindled brain,
And with a strange venom shot from vein to vein.
Whatever charms he saw in other bow'rs,
Were here combin'd, fruits, musick, odours, flow'rs,
A couch besides with softest silk o'erlaid,
And sweeter still a lovely yielding maid;
Who now more charming seem'd, and not so coy,
And in her arms infolds the blushing boy:
They sport and wanton, till, with sleep appress'd
Like two fresh rose-buds on one stalk, they rest.

When morning spread around her purple flame,
To the sweet couch the five fair sisters came;
They hail'd the bridegroom, with a cheerful voice,
And bade him make with speed a second choice.
Hard task to choose when all alike were fair!
Now this, now that engag'd his anxious care:
Then to the first that spoke his hand he lent;
The rest retir'd, and whisper'd as they went.
The prince enamour'd viewed his second bride;
Then left the bow'r, and wander'd side by side,
With her he charm'd his ears, with her his sight,
With her he pass'd the day, with her the night.
Thus all by turns the sprightly stranger led,
And all by turns partook his nuptial bed;

Hours, days and months in pleasure flow'd away,
All laugh'd, all sweetly sung, and all were gay.

So had he wanton'd threescore days and sev'n,
More blest, he thought, than any son of heav'n;
Till on a morn, with sighs and streaming tears,
The train of nymphs before his bed appears;
And thus the youngest of the sisters speaks,
Whilst a sad show'r runs trickling down her cheeks.

"A custom which we cannot, dare not fail,
(Such are the laws that in our life prevail)
Compels us, prince, to leave thee here alone,
Till thrice the sun his rising front has shown:
Our parents, whom, alas, we must obey,
Expect us at a splendid feast to-day;
What joy to us can all their splendour give?
With thee, with only thee, we wish to live.
Yet may we hope, these gardens will afford
Some pleasing solace to our absent lord?
Six golden keys, that ope yon blissful gates,
Where joy, eternal joy, thy steps awaits,
Accept: the sev'nth (but that you heard before)
Leads to a gloomy dungeon, and no more,
A sullen, dire, inhospitable cell,
Where deathful spirits and magicians dwell.
Farewell dear youth; how will our bosoms burn
For the sweet moment of our blest return."

The king who found it useless to complain,
Took the sev'n keys, and kiss'd the parting train.
A glitt'ring car, which bounding coursers drew,
They mounted straight, and through the forest flew.

The youth, unknowing how to pass the day,
Review'd the bow'rs, and heard the fountains play;
By hands unseen whate'er he wish'd was brought,
And pleasures rose obedient to his thought.

Yet all the sweets that ravish'd him before
Were tedious now, and charm'd his soul no more:
Less lovely still, and still less gay they grew;
He sigh'd, and wish'd, and long'd for something new:
Back to the hall he turn'd his weary feet,
And sat repining on his royal seat.
Now on the sev'nth bright gate he casts his eyes,
And in his bosom rose a bold surmise:
"The nymph," said he, "was sure dispos'd to jest,
Who talk'd of dungeons in a place so blest:
What harm to open if it be a cell,
Where deathful spirits and magicians dwell?
If dark or foul, I need not pass the door;
If new or strange, my soul desires no more."
He said, and rose; then took the golden keys,
And op'd the door; the hinges mov'd with ease.

Before his eyes appear'd a sullen gloom,
Thick, hideous, wild; a cavern, or a tomb.
Yet as he longer gaz'd, he saw afar
A light that sparkled like a shooting star.
He paus'd: at last, by some kind angel led,
He enter'd, and advanced with cautious tread.
Still as he walk'd, the light appear'd more clear;
Hope sooth'd him then, and scarcely left a fear
At length an aged sire surpriz'd he saw,
Who fill'd his bosom with a sacred awe;
A book he held, which, as reclin'd he lay,
He read, assisted by a taper's ray;
His beard, more white than snow on winter's breast,
Hung to the zone that bound his sable vest,
A pleasing calmness on his brow was seen,
Mild was his look, majestick was his mien.
Soon as the youth approach'd the rev'rend sage,
He rais'd his head, and clos'd the serious page,
Then spoke: "O son, what chance has turn'd thy
  feet
To this dull solitude, and lone retreat?"

To whom the youth : " First, holy father, tell,
What force detains thee in this gloomy cell ?
This isle, this palace, and those balmy bow'rs,
Where six sweet fountains fall on living flow'rs,
Are mine ; a train of damsels chose me king,
And through my kingdom smiles perpetual spring.
For some important cause to me unknown,
This day they left me joyless and alone,
But, ere three morns with roses strow the skies,
My lovely brides will charm my longing eyes."

" Youth," said the sire, on this auspicious day
" Some angel hither led thy erring way :
Hear a strange tale, and tremble at the snare,
Which for thy steps thy pleasing foes prepare.
Know, in this isle prevails a bloody law ;
List, stripling, list! (the youth stood fix'd with
    awe)
But sev'nty days the hapless monarchs reign,
Then close their lives in exile and in pain,
Doom'd in a deep and frightful cave to rove,
Where darkness hovers o'er the iron grove.
Yet know, thy prudence and thy timely care
May save thee, son, from this alarming snare.
Not far from this a lovelier island lies,
Too rich, too splendid, for unhallow'd eyes :
On that blest shore a sweeter fountain flows
Than this vain clime, or this gay palace knows,
Which if you taste, whate'er was sweet before
Will bitter seem, and steal your soul no more.
But, ere these happy waters thou canst reach,
Thy weary steps must pass yon rugged beach
Where the dark sea with angry billows raves,
And, fraught with monsters, curls his howling waves ;
If to my words obedient thou attend,
Behold in me thy pilot and thy friend.
A bark I have, supplied with plenteous store,
That now lies anchor'd on the rocky shore ;

And, when of all thy regal toys bereft,
In the rude cave an exile thou art left,
Myself will find thee on the gloomy lea,
And waft thee safely o'er the dang'rous sea."

The boy was fill'd with wonder as he spake,
And from a dream of folly seem'd to wake:
All day the sage his tainted thoughts refin'd
His reason brighten'd, and reform'd his mind:
Through the dim cavern hand in hand they walk'd,
And much of truth, and much of heav'n they talked.
At night the stripling to the hall return'd;
With other fires his alter'd bosom burn'd:
O! to his wiser soul how low, how mean,
Seem'd all he e'er had heard, had felt, had seen!
He view'd the stars, he view'd the crystal skies,
And bless'd the pow'r all-good, all-great, all-wise;
How lowly now appear'd the purple robe,
The rubied sceptre, and the iv'ry globe!
How dim the rays that gild the brittle earth!
How vile the brood of Folly, and of Mirth!

When the third morning, clad in mantle gray,
Brought in her rosy car the sev'ntieth day,
A band of slaves, that rush'd with furious sound,
In chains of steel the willing captive bound;
From his young head the diadem they tore,
And cast his pearly bracelets on the floor;
They rent his robe that bore the rose's hue,
And o'er his breast a hairy mantle threw;
Then drag'd him to the damp and dreary cave,
Drench'd by the gloomy sea's resounding wave,
Meanwhile the voices of a num'rous crowd
Pierc'd the dun air, as thunder breaks a cloud;
The nymphs another hapless youth had found,
And then were leading o'er the guilty ground,
They hail'd him king (alas, how short his reign!)
And with fresh chaplets strow'd the fatal plain.

The happy exile, monarch now no more,
Was roving slowly o'er the lonely shore,
At last the sire's expected voice he knew,
And to the sound with hasty rapture flew.
A little pinnace just afloat he found,
And the glad sage his fetter'd hands unbound;
But when he saw the foaming billows rave,
And dragons rolling o'er the fiery wave,
He stop'd: his guardian caught his ling'ring hand,
And gently led him o'er the rocky strand;
Soon as he touch'd the bark, the ocean smil'd,
The dragons vanish'd, and the waves were mild.

For many an hour with vig'rous arms they row'd
While not a star his friendly sparkle show'd;
At length a glimm'ring brightness they behold,
Like a thin cloud that morning dies with gold:
To that they steer; and now rejoiced they view
A shore begirt with cliffs of radiant hue.
They land: a train, in shining mantles clad,
Hail their approach, and bid the youth be glad;
They led him o'er the lea with easy pace,
And floated as they went with heav'nly grace.
A golden fountain soon appear'd in sight,
That o'er the border cast a sunny light:
The sage impatient scoop'd the lucid wave
In a rich vase, which to the youth he gave;
He drank; and straight a bright celestial beam
Before his eyes display'd a dazzling gleam.
Myriads of airy shapes around him gazed;
Some prais'd his wisdom, some his courage prais'd,
Then o'er his limbs a starry robe they spread,
And plac'd a crown of di'monds on his head.

His aged guide was gone, and in his place
Stood a fair cherub flush'd with rosy grace;
Who smiling spake: " Here ever wilt thou rest,
Admir'd, belov'd, our brother and our guest;

So all shall end, whom vice can charm no more
With the gay follies of that per'lous shore.
See yon immortal tow'rs their gates unfold
With rubies flaming and no earthly gold !
There joys before unknown thy steps invite,
Bliss without care, and morn without a night,
But now farewell! my duty calls me hence,
Some injur'd mortal asks my just defence.
To yon destructive island I repair,
Swift as a star." He speaks, and melts in air.

The youth o'er walks of jasper takes his flight,
And bounds and blazes in eternal light.

## THE MARBLE TEMPLE

### BY SYR DHANVI

O MY Goddess of Peace! O my Beautiful One! I seek sanctuary in thy garden from the lurid flashes and turmoil of war. But thy roses are withered and the fountain leaps no more with joy of life. Art thou in thy white marble Niche? O my Idol of Idols !

Or has desolation come upon thy shrine and the dust of the arena powdered thy tresses? Ah! sorrow hangs on thy brow and low! I perceive a mark impressioned on thy cheek, as though by the fangs of a dragon of Conflict. O my Idol of Idols, why art thou forlorn?—Or is it only mine eye that painteth this dismal view?

Do I not remember the lofty crest of thy Temple which rose in splendour? Its glittering pinnacles touched the skies—O my Idol of Magnificence! O My Sublime! Why art thou so changed? Why dost thy glory—which once was enthroned by adoring hands—totter under the veil of oblivion?

Be this the mirror of mankind, reflecting their vanity and showing all life as a farce, and time a masquerade. But, O my Idol of Idols! the sun of thy grandeur will pierce the darkest clouds of human vice, and what is noble will for ever remain : so shall thy torch of happiness glow, till existence furl its wings, O my Beautiful One ! O my Supreme One !

## " YES," CAME A " VOICE "

$\mathcal{T}$HE night was dark and furious—the rain fell in torrents —vivid flashes of electric fire lashed their forked blazes across the gloom, for a moment illuminated the surrounding objects, and partially revealed the awful horror of the scene. The deep-toned thunder rolled in long and terrifying peals through vaulted concave of heaven—as dying man fumbled in his lonely chamber, and lit a candle. Taking a pen he wrote :

" MY FRIEND,—Death seizes my throat, but my heart still survives, and I send you my present thoughts. While you may be reading these lines I shall be groaning under the agonies of absolute despair, for my past life earned me nothing more.

" I see the vast gulf of uncertainty yawning ; who can express the anxiety of my soul ? It flutters impatiently in its earthly cage. No words can paint my dread, as it wears a face appallingly fearsome. Looking back, the pages of life are dark and vacant, though the blanks are filled in by disgrace and ill doings.

" But yet I have a faint beam of hope, which darts across the tremendous obscurity and may be called a faith in the mercy of my Creator. I . . . I wish to write more, but my hand fails me, so good-bye."

" What, I ! " said the amazed soul, " I doubled with the burden of sins and defiled with the black stains ; I in this celestial light ! "

" Yes," came a voice. " Forgiveness knows no bounds. Go, Mercy calls thee to rest."

## A TEAR IN A SAPPHIRE VESSEL

*T*HE night was beginning to unfold her ebony wings, and I in the glow of the fire sat reflecting in my silent chamber. There was a humble apartment across the road, lit by the feeble beams of a candle, where sat a poor old woman at her work. Her hair was white as snow, her face wrinkled and full of care.

From her movements, from her dress, from a mere nothing I imagined her mournful story; and any human heart wil¹ melt and weep on its recitation. Presently some-one handed her a letter; her hands trembled as she opened it. She read, she fell back, she fainted—and people rushed to her aid.

One day the black carriages drew up at the door where I had seen the old woman, and carried their burden. The rain pattered on my window panes, and I gazed in my fire. All was dark, all was still and sad around: my thoughts rose high, and I was dreaming.

I was led to the first gate of the heaven. I saw many sights and heard sweet sounds, like the voices of angels hymning to their lyres. And Seraph Gabriel was with me, as he was conducting me in the paths of infinite. The light of heaven dazzled my eyes on our approach to the second portal; and would have sunk me beneath its insufferable splendour had not the angel shaded me with his ambrosial wings, and touched my eyes with balm of amaranth, which grows only in heaven.

And lo! at the gate of heaven stood a pedestal of Jasper, and on this a vessel of pure Sapphire, encircled with gold —in this vessel lay a tear, which did not evaporate in the celestial lights, but remained the same for ever.

" This tear that you see," said the angel on my inquiry, " dropped from the eye of an earth-born, virtuous old woman. It was shed in her affliction for her son's mutila-tion by a horde of blood-shedders."

Thence we advanced to the cities of diamonds. The spires looked as if they met and touched each other up above, and passing through an emerald glade I saw two human forms—an old woman and a youth : both were dressed in white, and sat talking on the bank of a rivulet. I hid myself behind trees, and crawled as near as I could, and I heard them speak.

" Do you see," said the old woman, " that small smoky speck far below ?—it is the earth."

" Is it the earth, where once we lived ? Can it be so ? " asked the youth in utter amazement.

" Yes, it is earth, my son," said his mother, " where, as you wonder, we once were—and can you not see the piteous pageant of human beings treading upon the skeleton hands of nations, still holding gore-stained swords ? "

" Yes, I can yet recall in the faint distance of time that there was something which was called suffering, but I can no longer remember what it was."

The vision disappeared, I awoke, and was sitting in the red glow of the fire in my lonely chamber.

## THE GARDEN

*S*HALL I soon behold thee again, O my garden of gardens, where the bamboo twigs frolic with one another all day long in the sunshine, and the lagging kine wind endlessly upwards the liquid river of life?

And the honey-birds dart between the flowerets, and breath of the winds passes onward, sweetened with the perfume of thy verdure?

Or is thy beauty made desolate for ever?

And the labour of the oxen all in vain?

And the pleadings of the birds, and the sighing of the wind?

Wilt thou nevermore delight the heart with the colours of thy raiment and the perfume of thy tresses, O my garden of gardens?

### II

Why art thou wilted, O my garden of contentment? Dost thou miss the loving hands that told thine every petal, and fed thee with the nurture of love, and tended thee ever in the joy of creation?

Or dost thou pine away in longing for the liquid music that the winds once wafted across thy bosom, till thy raiment shone as the noonday sun in the glory of it, and the honeybirds forgot their thirst and the oxen their weariness?

Shall thy ruined cisterns never more echo with the ripple of laughter?

Nor thy groves watch the healing of the sick and sorrowful?

My heart is sore for the anguish of thy passing, O my garden of contentment.

### III

But though thou art passed away and withered, O my garden of gardens, O my Beautiful One, yet shall the seed of love that was planted in thee flourish in the hearts of those who know thy glories, and shall spread its branches of compassion till the world be sheltered in the shadow of it.

And thy memory shall live for ever, and the perfume of thee shall be wafted throughout the whole earth, and at the presence of it all evil shall be dried up.

For what good has been, is for ever, O my Beautiful One. So is thy loveliness everlasting, O my garden of gardens.

## TWO PHASES OF THE MOON

THE moon one night descended her staircase of white clouds, and passed through my window panes. Her phosphoric rays stared in my eyes, and I awoke from my sleep.

O, what a heavenly night!

The silvery scene charmed me out of my chamber. The garden swooned under the Lady Moon, as might a youth in love. Unlike the humans, the ecstasy was expressed by a sublime stillness; and the very water in the marble-bottomed pond seemed in slumber.

The tea-rose petals sang a song without a voice, and the beautiful pansies vainly tried to borrow the variegated effect from the starry sky. Bunches of daffodils in a corner blew their trumpets in rapture, while vapours arose from the mignonette to offer the gift of their perfumes to the Lady Moon.

But ah, what a change!

The air ruffled my hair, the moon hid her fair face behind a shroud of black clouds. The wind rose high; it became distinctly chilly, and I hurried in. Drops followed drops; rain, mingled with lightning, lashed my window. The blue flashes were fearsome, and presently the thunder crashed at the top of the lofty temple.

The interior was lit as if by a thousand candles, and all was again silent, but it was the grim silence of Death.

## IN FADING RAYS

*I*N my sleep I saw a vision, and on waking found myself more able to battle with the difficulties of life : for I had heard the last of the Adamic family converse with the sun.

The rays of the sun were feeble, the earth was worn out with age. The bones of the manhood of nations still held the rusted swords in their skeleton hands, while other humbler remains of those who had died of famine or disease could also be seen scattered here and there.

No echoes resounded in the mighty cities of the world ; ships loaded with the dead glided mysteriously towards silent shores. Still in the midst of it all stood the lonely man. His words shook the autumn leaves from the trees, just as though a wind had passed through them.

" Proud sun," said he, " you and I are now left alone, but your race is run, and mercy calls you to rest. Your eyes now dimmed have witnessed the mournful flow of human tears—for ten thousand years or more—but you have seen the last.

" For ages, O sun, you were privileged to participate in the greatness of man. Nations rose and fell beneath you, all glory was yours ; but your sway had its limits : for did you ever heal an aching heart or add balm to a wounded soul ? "

" Go, then, and let the dark curtain of forgetfulness fall on the stage of human existence, lest your rising light may recall the pitiful pageant of mankind and establish life's tragedies once again.

" Even I long to see the last of your fading rays, and you, who have for long been spectator of the world's agonizing phases, must not wait till my breath escapes. You will not boast to perceive the death of this tongue that speaks, but the sympathetic night will receive my spirit, and I shall return to the realms of light. When your beams will be no more, I shall glow in the celestial radiance.

" Lose your lustre and go, O sun, while I have but a

little time yet in my worldly exile, and gladly await the death which will free me from earth's cruel bondage.

" Go—go, and tell the night, who covered your face every evening with her black wings, that you saw the last of Adam's race standing on worldly ruins, and nothing shook his unflinching faith in immortality."

## VISIONS OF A RECLUSE

*E*ARTHLY pleasures I had all, but none opened my heart. Wine, gold, and kingdom are chimerical, and nothing more than illusions devoid of reality.

Here, look my heart! you have all for nothing. The lordly deodars your roof, the velvety grass your carpet, the majestic Jumna to play music, and the gorgeous lamps of nature your light. What more do you desire ? Though once a king of men, yet now I have a domain over the guileless jungle, and reign in happiness of solitude. Here I stay, and perchance my blackened disc of mind may yet get bright in contemplation.

The world's reminiscences are repugnant to my soul, and here I shall recall nothing of life's bitterness. Peace and joy will now abide with me, and I shall be alone, yet not lonesome.

Days go, and shadows of night fall; I listen to the sweet music of Jumna, and roam unhurt amongst my wild friends. No human voice penetrated the wall of mighty hills, no man floated his barge on the river, and I gloried in my lonely splendour.

One divine summer evening the perfumes of wild flowers filled the air, all was calm, all was lovely and peaceful, and I was kneeling at my prayer. Soon a stupor came upon me, and I knew not where I was.

But lo! the scene had changed. It was cold; the Jumna, the jungle, and the hills were all gone, the very shape of my hermitage was altered, and I was in a strange land. The stream was small and leaped furiously from stone to stone, the forest was thick, and black clouds threatened a shower.

I wondered, however, not long on my environment, but I heard a sound as if lightning had struck a building and shaken the very foundation of the earth. It was not, as I thought, thunder, but some phenomenon which I had never before seen or heard. A huge tree fell with a crash, and a few pieces of metal, after striking the rock, rebounded and whizzed past my face.

"What a forcible power!" said I, "that can rend asunder big trees, and can throw metal in this fashion. What can it be? Where am I? . . ."

Not long had I waited when I heard horses in full gallop, and in the distance thunder booming. O Lord and Master! which planet is this? I muttered my prayers. Am I thrown in the pits of demons? Is it not the destination of all sinners after death? A shriek from a thousand voices interrupted my prayer, and horsemen drove down the valley like a hurricane. "Ah, cruel monster! spare our lives. . . ." A deep moan and a death-like silence once again. The noise startled me, and presently an old man stumbled over stones on my right.

"Protect me! hide me!" uttered the old man in agonizing. tones. "They are killing us. Here is my gold, and hide me."

"Come, father!" said I. "I seek neither gold nor silver, but am in quest for the peace of the soul. Your age demands respect; come and hide here; none will disturb the tranquillity of your pious years." He hid himself under my straw bed, as would an ostrich in a desert sand.

He could not speak, his arms were bleeding, and he bore a wound on his face, but after a while he said, "Good hermit, fly for your life; they have drained the wells of brutality to a drop, and the nails of their heels have ejected fountains of blood from the panting necks of the vanquished." My blood boiled with rage. "Where are they?" I asked. "What are they?"

"They are," said the old man, "dancing with mirth and glee in the red glow of their blood-stained swords yonder up that hill." "But who are they?" interrupted I. "Tell me, tell me, what kind of animals are they?"

"They are a race of men called the Dragons of War, and come from the North." "A race of men; surely, reverend friend, not men!" "Yes, men," replied he, "in shape and form—and heaven help us if we are discovered."

"Ay, ay," said I. "I understand you now, and all is

clear to me. This place—I wondered if it were an abode of demons; it is not, it is earth, and I have heard of these hordes of whom you speak. Wait here, father, and rest your limbs. To kill may be theirs, yet wrong shall be avenged and. . . ."

I had not finished talking, when lo, two men clad in a peculiar garb approached us, and interrogated me whether I had concealed an old man. "Concealed!" said I, "no! Besides what brings evil messengers to the resting-place of a hermit?"

"A priest! Ha, ha!" laughed one. "A priest? A coward—to dress in the guise of a hermit to escape punishment. Feel the edge of this weapon."

"My order," said I, "prohibits shedding human blood, and I am no coward, but have fought and won, and do not hide behind a priestly cloak. The old man whom you seek is here, but you will cross my corpse to pollute his worthy person. I have said that my order prohibits killing human beings, but you are no humans; so villains, come and let us measure swords. My fingers have not as yet lost their touch of the sword." They spoke no more, and hurriedly retraced their steps. The old man sat in tears, and at last fell dead with wounds, and I knelt over him. Then I awoke.

The water of Jumna was like a sheet of melted gold, and its flow was serene. The evening breeze, loaded with fragrance, produced a music as it glided through the deodar leaves, and the sun was just disappearing behind the mountain chains. The sky was painted red, as I sat on the bank of Jumna meditating over my vision, and thought whether the colour in the sky was not the particles of innocent blood agglomerating up above to supplicate and invoke the wrath of heaven on the offenders in the land of my vision. But visions are visions; there are no such peoples on God's earth, and I was again at my prayer in my peaceful hermitage.

## THE HERMITAGE OF SANKARA

ON the sacred banks of the Gomtee, in a solitary part of the jungle containing fruits of every kind, continually resounding with the songs of innumerable birds and the light step of the stag or the timid gazelle, far away from the habitation of man, the hermitage of Sankara was situated.

In this delightful retreat the holy person was entirely devoted to fasting, praying, privation, and many painful duties. When summer reigned in all its terrors he surrounded himself with fires and sat bareheaded in the scorching sun ; in the rainy season he lay down in the water; and in the depth of winter he enveloped himself in wet garments, when he was already benumbed with cold.

The Devas, the Gandharvas, and other divinities of India, were struck with admiration. " Oh," they cried, " what an astonishing firmness ; what an endurance of pain! " These were witnesses to the appalling rigours capable of ensuring Sankara the conquest of the three worlds.

Their admiration being of a jealous kind, it yielded to fear that the will-power thus acquired would make him greater than themselves. They wished to make the pious hermit lose the reward of his long penance, and with this intention they went to their master to seek advice. Indra, the god of the elements, had also noticed the virtuous character of Sankara, and acceding to the request of the others, he addressed the nymph Pramotoncha, distinguished for her beauty and youthful grace.

" Go, Pramotoncha," commanded he ; " go like lightning to the abode of Sankara ; employ all your powers to make him break his penance."

" Powerful Divinity," answered the nymph, " I am ready to obey your orders, but I tremble for my existence ; I fear that illustrious solitary whose looks are so terrible, for his countenance is as radiant as the sun. He in his anger may load me with imprecations, if he should know the object of my mission. Why not, oh Mighty Power, choose another for this perilous enterprise?"

"No," replied Indra, "other nymphs will remain with me. On your celestial beauty I place my hopes. I shall, however, give you Love, Spring, and Zephyr for your assistance."

The sweet-smiling nymph, much flattered by these words, immediately traversed the air with her three companions and alighted in the jungle near the hermitage of Sankara. They wandered for a time beneath those immense shades, which recall to one's mind the eternal verdure of the gardens of Indian hills. On every side Nature smiled, and they were surrounded with fruits, flowers, and singing birds. Perched on the swaying branches, the birds, as various in plumage as in song, equally delighted the ear and the eye. Here and there were pools, clear as crystal, the surfaces of which were dotted with graceful swans of snowy whiteness and a flock of aquatic fowls that love shade and coolness. Pramotoncha and the others could not sufficiently admire the scene. She, however, reminded her assistants of the object of their journey, and called upon them to act in concert to achieve the success of the undertaking, while she began to devise plans to alienate the thoughts of the pious man from his devotions.

"Ah, ah!" she exclaimed, "we are to see this intrepid conductor of the car of Brahma, who boasts of having under the yoke the fiery coursers of the passions. Oh! how I pity him, that in this encounter the reins will drop from his hand; yes, were he Brahma himself, his heart will this day feel the power of the mighty shaft of Love!"

As she concluded these words she advanced towards the hermitage, where by the influence of the holy anchorite the most savage beasts were deprived of their ferocity. Withdrawing to a distance on the bank of the river, she mingled her enchanting voice with the sweet songs of the lonely kokila and swelled the air with a rapturous melody. At the same time Spring diffused new charms over all Nature. Kokila sighed with great softness, and by an ineffable harmony threw the soul into a voluptuous languor. The trickling pearly drops of the bloom-shaded brooklet made music. The gentle breezes, laden with the perfume of the wild flowers, moved with dancing steps. Zephyr's craft being now so well established, Love, armed with her burning arrows, approached the priest to infuse into his veins a consuming fire.

Struck with the melodious songs and the sudden change in the freshness of the atmosphere, Sankara hastened to the spot whence the sound of the music was coming. He was confounded; the musician could nowhere be seen, yet the music was everywhere. While he thus still wondered, he saw a majestic banyan tree split in half; a most beautiful feminine figure appeared in the cleft, and in an instant the tree closed again, the form vanished. Sankara rubbed his eyes, thinking he was dreaming, but as he opened them the vision was there. Amazed and bewildered, he fell unconscious to the ground, and on recovering his senses he raised his hands towards the skies in supplication. Pramotoncha, assuming mortal form, drew near him. "Who art thou?" asked he. "What is thy origin, O adorable woman? Thou, whose graceful form, whose eyebrows so delicately arched, whose enchanting smile no longer leave me master of my reason. Tell me, oh, tell me, sweet creature, who art thou?"

He tried to touch her, but as soon as their hands met, Pramotoncha smiled and made herself invisible. She called to her sisters to wind up their magical spell till the next day, explaining that the next stroke would entirely captivate the hermit, and that they should then weave the thread inextricably round him.

Sankara reeled in the dust and was afraid that his reason was gone. Whether he was changed and the whole universe was altered with him, whether he was dead or alive, he did not know. Stupefied and at his wits' end, the hermit sought his retreat. But every thought was centred in the image of her he had seen; he found sensations springing up in his mind that he had never felt before; he became agitated and sought in vain for repose; he believed he had only begun to exist from the moment his eyes had met hers—beyond this all was void. Alas! he dared not think of the future; his destiny was irrevocable.

The day dawned in all its splendour, the nymphs were again at work, the birds sang in Sankara's ears, and aroused him from his trance—for trance it was, as he did not sleep. He placed his hand behind his ear, and the same music vibrated in the air; he ran to the spot where he had seen the woman, the same tree opened, and the very same charmer stepping out, advanced towards him.

" Oh, can I believe mine eyes? Can it be thou, again, fair lady? Have compassion on me and tell me what is thy station?" spoke the bewitched hermit.

" Since you ask," replied Pramotoncha, " I am the most humble of all maids, and make my living out of gathering these wild flowers; my station, holy hermit, is now nothing, though once my father swayed the sceptre of four kingdoms. My story is sad, and ill-suited for a reverend ear like thine, so let me detain thee no more and take thee away from thy godly pursuits."

" I implore thee," said the hermit, " to tell me why thou art reduced to thy present state, and if it may be in the power of a poor man, he may, perhaps, lighten thy care and advocate thy cause."

" My cause is in the cold caress of the grave," replied the nymph. "As to my story, listen: I am the only daughter of Raja Bishn! He elicited the wrath of a witch, and not only paid for his own life, but the wicked witch placed an eternal curse upon me, by converting me into an ever-roaming form. And this is why I had to become invisible to thee yesterday, for the witch called on my soul to change my place, lest I should have the pleasure of cherishing thy affection."

" Then thou dost reciprocate my sentiments. Come with me thou, the light of my heart; I shall evoke all the powers of heaven and earth and relieve thee of the base wiles of the witch."

With these gentle words all the firmness of Sankara forsook him, and taking the young nymph by the hand, he conducted her to his hermitage—a hermitage where no woman had before set her foot. Then Love, Spring, and Zephyr, judging that their ministry was no longer needed, returned to the ethereal regions and related to the delighted gods the success of their strategy.

Meantime, Sankara, by supernatural power, which his austerities had procured him, instantly metamorphosed himself into a young man, endowed with divine beauty; celestial garments, garlands like those with which the gods adorned themselves, heightened the lustre of his charms.

Fastings, ablutions, prayers, sacrifices, profound meditation, duties to the gods, were all neglected. Solely taken up with his passion, by night and by day, the poor hermit never thought of the shock given to his penance. Plunged as he was in pleasure, the days succeeded each other without his perceiving it. He did not leave her an instant.

She was therefore greatly surprised when one evening he suddenly rose from her side and hastened towards the consecrated grove. "What is the matter?" she asked inquiringly.

"Dost thou not see," answered Sankara, "that the day is drawing towards the close; I hasten to offer my evening prayers for fear of committing the least fault in the accomplishment of my duties."

"Oh, man of consummate wisdom! what does this day signify to thee, in preference to a hundred others? Come! come!" said the nymph, "if this should pass uncelebrated like all those which thou hast allowed to pass away for these many long months, tell me, I pray, who would pay attention to it or take offence?"

"But," replied the anchorite, "it was this very morning, O charming woman, that I first saw thee on the bank of the river; and when this is the first evening that witnesses thy presence in this place, tell me, what dost thou mean by such bold remarks and the derisive smile that I perceive upon thy lips?"

"And how," she said, "can I avoid smiling at thy error and forgetfulness, when, since the morning of which thou dost speak, one revolution of the year is nearly complete?"

"What! can it be truth? Thou seducing nymph! Or is it a mere joke?"

"Oh!" ejaculated the sorceress, "how can you suspect me of such falseness? I will not tell a lie to a venerable Brahmin, to a holy hermit who has made a vow never to deviate an instant from the path followed by the wise; but now know me as Pramotoncha, who was sent by the god of the elements to break thy pious life, and I have done it."

"Oh, woe to me!" cried the unfortunate Brahmin, whose eyes were at length opened. "Oh, lost fruit of my long penance! All those meritorious works! All those actions conformable to the doctrine of the Vedas! Are they, then, altogether annihilated?

"Nay, nay! The ever-watchful eye of the All-seeing is open upon us, and I make Him witness. Fly! fly far from me! That power of concentration, won by austerities, which made a year of pleasure seem but as a day, that power is still with me. Go, woman! Go! Thy mission is accomplished. Yet even from thee have I learned something. With greater will, because with greater love, I turn once more to Him who is All-power, All-love, and bow my pride unto His feet."